Dervla Murp

Dervla Murphy was born in 1931 in Co... Dublin parents. Since 1964 she has been regularly publishing descriptions of her journeys – by bicycle and on foot – in the remoter areas of four continents. She has also written about the problems of Northern Ireland, the hazards of nuclear power, and race relations in Britain. Her most recent books are *Through the Embers of Chaos: Balkan Journeys* and *Through Siberia by Accident*. She still lives in County Waterford and is accompanied by many animals.

Silverland

A Winter Journey Beyond the Urals

DERVLA MURPHY

JOHN MURRAY

First published in Great Britain in 2006 by John Murray (Publishers)
An Hachette Livre UK company

First published in paperback in 2007

1

© Dervla Murphy

The right of Dervla Murphy to be identified as the Author of the Work has been asserted by her in accordance with the Copyright, Designs and Patents Act 1988.

A CIP catalogue record for this title is available from the British Library

ISBN 978-0-7195-6829-9

Typeset in Monotype Bembo by Servis Filmsetting Ltd, Manchester

Printed and bound by Clays Ltd, St Ives plc

John Murray policy is to use papers that are natural, renewable and recyclable products and made from wood grown in sustainable forests. The logging and manufacturing processes are expected to conform to the environmental regulations of the country of origin.

John Murray (Publishers)
338 Euston Road
London NW1 3BH

www.johnmurray.co.uk

For Lovina and Nico –
Always there when needed
and often needed

Contents

Acknowledgements

In Moscow Anna Zvegintzov and Clem Cecil provided valuable insights, much practical help and generous hospitality.

In Severobaikalsk Rashit and Raia Yasin did likewise.

Rachel Murphy as usual provided shrewd editorial advice.

Lovina Wilson struggled through a tangle of semi-legible manuscript corrections to achieve a flawless typescript in record time.

To all, my gratitude.

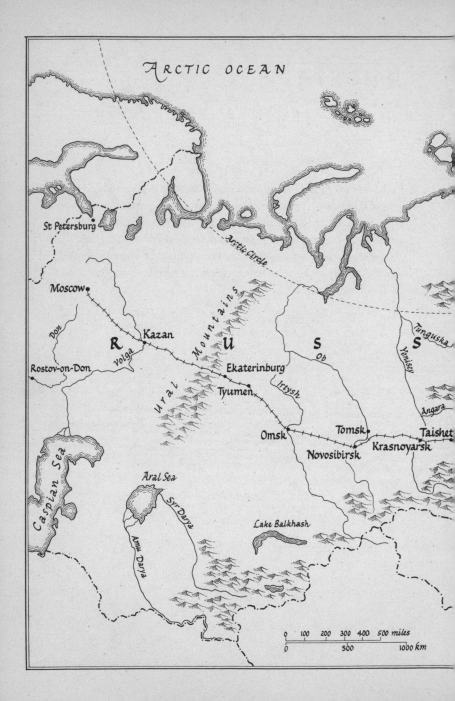

ARCTIC OCEAN

Arctic Circle

St Petersburg

Moscow

Don

R

Kazan

Volga

Rostov-on-Don

U

Ural Mountains

Ekaterinburg

Tyumen

S

Ob

Irtysh

Tunguska

Yenisey

Angara

S

Omsk

Tomsk

Novosibirsk

Krasnoyarsk

Taishet

Caspian Sea

Aral Sea

Syr Darya

Amu Darya

Lake Balkhash

| 0 | 100 | 200 | 300 | 400 | 500 miles |
| 0 | | 500 | | | 1000 km |

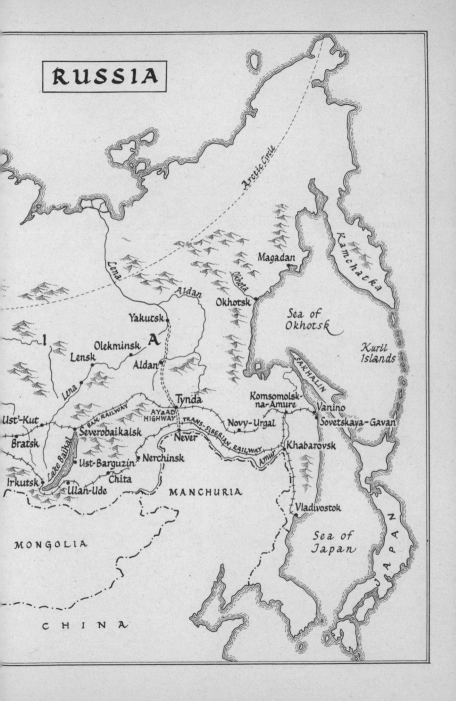

Foreword

Given my destination, Victoria Coach Station seemed an unlikely starting point; I associated it with going home to Lismore (how many times in the past half-century?) via Fishguard–Rosslare on Eurobus service 890. Now, waiting for an overnight coach to Cologne, I viewed my many fellow-passengers and felt a regrettably snobbish frisson. Certainly no one else in that crowded concourse was setting out for Vanino, two whole continents away. From Cologne a train would take me to Moscow, in thirty-six hours, for the modest sum of €165. And from Moscow BAM trains would take me by easy stages to the Russian Far East. The notion of travelling overland from the Channel port of Calais to the Pacific port of Vanino had a pleasingly nineteenth-century flavour.

My luggage was more than usually weighty and complicated: a large rucksack full of garments appropriate to mid-winter Siberia, plus two empty pannier-bags strapped to a gigantic suitcase containing gifts (mainly books) for the many friends who in 2002 had cherished me when I was maimed. Never before had I travelled with a suitcase of any dimension and this monster discombobulated me. From Lismore to London its contents had been packed in the pannier-bags and in a decrepit golfer's bag, all three items securely roped to slightly buckled wheels. A London friend took one horrified look at this construction, then generously presented me with a luxury suitcase, the sort you lead around like a dog, not noticing the weight – until you have to escort it down an escalator when it becomes life-threatening to those ahead of you. In Cologne railway station the Dog ran out of control and felled a young woman who was graciously forgiving. An older woman might have had broken bones.

My coach companion was a handsome young Nigerian, resident in Brussels, who had gallantly helped me heave the creature aboard. My pannier-bags puzzled Steve, as did my destination. 'But it's *January*,' he protested – then looked increasingly bemused as I explained the convoluted genesis of this mid-winter journey.

In October 2002 I had left my bicycle with a friend in Severobaikalsk on the northern shore of Lake Baikal, intending to return there in July 2003. But nowadays my plans have to be flexible because of granddaughters (three) and animals (eight). The former came to stay in April 2003 and again in July, while their parents were moving from the west of Ireland to the north of Italy. As a result *Through Siberia by Accident*, my last book, was not completed until November – when Christmas looms and it's hard to find an animal-sitter. Thus it came about that on 16 January 2004 I was bound for Siberia and my delayed return had required a major change of plan. Groups of foreigners do cycle there in mid-winter, as a sort of stunt, but even in my salad days pedalling in such extreme conditions didn't appeal to me – hence the railway marathon. In March, when the thaw came to southern European Russia, I would take a train from Severobaikalsk to Rostov-on-Don and spend a month cycling to Moscow on third-class roads, staying in villages overnight.

Steve stared hard at me for a silent moment. Then he said, 'I think you're mad. Russia now is full of criminals. If you don't freeze to death they'll kill you.'

The *Siberian BAM Guide*, by Athol Yates and Nicholas Zvegintzov, tells us that the Baikal–Amur Mainline (universally known as BAM)

> was the largest civil engineering project ever undertaken by the Soviet Union and probably by any country in the world. It devoured the same gigantic amount of resources as were used to conquer space in the 1950s and 1960s . . . In the 1970s, probably 20,000 people lived in the BAM Zone . . . Today over one million live in the Zone's three new cities and 100 settlements.

The construction of this 2,125-mile railway began in 1933 and con-tinued, on and off, for sixty years – almost the lifespan of the Soviet Union. At various stages it involved an extremity of Stalinist cruelty, bureaucratic bungling on a cosmic scale, ferocious infighting among Moscow's scientific elite, potentially lethal confrontations between rival factions of the Kremlin's top economists, awesome displays of innovative engineering skills, astounding logistical ingenuity and heroic feats of courage and endurance in anti-human terrain at anti-human temperatures. By now a distinctive sub-species has evolved: 'New Siberians', the BAM-builders and their descendants. These thousands of men and women, originally recruited from all over the Soviet Union, maintain the railway and rolling stock and run the services. They are understandably proud of themselves as pioneers who opened up much of Eastern Siberia and they display a touching loyalty to and affection for BAM as an institution. In 2002 many of them became my friends – and not only because I share their possibly biased view of the world-famous Trans-Siberian Railway as, by comparison, a minor achievement.

I

A Few Digressions and One Detour

A N ODD THING happened as our coach drove slowly along Cologne's Rhine embankment. I had been thinking about the immediate future, not the distant past, yet suddenly and vividly I saw an eighteen-year-old girl cycling along this same embankment displaying on her shirt front two badges – the gold and blue of the CTC (Cyclists' Touring Club), the green and white of An Oige (Irish Youth Hostels Association). The bicycle, named Cleopatra, was grossly overloaded; this being my first tour abroad I hadn't yet learned how to travel light. In May 1949 much bomb damage remained visible and I marvelled to see construction workers active on a Sunday and to hear that most Germans were doing night shifts to put things together again as quickly as possible. When the cathedral appeared, almost intact though surrounded by ruins, its survival seemed proof that Europe's recent regression to barbarism had not been total. That evening, in a letter to my parents, I wondered, 'Is it silly or wrong to feel so reassured by a beautiful building's survival? The same air force that spared it killed thousands of civilians for no reason in Dresden etc.' I still haven't found an answer to that question. It doesn't go away. Was it silly or wrong of me to feel as distressed by the Taliban's destruction of the Bamian Buddhas as by the US air force's killing of Afghan civilians?

Platform No. 3 was almost deserted, and so long one couldn't see either end where I emerged from the lift. On other platforms, Cologne's Saturday evening shoppers were gathering – expensively dressed and shod, laden with sleek parcels, glossy carrier bags, gay bouquets: a thriving, confident population, the majority unborn when I first visited their city. Cologne's less fortunate residents were not, I had noticed earlier, allowed into the railway station, or the cathedral.

Soon the lift delivered a few groups of Poles, hauling enormous cardboard cartons. The only other lone traveller was a friendly young

German named Andreas who looked rather unhappy. 'You're going all the way to Moscow?' I asked.

Andreas nodded, pulling his woolly cap over his ears. 'There is my first job, working with a big German construction company, interpreting. I speak good Russian. My generation, looking at the world, think it's a most useful language, there's a lot happening in Russia, they need help, there will be well-paid jobs.' He paused. 'My parents are angry, wish me not to go, say I should stay here using my Russian in a safer job. They think Moscow is so mafia-run I'll be corrupted or murdered!' Another pause, a quick sideways look, small nervous hand movements. 'Do you know about the Moscow mafia, how they operate?'

As I was confessing my ignorance our train approached, a ponderous antique in contrast to Germany's swift streamlined models. 'Let's travel together,' said Andreas. But we couldn't; on Russian trains passengers are predestined to occupy a specific bunk in a specific coach and no personal rearrangement is permitted. When Andreas tried to board my coach, simply to help me with the Dog, he was barred by my *provodnik*.

The *provodniki* institution is, I think, unique to Russia's railways and their international tentacles, such as this train. Each long-distance coach has two (male, *provodnik*; female, *provodnitsa*) and these multi-talented people serve as conductors, cleaners, clerks, dispensers of bedding, tenders of the communal samovar, keepers of the lavatory key, controllers of the lighting and piped music, auxiliaries to the Railway Police. You don't argue with your *provodnitsa* (they are usually female) and should you inadvertently break a rule – go barefooted down the corridor, not tidy your table after a meal, become obviously inebriated, light a cigarette – you must humbly accept a tongue-lashing. Its meaning will be perfectly clear though you know not a word of Russian.

Employment on international trains is a perk, which perhaps explains why my coach had a *provodnik*. Mikhail was middle-aged, undersized, monolingual but amiable; his close-set eyes, beaky nose and absence of chin gave him an oddly avian appearance. He insisted that I must at once lock my door and keep it locked.

In one way it was disappointing to find myself alone in a three-berth, second-class coupé; I had hoped for English-speaking (or even German-speaking) Russian companions. However, given the space available – far less than on the Trans-Siberian or BAM lines – this coupé would have felt cramped with two passengers and seriously overcrowded with three. Punctually at 18.18 we pulled out of Cologne into the half-darkness of night in an industrialized zone and soon I was asleep.

Dawn over Poland: fast-moving ragged pale grey clouds and amidst them a freakish formation, a static circle of vaporous copper, soon turning to red-gold, keeping itself separate from the dullness all around – like a molten volcanic crater, inverted. Then the meridian brightened to pale blue and dark snow clouds massed along the horizon.

Poland's mid-winter landscape is unexciting; an endless plain, lightly snow-covered, its ponds and streamlets frozen over, its rivers iced only near their low banks. Usually farmsteads were visible, stone and wood dwellings smaller than their outbuildings, surrounded by neat little fruit orchards with miniature plastic tunnels between the trees. Rarely, lines of puny misshapen pines or frail birches provided windbreaks. This was a still-life landscape – apart from Eurasia's omnipresent crows – until a few cyclists and pedestrians appeared on the rutted, black-iced tracks linking hamlets and motor traffic began to trickle along a narrow tarred road in the distance. Each village station had a blue wooden shrine, like a sentry-box, with electric 'candles' glowing before its statue of the Virgin Mary. Approaching Golabwi the road drew closer and carried many more vehicles than I remembered from my six-weeks' cycle tour of Poland in 1981 (its highlight the now famous Solidarity conference in Gdansk).

Our first stop was at a big town (or small city?) whose name escaped me. Its dingy seven-storey apartment blocks and industrial sprawl contrasted comically with two brand-new free-market flourishes – one a tall octagonal building, mainly constructed of blue glass, with no legend visible to explain its function. Then, approaching Warsaw, patches of woodland appeared and the embankments' blanket of dirty snow was thicker. In Warsaw station the last fall had been shovelled into hillocks in the middle of platforms – but inefficiently, leaving treacherous slabs of ice.

At noon Mikhail delivered long forms, in Russian only, for all passengers to fill in and present to the Belorussian immigration officers at the Brest border station. When I requested a non-Cyrillic version Mikhail looked apologetic while saying 'Nyet!' Soon after, numerous immigration officers swarmed onto the train in military fashion; ours was young, slim, handsome, hard-faced – let's call him Stan. He glanced at my form, filled in by guesswork, then scrutinized my passport and beckoned me off the train. Without a transit visa I could not proceed on the eight-hour journey through Belarus. To emphasize his point he pulled my rucksack off the top bunk and flung it into the corridor.

Mikhail was hovering in the background, looking agitated. I begged him to find Andreas since Stan apparently spoke no English. He rushed off but by the time Andreas came sprinting from his distant coupé I had been forced to heave the Dog onto the platform, unaided by Stan. Quickly I explained that I had visited Belarus's London embassy, passport and wallet in hand, asked for a transit visa and been told none was necessary if I remained on the train.

Stan shrugged and said the embassy had got it wrong. Now I must return to Poland and obtain a visa from the nearest Belorussian consulate, some fifty miles away in the large industrial town of Bialystok.

I whispered to Andreas, 'Should I try a bribe?' He whispered to Mikhail who shook his head. Stan might be tempted but he daren't relent; if I tried to leave Belarus without a visa he could get into trouble, whatever the London embassy said. The dollar is not always and everywhere mighty.

Mikhail, muttering sympathetically, helped me to shoulder the rucksack and Andreas called 'Good luck!' as Stan – my passport peeping out of his jacket pocket – led me away.

Brest's station covers acres and the Dog's limitations were exposed by three long underpasses, with broken concrete floors and many steep steps. Obviously such suitcases are designed to glide over the smooth plastic of airport tiles. When Stan realized that I was physically incapable of coping with those steps he took over and I tried to establish a less confrontational relationship. I was his victim, but he too was a victim – of a regime still, in 2004, exhibiting some of the Soviet Union's most tiresome features. However, my smiles and effusive thanks, on each top step, bore no fruit; I was left to drag the Dog over the next rough stretch. Meanwhile I was worrying about my friend Anna; at dawn on the morrow she would be waiting for me in Moscow's Belorusskaja station. Also I was fretting mildly about wasted money, assuming I would now have to buy a Brest–Moscow ticket. In the customs and immigration hall Stan abruptly vanished with no gesture of explanation. The echoing expanse of parquet flooring was furnished only by a long wooden trestle table, crudely made, and two small daises; on each sat a quartet of black leather-jacketed youngish men, chain-smoking while filling in endless forms, with long pauses for chats. At intervals an elderly head-scarved woman in frayed garments, wielding a grass broom, swept up their cigarette ash and smouldering butts. Men in green or blue uniforms occasionally sauntered to and fro with guns in their belts and files under their arms. No one had even glanced in my direction when I arrived and everyone continued to ignore me – I might have been invisible.

Sitting on a solitary metal camp chair in a corner I speculated about the original status of this extraordinary chamber. Pinkish marble pillars supported a high baroque ceiling, recently repainted blue and white; some of the painters' ladders remained in situ. A wide gallery, with exquisitely carved wooden balustrades, ran around three of the greenish marble walls. The many windows, most now sealed with concrete blocks, looked vaguely Gothic. Had this been a waiting-room for the czar and his entourage? But did czars ever have to wait for trains?

Time passed visibly; a large clock, high on the wall opposite me, recorded its passing as the minute hand jerked from 2.10 to 3.45. I wondered if Stan enjoyed having a foreigner trussed up in red tape. Anyway I had no reason to feel uneasy, I was just being given a harmless taste of what so many endured in Soviet times – intimidation by threatening looks, nothing clarified, no explanations heeded, the individual crushed under the steamroller of the State.

The disparity between London's visa rules and Brest's should not have surprised me. Belarus is where you might expect quirky things to happen. In itself it is an oddity, a stray bit of the broken Soviet jigsaw which has always been part of someone else's jigsaw and lacks any previous experience of nationhood. Dangerously located, always coveted by stronger neighbours, its low-lying territory (slightly smaller than Britain, with a present population of 10.3 million) was settled in the sixth century by East Slav slash-and-burn peasants whose descendants have never had a chance to develop a clear national identity. Nor, until recently, did they yearn for independence. Nobody even knows the origin of the name 'Belarus' (White Russia) and because this territory didn't become part of Russia until 1796 some of the new-hatched nationalists resent it.

The region's earliest principalities – Pinsk, Minsk, Turov and Polatsk, set up by Norman and Greek traders – were taken over by the Rus soon after they had founded the state of Kiev in the ninth century. In 1240 the conquering Mongols arrived and Belarus's princes briefly became Tatar vassals. During the following century Lithuania gradually gained control but allowed Belarus considerable autonomy, even for a time using Belorussian as its own official language – a telling measure of the prevailing confusion in that corner of Europe. When the Polish and Lithuanian crowns were united in 1386, in a power-sharing agreement, Lithuania became officially Roman Catholic but Belarus's peasants remained Orthodox.

In 1569 power-sharing ceased, Poland became the dominant partner, Lithuania's nobility adopted the Polish language and culture and subsequent agricultural 'reforms' condemned Belarus's peasantry to serfdom. Twenty-seven years later the Union of Brest, engineered by the Poles, established the hybrid Uniate Church, sometimes described as 'Greek Catholic'. This compromise required the Belorussians to accept papal authority while retaining their Orthodox rituals.

For the next two hundred years Poles and Jews controlled Belarus's trade, such as it was, and the peasants suffered extreme poverty. Then came the Partitions of Poland, when Austria, Prussia and Russia each grabbed chunks of Polish territory and Belarus found itself part of the czar's empire. At once St Petersburg imposed 'cultural Russification', banned publications in the Belorussian language and, in 1839, ordered Belarus to revert to Orthodoxy. Most meekly obeyed and the Uniate Church was in theory abolished. (In practice it survives to this day.) Belarus then became part of the Pale of Settlement, that area to which Russian Jews were confined in the nineteenth century, and soon Belorussians were outnumbered in their towns and cities by Russian settlers and Jews. A few small industries were set up but rural poverty worsened, driving 1.5 million Belorussians to migrate to Siberia or, if they could raise the fare, to the United States.

The First World War saw much Russian and German blood shed on Belorussian battlefields and left the entire area devastated and starving. In March 1918 the Treaty of Brest-Litovsk allowed Germany briefly to take control of the Baltic states, Poland and most of the

Ukraine and Belarus. This left the city of Brest – eastern Europe's most important road–rail junction – within Poland where it remained until August 1939 when that unfortunate country was yet again carved up, this time by Hitler and Stalin. Now Brest was back in Belarus, almost on the new border, with the Buh river separating the Nazi and Soviet armies.

In 1918 German-occupied Belarus had declared itself an 'independent democratic republic' but no one took the gesture seriously and in 1921 the Treaty of Riga gave the western third (approximately) of present-day Belarus to the Poles. Their promptly launched programme of 'Polonization' nourished Belarus's infant nationalism, provoking a minority of young men ineffectually to take up arms.

A year later eastern Belarus became a Soviet Socialist Republic, a founder member of the USSR. During the 1930s collectivized farms, artificial famines, heavy industries and Stalinist purges arrived; no one knows how many mass slaughterings took place. In the Kurapaty Forest, near Minsk, the bodies of more than 100,000 men and women were exhumed in 1988.

In 1941 the Germans rapidly overran the territory though Brest's Soviet garrison put up a heroic defence, still recalled with pride. Subsequently several major battles were fought in Belarus, and Minsk was reduced to rubble. Between 1939 and 1945 Belarus lost more than 25 per cent of its population: at least two million people. Some were victims of Stalin; the rest, including Belarus's many Jews, died in the Belarus-based Nazi concentration camps – which numbered more than two hundred.

After the war hectic reconstruction and industrialization brought about massive immigration from Russia and Belarus became one of the most prosperous Soviet republics. Until about 1980 its political leadership – increasingly senile – was drawn from that honoured army which eventually defeated the Nazis. As a group, these men shrewdly combined loyalty to the Kremlin with pride in Belarus as an embryonic nation.

Since czarist times the Russians had sought to emphasize the closeness of the three Slav peoples of Russia, Ukraine and Belarus, who together made up nearly three-quarters of the empire's population, the Russians on their own contributing slightly less than half. Following St Petersburg's example, Moscow now imposed Russian as the official language of Belarus and most parents accepted this, thinking it sensible not to limit children to what Moscow described as 'a domestic dialect'. Their compliance angered the small minority of fervent nationalists, Belorussian having long since developed into an authentically separate language, though one easily enough understood by Russians and Ukrainians. Until 1988 some 83 per cent of pupils were taught only in Russian.

In 1986 the Chernobyl disaster happened just over the border in Ukraine but did most damage in Belarus, heavily contaminating one-fifth of the countryside. Of all the Slav Soviet republics, Belarus was seen as the least likely to welcome Mikhail Gorbachev's reforms and probably nothing less than Moscow's scandalously irresponsible mishandling of the Chernobyl crisis could have stimulated an active political opposition to Belarus's crypto-Stalinists. In 1988 Zjanon Paznjak, the archaeologist who publicized the Kurapaty mass graves, became leader of the new Belarus Popular Front (BPF). Its public meetings to consider the Chernobyl fallout, in every sense, and the near-extinction of the Belorussian language, were well supported. But in October 1988, after the Kurapaty revelations, it went too far by organizing a non-violent anti-Stalin demonstration. Riot police moved in with water cannon, tear gas and truncheons – as good a way as any, in the heady days of 1988, to increase support for the BPF, which won some 20 per cent of the seats in the March 1990 elections. Four months later came Belarus's declaration of regional sovereignty, inspired by the Minsk soviet's anxiety to avoid further contamination by *perestroika* from Moscow. Shortly after, Belorussian replaced Russian as the official language, a move which caused such intolerable confusion that Russian was given equal status in 1995.

Minsk's hardliners of course supported the attempted coup against Gorbachev in August 1991. When it failed the Belarus Communist Party did a fast U-turn and declared full national independence, changing the country's name to the Republic of Belarus. The Supreme Soviet then chose as the new head of state a BPF-backed physicist, Stanislau Shushkevich, who in 1986 had publicly criticized the authorities' criminal post-Chernobyl negligence, bravely supplying shocking sets of facts and figures. However, hardline Communists continued to dominate in Minsk and the KGB remained operative. The hardliners blocked most moves towards moderate economic reform, favoured by Shushkevich, and over time became increasingly antagonistic. In January 1994 he was dismissed and replaced by a retired senior police officer, Mechislau Gryb.

Six months later Belarus held its first direct presidential election and a non-Party man, Alexander Lukashenko, won easily. He had vowed to stop price rises and privatization, to defy the mafia and move closer to Russia. Sometimes charitably described as 'eccentric' or 'individualistic', he had been a collective farm director though never a Party member. In 1996 a manipulated referendum castrated the parliament, giving him dictatorial powers, and his antics on the international stage caused some amusement among those not subject to his rule. When he accused the Soros Foundation of owing Belarus $3 million in back taxes, though Mr Soros had recently donated $13 million to Belorussian hospitals and schools, the Foundation diverted its dollars elsewhere. A Russian journalist, imprisoned on suspicion of having 'violated the border' with Lithuania, was held without trial for three months. In June 1998 several ambassadors from EU countries and the United States were locked out of their shared diplomatic compound without warning – not even being allowed in to collect pyjamas and toothbrushes – allegedly because the buildings needed repairs. The EU group left Minsk in a justifiable huff and didn't return until January 1999.

When Lukashenko's five-year term as president expired in May 1999 the opposition parties, condemning the 1996 referendum as illegitimate, staged an election. But their candidates were handicapped by living in permanent exile (Zjanon Paznjak) and being in jail (Mikhail Chigir) and that blatantly fixed poll could claim no more legitimacy than the referendum. Five years later, when Poland joined the EU on 1 May 2004, Lukashenko remained in power.

By then several recklessly defiant journalists had disappeared, all independent media outlets had been muzzled and the occasional staging of show trials kept the population on edge. However, the CIA-funded 'Orange Revolution' in Ukraine unnerved Lukashenko: could Belarus's 400,000-strong Polish community become the breeding-ground for something similar? The country's largest NGO was the Warsaw-backed 'Union of Poles in Belarus' which for years ran its own obliquely anti-Lukashenko Polish-language newspaper, now suppressed. After 1 May 2004 hundreds of Poles were arrested and detained without trial but the EU ignored Warsaw's plea for Brussels to impose sanctions on Minsk.

Small wonder Belarus's London embassy and Brest's immigration officers differ on transit visas.

At 4.15 a policeman opened a door at the far end of the hall and fifty or so peasants rushed in bearing passports to be stamped and bits of paper to be signed. Each carried a few sacks, nylon bags or cardboard cartons, all empty. As they queued beside the trestle table a scared-looking young man was hustled in by a complacent-looking customs officer who curtly ordered him to unpack his large grubby rucksack. It contained very many cartons of cigarettes. A policeman was summoned to handcuff the culprit and remove him while the customs officer sealed his loot in a tin trunk and locked it in a space under one of the rostrums.

Then Stan appeared in a distant doorway, beckoned me, and led me through the snow-powdered dusk along unlit platforms to a two-coach train. Presumably this would take me to Bialystok. Stan stood watching while I hoisted the Dog on board, then returned my passport and strode away. His impassivity chilled me; at no stage had he allowed eye contact.

My little coach had slatted wooden seats, a collapsing ceiling, a floor patched with bits of corrugated iron. An elderly conductress was stoking its coal stove with arthritic hands; she ignored my greeting. For some time I was alone, then the peasant cohort arrived – a jolly group, despite their evident poverty. They considered me with apprehension-tinged curiosity: what was a foreigner doing on their exclusive cross-border service? Nobody returned my tentative smiles.

We moved at something between walking and cycling speed and beyond the narrow Buh, a tributary of the Vistula, stopped briefly for two Poles to come aboard: police and customs officers, all amiable young men. Strolling through our coach they glanced casually at a few of the proffered passports, then squatted down by the open stove to warm their hands while sharing a packet of biscuits with the conductress.

An hour later, at an unlit halt, everyone else disembarked. When I remained seated the conductress shouted at me, indicating the exit; here was the end of the line. But this couldn't possibly be Bialystok –

so where were we? By the time I'd extricated myself and my gear the conductress and the officers had vanished and the peasants were hurrying into a small building at the end of a rough path running between the track and a field. It was dark and snowing steadily with black ice underfoot. In the empty station, its ticket office closed, I hesitated; the building was warm, perhaps I could sleep there overnight? Beyond, a few feeble street lamps illuminated a small silent village, none of its inhabitants visible. It was, I think, called Kleszczele – but I could have got that wrong. Then I noticed, parked nearby, an army jeep. Hopefully I asked the two young soldiers, 'Hotel?' and the driver wordlessly directed me across a T-junction. Proceeding cautiously, looking for a 'HOTEL' sign, I saw instead a tiny board at waist height saying 'Zimmer – Chambre – B&B' and pointing up a long slippery path to a new two-storey house.

When Mrs Chojecki opened the door I knew my luck had turned. Middle-aged and fubsy, she had crinkly fair hair, dark eyes, a kind smile, an instant welcome. Then Mr Chojecki appeared, tall and well-built and courteous in an old-fashioned way. As I began to explain myself he nodded, immediately recognizing the problem; this B&B owes many of its foreign guests to Belorussian immigration officers. In German my host advised me to have my Cologne–Moscow ticket stamped without delay at the local station, giving the time of my arrival; this would validate it for the next day's onward journey.

Perhaps the station should have been staffed, even at 8.0 p.m., but my knockings and callings went unheeded. So Mr Chojecki wrapped up well and gallantly went forth to seek the clerk. When he returned with my stamped ticket he had also booked a taxi for 7.0 a.m. It was twenty-five miles to Bialystok and the bus would not get me back in time to catch my return train to Brest.

By then I was relaxing in an overheated living-room dominated by a tall Christmas tree gaudy with baubles; on 18 January it seemed irritatingly superfluous. Near the stove sat Krystof, the Chojeckis' only child, a cheerful twenty-year-old paraplegic, confined to his bath chair. He spoke some English so my arrival delighted him and his parents beamed proudly as he and I conversed. This was a home adapted to his needs, a sad home in one way, yet happy because of the amount of love around.

Mr Chojecki owned and managed a small but flourishing furniture factory in a nearby town. He made a point of being in his office by 7.0 a.m. six days a week; to get the best out of employees, their boss must be seen to work hard. He was ambivalent about the EU. It would widen his market but he feared that Brussels' regulations would handicap family firms. Mrs Chojecki also felt uneasy; when EU attitudes took over, would the state continue to help Krystof or would his present free day-care service be privatized? Tea was served before Mrs Chojecki showed me to my room. A huge TV set bulged from one corner and the two wide windows were overdressed – lace curtained, with sweeping drapes of pale green nylon restrained by silver bows. As in Russia, potted plants abounded; the fronds of one exuberant palm tree had to be dodged at the top of the stairs and swathes of a prettily mottled vine brushed my cheek as I entered the bathroom.

At 4.30 a.m. the family alarm clock rang and thirty minutes later I was called from downstairs – a nice coincidence, this being my customary breakfast time. Numerous dishes crowded the long table: locally made sausages and salami, cold roast lamb, pork jelly containing minced meat and chopped vegetables, brown and white bread, shiny slices of processed cheese and a butter substitute. The array of sweetmeats mandatory in Russia was absent but everyone sugared their pink herbal tea. Mr Chojecki began the day with one quick shot of plum brandy, then as an afterthought offered me a shot. His wife looked slightly shocked when I tossed it back.

Krystof's day-care centre opened at 6.0 a.m. and while his parents were manoeuvring him into the car – a slow and difficult process – I again tried to telephone Anna, having failed the previous evening. At 6.30 I gave up; it later transpired that her computer was occupying the line.

The unmarked taxi owned by Jerzy, a friend of Mr Chojecki, arrived a quarter of an hour early. Jerzy – once employed in Warsaw by 'an important American businessman' – spoke broken English fluently and was an outgoing character, curious about me and informative about himself. His two married daughters, in their twenties, had a toddler each and shared the mothering. Since 1999 they had been taking it in turns to work for six months as domestic servants in Brussels. Rich NATO or EU officials paid them lavishly, by Polish standards, and they spent only a fraction of their wages. Soon they and their husbands – both now employed by Mr Chojecki – would be able to set up together in business. Maybe open a café, or a car repair service-cum-video shop? Once you had the initial dollars, anything could be built. As for the toddlers, they were thriving – not sure which sister was their mother or aunt but none the worse for that. And the husbands, being devout Catholics, coped chastely with their intervals of celibacy – or so Jerzy asserted.

In 1981, on my way to Bialowieza Forest, I had avoided Bialystok, a city industrialized since the nineteenth century; its many factories now competed in the pollution stakes. On the ring road we met a convoy of loggers' trucks loaded with tree trunks up to forty metres in length and of massive girth – some magnificent oaks, the rest pine and spruce. The fringes of Bialowieza Forest have long been exploited by timber merchants but most of its 1,290 square kilometres (580 of those in Poland) were rigorously protected until the free marketeers arrived. In 1981 I was restricted to the small tourist area; only scientists with special passes could enter this last refuge of the European bison. Bialowieza's other inhabitants include elk, red and roe deer, lynx, boar, otters, beaver and wolves. Now a mere 8 per cent of the total area is protected.

The Belarus consulate is one of a row of substantial bungalows set in spacious gardens on the northern edge of Bialystok, opposite wide fields. Jerzy deposited my luggage by the locked gate and looked concerned on noticing that opening time was not until 9.0 a.m. – it being then 7.25, with the thermometer on the gatepost reading −7°C. Soothingly I explained that travellers are inured to such temporal lacunae. As we said goodbye he gave me a packet of chewing gum. 'While you wait, it's easier if you chew.'

Briskly I walked to and fro while a heatless sun appeared, turning to pale gold the few flimsy clouds above the horizon. Commuting motorists passed, each car packed with workers; the only pedestrians were schoolchildren, well groomed and neatly uniformed with stylish satchels. Near the consulate entrance Belarus's contentious national flag hung limply in the still air. The first, 1990, version had shown two thick white stripes, symbolizing purity and freedom, separated by a narrow red band symbolizing valour. Under President Lukashenko this was replaced by an emended version of the flag flown in Soviet times – mostly red, above a green stripe. The emendation removed a small hammer and sickle. To fly the 1990 flag was now illegal, in practice as well as in theory. Citizens rash enough to display it were routinely arrested.

As I walked I anguished about those loggers' trucks, their tragic significance. According to the ecologist Dr Thomasz Wesolowski of Wroclaw University, who since 1976 has been spending three months each year in Bialowieza Forest, the timber industry has recently done immense damage. As he told Ros Coward of the *Guardian*:

> Foresters are taking more and more of the mature trees, claiming they have to clear them because of wood-boring beetles. They are using huge machinery, cutting roads deep into the forest, changing its nature, opening up the protected area to invasive species and diseases . . . Unbelievably, the Polish government has said the site should be listed, but should be managed by the foresters. That's like asking the wolf to look after the sheep.

At 8.05 a young woman clerk came hurrying towards the consulate and stared suspiciously at me and my gear. She was fat, pale, dark-eyed and heavily made-up, wearing a rabbit-fur hat and an ankle-length black leather coat. As she fiddled with the gate's security buttons I asked permission to wait inside but she frowned, shook her head, stepped inside, slammed the gate – then five minutes later reappeared on the verandah and beckoned me in. Fair enough; underlings can't take responsibility for breaking the rules, least of all in Belarus.

From the sparsely furnished visa office I could see, through a high plate-glass barrier, two other young women settling down to drink coffee while poring over a German fashion magazine. The consul emerged from his lair at 8.50, a surprising ten-minute concession to the foreigner. (No doubt he needed time to put my dollar bills through an anti-forgery test.) He had sleek straight dark hair, pasty cheeks, cold pale eyes, thin lips and a harsh manner. The fee for traversing his country by train was $55 or $100 for a two-way visa. As I filled in my form the wall clock chimed nine and a dozen poorly dressed Polish men came bustling in, loudly vying for attention until the consul barked at them, when they formed a fidgety queue. While filling in multiple forms per person they engaged the clerks in complicated disputes, their tones and expressions aggrieved.

My form and passport went to the consul for processing and fifteen minutes later he emerged to glare at me. 'You give no telephone number, why?'

'My number is ex-directory.' I refrained from asking why any Belorussian official might wish to ring me in Ireland.

'You give no husband name, why? Even if dead you must give name.'

'I've never had a husband.'

'Yes, you give child's name, name of child is your husband. Divorce or not, give husband's name.'

I smiled condescendingly. 'In some countries women without husbands have children. It's easy.'

The consul coloured momentarily and then snapped, 'Postcode, you give no postcode, why?'

'Because Ireland has no postal codes, outside of Dublin.'

'You give no street name, no apartment numbers – why?'

'I don't live in an apartment and my town is really a village and doesn't have street numbers and anyway I live behind a street.'

The consul was in no position to dispute those facts of Irish life but as he glowered down at my form, a fist clenched on either side of it, his disbelief was obvious. Yet my visa soon appeared, with a triple-stamped receipt for $55. When I requested a taxi it arrived so promptly that I assumed it to be consular-related.

The dour, middle-aged driver smelt unwashed and chain-smoked all the way back to the railway station. There he spoke for the first time, to demand $40. I gave him $20 – Jerzy's charge – and left him red with rage, shouting abusive things about Ingleezi, while I dragged the Dog through deep new snow into the ticket office. To my bewilderment the young woman clerk gave me a free ticket back to Brest. Does the Polish railway have a compassionate policy towards the victims of Belarus's unpredictable visa requirements?

I boarded the empty little train at 10.45 and, perched near the stove, reflected that the consul and Stan seemed set in the same mould: no eye contact and that scary facial immobility which suggests the stunting of a person's individuality. Of course I had met them both as officials – how different would they have been if we'd met socially? Could we then have encountered each other as human beings? Or are such people so conditioned that they can have relaxed relationships only with their own sort?

Towards noon the peasant cohort arrived, their bags and sacks and crates now overflowing with basic household goods – soap, salt, kerosene, tea – and with preserved fruits and vegetables bought at the Monday morning market near the railway station. Then suddenly uniformed Poles were everywhere, checking passports and handing out long bilingual forms (in Polish and Russian) to be filled in en route. I was considering mine with trepidation when Julia appeared. In her early twenties, she carried a worn leather monogrammed briefcase and a large shoulder bag full of books. I could see one English volume, a P. D. James paperback, and my spirits rose: here was a form-filler.

Julia had short straight tawny hair, remarkable jade-green eyes and strong bony features. After a year in London as an au pair she was studying medicine at Warsaw University. She described herself as 'a hybrid – doesn't that sound better than "mongrel"?' Her mother was half-Polish, half-Ukrainian, her Belorussian father had a German maternal grandmother whose own mother was Lithuanian. 'This is how history has mixed me up,' said Julia cheerfully. 'This is why I like the EU idea, let's all be Europeans not thinking about past conflicts and muddled genes.'

'So what's your native language?' I asked.

Julia laughed. 'I don't have one! I grew up bilingual, Polish and Russian. I've learned English and German because those are the important languages of science and communication. The French think that French is important but I can learn what I need without French. If you really speak only one language, that must make problems as you travel!'

'Yes,' I said, 'like the form-filling problem I hope you'll now solve for me.'

As Julia complied she chuckled over her task. 'Are you carrying weapons, explosives, dangerous chemicals, illegal drugs or more than two hundred cigarettes?'

I admitted to carrying three hundred mini-cigars, not an excessive ration for three months in cigarless territory. 'We'll ignore those,' decided Julia. 'No one will search you; you don't exactly look respectable, but you do look harmless. You know it was silly to buy cigars in London, they're much cheaper in Moscow. I smoke them, too; my friends in London said they were less dangerous than cigarettes.'

Julia's parents lived in Minsk; both were 'redundant' academics, now scratching a living as translators. 'My father is an idealist, wanting to bring democracy etcetera to Belarus. My mother thinks he's crazy and wants to live in Warsaw but she loves him so there they stay. I'm going now to my brother's wedding. He's an electrical engineer wanting to be a poet. He's marrying a mad Russian artist who only paints insects at work – as examples, she says, of how humans should organize the world. So we'll have more muddled genes!'

I glanced around at our fellow-passengers, animatedly conversing, and asked, 'What are they talking about?' Julia listened for a moment before replying, 'Prices, how much the Brest poor can gain by crossing the border. That's how they organize their world. I'm sorry for the Belarus people – always pushed around, still not knowing where they're going – or if they do, not knowing how to get there. You can see they're afraid to let go of the Soviet framework. Their past gives them no light for the future. My father says their nobles always deserted them, went over to the latest conqueror. They've no glorious peasant leaders to inspire them, no great military heroes. They've never had a chance to get an identity to be proud of, that's why my father feels it's a challenge and a duty to stay in Minsk.'

I wondered why my companion was so far off the Warsaw–Brest mainline – then regretted asking. Julia went tense, looked away, was distressed. Clumsily I tried to retrieve the situation, peering through the window, exclaiming at the overnight snowfall, remarking that in Ireland snow is a rarity.

Julia said, 'It's OK, a normal question. I've been to comfort the family of a close friend. He killed himself two weeks ago. A brilliant student, no motive except he thought too much about the future. Not his personal future – that was bright – but everyone's dark future. Looking down the vista of the new century terrified him. He didn't want to be there – that's what he said in his note.' As she spoke we were approaching an obscure platform at the perimeter of Brest station. 'Hurry!' urged Julia. 'Let's get out before the others – I can see my aunt waiting.'

Aunt Liza had sad eyes and a kind expression; long, voluminous fur-lined garments and a towering *shapka* emphasized her height. She lived in Brest, spoke no English and initially seemed ill-at-ease with her niece's unexpected companion. 'Not used to meeting foreigners,' Julia murmured apologetically while helping me drag the Dog through a labyrinth of shadowy passageways, tunnels and corridors.

We came to rest in a cavernous ticket hall-cum-waiting room, adjacent to the customs and immigration hall but resembling a barn rather than a salon. One wooden bench, seating six at a squash, stood against the wall near massive oak double doors, their fittings of tarnished brass. Aunt Liza noted bitterly that if young people get to this bench first they don't nowadays stand up for their elders, several of whom were leaning wearily on the antique radiators.

It was now 1.30 p.m. Julia's train departed at 3.0 and mine (the Prague–Moscow service) at 4.20. Many convoluted processes were involved in transferring me from the Cologne–Moscow service and the only clerk who could cope with all those telephone calls and sheaves of documents took her lunch-break at two o'clock. By the time she returned I had said goodbye to Julia – and, as I thought, to Aunt Liza. She, however, returned from the Minsk platform at 3.10 – to protect me, if necessary, from the bureaucrats and guide me to the correct platform. Without her, I might well have missed that train. Brest station lacks direction signs, in any language, and is disconcertingly unpopulated, at least in mid-winter. Between the waiting-barn and my platform we met no railway staff, no passengers, nobody.

This service had been through a severe blizzard; before the doors could be opened and the steps put down each coupé's *provodnitsa* had to hack off layers of frozen snow. Then a score or so of men appeared, armed with mallets and what looked like giant chisels, and spent forty minutes dislodging the long train's external cargo, giving the engine special treatment.

I was the only passenger embarking. Aunt Liza saw me into my empty four-bunk compartment and before I could prevent her had paid for my bedding – two sheets, a pillowcase and a towel in a sealed cellophane bag. (The cost is less than a dollar but every dollar counts when you live in Belarus.) Not realizing that I knew the ropes, she pulled a rolled-up mattress and blanket from a top bunk and made my bed. When I attempted to accompany her to the coupé door she shook her head and gestured eloquently: I must stay with my possessions. So we hugged in the corridor. As I had discovered on my previous journey, the Russian habit of hugging is very useful when gratitude has to be expressed without words. Aunt Liza and Julia more than made up for Stan and the consul.

True to form, we departed at 4.20 precisely, despite the blizzard. All the rolling stock parked on Brest's side tracks looked rusty and under-used – hundreds of freight wagons and scores of carriages. On Belarus's main track the train rocked too wildly for me to write my diary. Already the sun had set but the flat featureless snowscape glimmered for another half-hour; crossing Belarus by night would not, I decided, be too frustrating.

Taking my tea mug to the communal samovar at the end of the corridor I noticed that most passengers were asleep – had perhaps been asleep all day. One however was awake and alert, observed my foreignness, joined me at the samovar. An elegant middle-aged Muscovite, she spoke fluent English. 'You're a tourist? From which country? From Ireland! What a coincidence! Come join me for supper and I'll tell you why.'

'As a sociologist' – said Eva, while carving a chicken – 'Ireland greatly interests me at this time. The EU has completely changed your country, yes?' I nodded. 'Soon I must visit Ireland to analyse those changes – you like them?' I shook my head. 'No? Tell me why not – is it because you are an older person?'

I made a few superficial comments; while appreciating her hospitality, I was not warming to Eva. She had been on a six-weeks' tour of the EU's new recruits and would soon be explaining to her students why those governments were so happy to join the EU and NATO, to become satellites of the capitalist great powers. 'This surprises some of my students,' said Eva, 'but I can understand. The West is rich and strong, those countries are poor and weak. Their governments feel insecure about being independent, alone. All those people are used to belonging to something bigger than themselves – the Russian or Austrian empires, the Warsaw Pact. Their independence after World War I had bad endings. Now they can relax, getting EU funding and NATO weapons.'

I asked, 'Why do they need NATO weapons? Who's threatening them?'

Eva frowned, looked puzzled, then laughed at my naivety. 'Now every country needs to be well armed – the Mussulman, the Islamic terrorists, they threaten us all!'

As soon as courtesy permitted I retreated to my bunk and slept through both border crossings. After all that visa hoo-ha, nobody, in the small hours, came aboard to inspect documents. Then at some Russian station I was woken briefly when the ceiling light went on and two grumpy old men settled on the opposite bunk to unpack a multi-course meal.

At 7.0 a.m. in mid-winter, Belorusskaja station is not where people linger. While I was struggling with the Dog my fellow-passengers disappeared, a pattern that was becoming familiar. Twenty-two hours previously (the Cologne–Moscow service arrives at 9.07) Anna would have been anxiously pacing this platform, seeking her guest – so I had no address to show a taxi-driver.

In search of a telephone, I roamed through the station's many gloomy deserted corridors. In warm corners groups of Moscow's 80,000 homeless children were curled up; at first I mistook them for bundles of discarded rags. Then a tall, burly taxi man overtook me and asked, 'American tourist?' Having put him right I begged, 'Please, can you show me the telephones?' He glanced at his watch and said, 'None here until 8.0 when workers come.' This ploy was merciful in the circumstances. My rescuer rang Anna on his mobile and soon we were speeding along one of Moscow's racetrack-like boulevards, infested even before dawn with death-dealing drivers. Builders' cranes reared above snow-laden roofs. And cottage-sized billboards, garishly proclaiming the triumph of consumerism, seemed to have been breeding in my absence.

The taxi man asked, 'You stay how long in Moscow?'

'Thirty hours,' I replied.

2

Five Days to Lake Baikal

JOYOUSLY, AFFECTIONATELY, I approached a very long, olive green
train, its engine bright scarlet – BAM's Moscow–Tynda service
which departs from Kazan station thrice weekly at 1.10 p.m. In 2002
I had become a BAM junkie, partly because these trains' favourite
speed is 20 m.p.h. Unlike the Trans-Siberian they tend to be exter-
nally shabby though internally their *provodniki* insist on high standards
of cleanliness and tidiness.

Watching the platform scene from my coupé, I remembered the
observations of John Foster Fraser, a young Englishman who in
August 1901 embarked for Irkutsk on what was then the Siberian
Express. The heterogeneous throng diverted him. Jolly young officers
sporting gold straps on the shoulders of white linen uniforms were
being seen off by bejewelled noblewomen with liveried servants in
attendance. Drunken mechanics, their eyes glazed, cheerfully singing,
lurched towards fourth-class carriages. Stolid peasants – hair matted,
red shirts open-necked – said awkward farewells to squat, short-
skirted, unattractive (to Mr Fraser) wives. Felt-hatted American businessmen each needed several porters to push their trunks. A blushing
beardless army conscript received frantic kisses from his tearful old
babushka. As the train moved off everyone, whatever their condition,
blessed themselves. I marvelled to think that such was the Muscovite
scene in my own father's childhood. A century later Moscow offers
equally extreme but less picturesque contrasts – though not among
BAM passengers, generally a homogeneous lot. If richer they would
fly, if poorer they couldn't afford a train ticket.

In 1901, before the completion of the Trans-Siberian, Mr Fraser's
'Express' covered the 3,371 miles to Irkutsk in eight days. More luxurious than the modern Trans-Siberian, it boasted a restaurant car,
ladies' boudoir, library, piano, observation car, bathrooms (with baths)

and electric light. The railway had started a boom beyond the Urals; but for the neurotically secretive Soviets, southern Siberia would now seem to us no more remote or extraordinary than Canada.

This same comparison fascinated Mr Fraser, one of my notional companions on this trip; just before leaving home I had read his *The Real Siberia* (1902). A hardy young Englishman with a jaunty journalistic style, he was diligently inquisitive and prone to fervent outbursts of late Victorian jingoism. Another such companion – Charles Hawes, author of *In the Uttermost East* (1903) – wrote a more erudite account of his pioneering journey far from the railway (or any other) track. By the 1890s adventurous young Englishmen, whose forefathers had been restricted to educational Grand Touring around Europe with a tutor, often included Siberia in their solo tour of the world.

With only moments to spare, two young women breathlessly joined me. Olga, going all the way to Tynda, was tall and slender with a prodigious amount of luggage bearing Egyptian Airlines labels. Our *provodnitsa* (Maria, middle-aged trying to look younger) reprimanded her for stacking cartons on the vacant upper bunk, then crossly accepted that there was no alternative. Olga seemed either unwell or emotionally distressed; at once she silently retired to her upper bunk and remained there for thirty-six hours, apart from occasional trips to the samovar or the loo.

English-speaking Tanya ('I get degree for marketing tourism') was on a short journey to Murom, a small but heavily industrialized city. Chubby and spotty and voluble, she invited me to view her latest photograph album as Russian rail travellers are wont to do. It portrayed a group of proselytizing Mid-West evangelists visiting Moscow to encourage and enlarge their local flock. Most were youngsters wearing ingratiating smiles and given to playing guitars and drinking Coca-Cola in assembly halls decorated with multicoloured bunting that spelt out CHURCH OF BROTHERHOOD WITH THE LORD. Their leader-preacher stayed in the background, sometimes linking arms with new recruits. Tanya featured in every photograph, looking blissfully integrated.

'I give you a good book to read' – Tanya was rummaging through her shoulder bag – 'to teach about the Brotherhood. In Russia we have a bad church, they want keeping us in the past. We want going into the future, like Americans. God blesses America because they are democratic. Russian church wants keeping every power, not democratic. Three years before, I am meeting this democratic church and becoming happy. I change, I feel free, I know the Lord is there for me. My sister the same, ten years older than me, no religion before, not happy. Two years she was living with boyfriend, Maxim, living together not married. Then she got fond of another and went away to Moscow. After two years with him she got sorry because the Lord claimed her. A friend took her to a big party at the Brotherhood church. Then she saw everything, all her life what she did and felt, in new ways with light from the Lord. The Brothers sent her back to Maxim, she told him the Lord told her they must marry. The Brothers and Sisters in Texas said they could get a honeymoon for wedding present in US with six-months' visas. Last November they got married in the Brotherhood church in Murom – it is house, not real church. Now Maxim works for us in Texas, telling how Russians need Brothers' help to follow the Lord truly. And how much danger we have. The Orthodox Church hates us. It's sad my sister must come back after two weeks to not lose her good bank job. She won't see Maxim before the middle of May. A baby was coming but not now, the bank gives no holidays for having babies.' Tanya handed me a bundle of booklets, one in English, the rest in Russian. 'Please give them to young people who need the Lord, this country has a big need of light from the Lord.'

I murmured 'Thank you', put the booklets on my shelf and opened a bottle of beer – strong beer, Baltika No. 9. There was something touching about Tanya's zealous longing to help her contemporaries and if people need the Lord it's not for me to scoff at – or even question – that need. What bothered me was not the theological content of her story but the political sub-text. I hold no brief for the Russian Orthodox Church – not many do, nowadays, outside its own divided ranks. Yet I resented the Brotherhood's manipulation of the national Church's flaws to alienate young Russians from their own culture.

On our slow way through Moscow's dismal suburbs the icicles hanging from factory eaves had been three to four feet long. At Gus'-Khrustal'nyy, our first stop, they were five to six feet – and thicker. In the freezing dusk many men and women, mostly young-ish, were desperately hawking glassware – jugs, tumblers, wine glasses, vodka glasses, huge 'joke' brandy glasses used as vases or ornaments. These employees of a failing local glass factory, paid in kind not cash, worked only three days a week and spent the other four around the station. As our train came to a halt they besieged it, their rivalry fierce – degradingly so. The bargaining was ruthless, quite often becoming abusive. Here was poverty in action. I bought from three women, paying the reasonable asking price which irritated Tanya. After much haggling she bought two dozen wine glasses, four boxed sets of six. 'At home I sell for twice what I pay. This way we live. Gus'-Khrustal'nyy workers have no money to get to where they can sell for more.'

So what's new in the New Russia? Pre-Revolution travellers quite often made passing references to ill-paid industrial workers selling the fruits of their industry on the streets, with or without their employers' knowledge. And H. H. Fisher, an American historian who wrote a grimly fascinating account of the post-Revolution 'American Relief Administration', *The Famine in Soviet Russia, 1919–1923* (1927), recorded:

> The factory worker, if lucky enough to find work, managed to live by taking articles manufactured in his shop and selling them surreptitiously in the market . . . The practice of taking one's pay through pilferage or petty graft [was] so general in all forms of employment at the time, that it could not be described as dishonest without indicting the whole population . . .

'Why did you want to come back to Russia?' wondered Vera, a Muscovite acquaintance. Not an easy question for me to answer honestly so I muttered something vague about Siberia's multiple attractions. Vera might have taken umbrage, or felt patronized, by an admission that Russia's in-built ambiguities and current problems intrigue me.

Eurasia is more than a geographical term; nineteenth-century Russian writers commonly referred to 'Europe' as a place apart from their own empire, then being extended to the south and east. Long before those extensions, the few Europeans who ventured into Russia were prone to comment knowingly on the natives' Asian component, as though their mostly Slav ancestry had been permanently modified – psychologically if not physically – by a hundred and fifty years of total submission to Mongol rule. In 1591 Giles Fletcher from England judged the Russians to be culturally inferior to the Golden Horde, in almost every way. Travellers agreed that in general they were an uncouth people, irremediably corrupt and cruel, cunning rather than intelligent. Having taken their religious cue from Byzantium, and missed out on the Renaissance and Reformation, they needed authoritarian rule, were too undeveloped to cope with any more sophisticated political or legal system. England's jury trial, for example – could anyone imagine that system working in a czardom? Even the Russians' virtues were regarded as primitive: inebriating hospitality, embarrassingly lavish generosity, reckless physical courage, a capacity for enjoying the moment without much thought for the morrow. Those early Eurocentric travellers had it all worked out to their own satisfaction.

Later observers tended to be more historically aware and less cocky; they appreciated the nuances and were fascinated by the complexities, accentuated when one tyranny gave way to another. For me those ambiguities, combined with the friendships I had made in Siberia, acted like a magnet – though without speaking the language no one can hope to penetrate far below Russia's surface.

Post-Communist Russia had scarcely drawn its first breath when the free marketeers arrived – the Cold War victors, as they loudly described themselves. Led by the IMF and determined to control the vanquished, they were equipped with an arsenal of discredited economic theories which had already brought ruin to what used to be known as the Third World.

While the Soviet Union was falling apart faction fighting had broken out behind the scenes in Washington, between those favouring 'shock therapy' economic reform and the 'gradualists' who would have urged Russia to learn from China's carefully planned, long-drawn-out transition to a market economy. Even at the time outside observers – ordinary people, equipped only with common sense, lacking any specialist knowledge of either Russia or economics – could foresee that the gradualists would do less damage. Yet the IMF shock therapists, egged on by the US Treasury, won decisively. What both factions dreaded was a regression to Communism, a revival of the notion that Gorbachev's *perestroika* could be made to work.

Stalin's regime had subjected countless millions to hardships and cruelties beyond description. But after his death in 1953, and Khrushchev's denunciation of Stalinism at the Twentieth Party Congress in 1956, two generations undoubtedly benefited from Soviet Communism even while its foundations were being eroded by corruption, incompetence and the arms race. Ordinary subjects of the czar had never enjoyed freedom to travel, freedom of speech and assembly, or any other 'inalienable democratic rights'. What Soviet citizens did enjoy was freedom from worry about jobs, housing, heating, education, health care, pensions. Although the implacable pursuit and punishment of dissidents continued after 1956, the mass of the population could then lead a notably less stressful life than their forefathers – not to mention foremothers – before 1917.

However, the IMF has always failed to realize that 'market reform' is not a free-standing phenomenon, a good thing of itself if efficiently implemented by highly trained economists. Human beings are involved, with all their varied needs and desires, prejudices and traditions, strengths and weaknesses, habits of mind and social institutions. Russia's plunge into national destitution began when the IMF and its allies dismissed as irrelevant all the advice offered by alarmed Russian economists, historians and social anthropologists. The Cold War victors proclaimed that only capitalism rampant could make things better for those just 'rescued from Communism'. Their shock therapy was another move (though even for its proponents' sake a mistaken one) in the globalizers' campaign to impose market forces on the whole world.

During the 1990s Moscow spent on the military only one-fifth of the former Soviet allocation – a saving which alone should have raised the general standard of living. But simultaneously Russia's gross domestic product was falling annually at a faster rate than during the Second World War. Industrial production fell by 24 per cent in the period 1940–46; in the 1990s it fell by 60 per cent.

So what was going on? Privatization, of course – and shock therapy allowed no time for the setting up of those legal and financial structures essential to control it. Thus the IMF, World Bank and US Treasury begat an unrestrained oligarchy eager to stamp on those seedlings of democracy – visible in corners of the Kremlin – which the West claimed to be nurturing.

People's savings vanished in 1992 when most prices were freed without warning and inflation took over at a gallop – then had to be curbed by dramatically raising interest rates. The IMF lent more billions to avert devaluation – $4.8 billion in July 1998, just before the rouble crashed and devaluation happened anyway. After that, contrary to IMF predictions, the economy began to show some slight signs of life.

Oil is among Russia's main exports and in 1992 one of the most important prices ('natural resources') was not freed. Since 1989 vulturine members of the Soviet nomenklatura had been gathering around the dying Soviet Union, hungry to strip the carcass of its assets. Their official positions gave them easy access to the national oil reserves and overnight millions – sometimes billions – could be made by buying cheaply and selling on to the West. Those vultures became founder members of the new oligarchy; at supersonic speed their loot found its way to the US stock market or into untraceable offshore bank accounts. No tax inspectors tried to dam this torrent; in newly 'liberated' Russia such creatures were unknown. 'Instant privatization' had also cleared the way for other crooks to take over numerous state institutions and industries and rapidly the oligarchy expanded. By 1998 Russia had qualified as the world's most indebted country and in April 2000 the *Financial Times* reported 'a conservative estimate that since 1993 between $130 and $140 billion have been lost to Russia'. Over the same period direct foreign investment came to $10 billion and IMF and World Bank loans to $25 billion.

Few Russians were surprised when Anatoly Chubais, the Kremlin's privatization director, was invited in 2000 to the home of Lawrence Summers, Deputy US Treasury Secretary. This invitation indicated (among other things) that the Treasury was 'in denial', still arguing that more loaned billions would enable Russia to take off, at last, in the required direction. By then other Washington factions were admitting that everything had gone horribly wrong in Russia and that the IMF and Treasury were tainted not only by their failure to prevent – or at least denounce – mega-scams but by the well-founded popular belief that several senior Western officials had participated in them. Long before the European and US media exposed all this, the Duma's Inspector-General had provided Washington with a detailed dossier, sending the administration into a cover-up frenzy. This included an attempt to bully an independent-minded senior World Bank official, Joseph Stiglitz, who in 1999 had been invited to Moscow 'to open a discussion unfettered by either IMF ideology or US Treasury's special interests'. Prompted by the Treasury, the World Bank president ordered Mr Stiglitz (the Bank's Chief Economist!) not to go. In *Globalization and its Discontents* (2002) Joseph Stiglitz explains: 'While Treasury would like to think of the World Bank as its own property, other countries can, when carefully orchestrated, outflank even the US Treasury secretary. And so it happened here: with the appropriate calls and letters from Russia, I proceeded to Russia to do what the Russians had asked.'

Mr Stiglitz is not the sort who marches with a banner when capitalists are conspiring on summits. However, having himself operated within the sordid engine-room of the capitalist ship, he has much of interest to say:

> For the majority of those living in the former Soviet Union, economic life under capitalism has been even worse than the old Communist leaders had said it would be . . . By siding so firmly for so long with those at the helm when huge inequality was created through the corrupt privatization process, the USA, IMF and the international community have indelibly associated themselves with policies that, at best, promoted the interests of the wealthy at the expense of the average Russian.

Quite so. Here lies part of the answer to that question so often asked in the US after 11 September 2001 – 'Why do people hate us?'

Beyond the Urals there was a considerable surprise: noticeably less snow than in European Russia. One visualizes Siberia as a vastness snow-smothered for most of the year. Not so, however. Snow there is, from October to May or September to June, depending on the latitude, but in many regions it is quite sparse and ice is the most conspicuous feature.

A certain camaraderie soon becomes apparent amongst long-distance passengers, those who are relaxed on the train because it will be 'home' for five or six days – or longer. Their journey is a whole chunk of life with its own distinctive rhythm to which people adjust on settling into the compartment, arranging possessions, defining personal interests, arriving at polite compromises if interests conflict. The short-distance passengers, on board for a mere eight, twelve or twenty-four hours, are usually more restless, impatient to get to their destination, regarding time on a train as a boring but unavoidable interruption of daily life. To the last category belonged those two young women who had replaced Tanya by the time I awoke next morning.

Lying on my bunk, I could hear the irregular clangorous thumping, up and down Izhevsk's platform, of frozen snow being knocked off wheels – an essential routine at every halt. Our coupé's temperature was mercifully lowered at night but on my way to the samovar I saw Maria stoking the coal stove; soon the pipes were too hot to touch and I was stripping to my T-shirt.

Izhevsk is a large industrial city with an imposing station building – high, long, severely handsome. Its façade, newly painted white, matched the new snow all around. This was a sunless dawn, crows wheeling against a low silver-grey sky.

An hour later we were crossing a wide river, smoothly snow-blanketed. Was this the Belaya, the Kama or the Kolva? Such a tangle of rivers wriggles across the map that I failed to identify it. Near a large village, schoolchildren were struggling through thigh-deep snow while their dogs merrily rolled in it. Alone on that short platform a recklessly ungloved man straddled his suitcase drinking from a thermos, awaiting a local train. Far beyond this village, in the middle of nowhere, a solitary woman wearing snowshoes toiled up the steep embankment carrying two lidded buckets. Then a blizzard came, obliterating the landscape.

Towards noon the compartment's newcomers awoke; neither spoke English but their boss did. They belonged to a six-person team commissioned by some dodgy Moscow-based company to promote alternative medicines in Western Siberia. Alexei, their extrovert leader, was very tall, sensationally good-looking and clearly pleased to be leading five personable young women into the wilderness; none had ever before crossed the Urals. This lively, gregarious group spent the rest of the day squeezed into my compartment, giggling and chattering and eating substantial meals linked by not insubstantial snacks.

For my benefit Alexei displayed his wares, guaranteed to cure constipation and diarrhoea, earache and backache, obesity and diabetes, lethargy and asthma, stress and acne – and other more exotic ailments unknown to me. There were brightly packaged herbal teas, tiny brown glass phials of strange-smelling liquids, bottles of lotions and tonics ('from Laos, Korea, Tibet'), sachets of powdered this and that (Alexei was reluctant to say what), pills of every size, shape, colour and texture – and, most innovative of all, a.m. and p.m. toothpastes in dumpy glass jars. Different formulae, it seems, are needed because our nocturnal saliva corrodes our teeth and p.m. toothpaste – the humdrum sort – only counters food corrosion. My impression was that the team genuinely believed in the efficacy of its wares – which impression, even if mistaken, must have improved their chances as salespersons.

When Alexei urged me to test the anti-lethargy cure I imbibed a phial of sticky brown liquid, odd to the palate but not unpleasant. However, lethargy is not among my problems so I was an unsuitable guinea pig. All these samples had been carefully arranged in a portable display-case (each of the team had one) and they made quite a pretty picture. Someone had invested a considerable amount in this enterprise. The labels were multilingual – the company hoped to expand its market to the US – and the precision of the English suggested help from a native speaker. Or was the entrepreneur a native speaker? The tonics and lotions had descriptions and directions in, allegedly, Tibetan. Alexei seemed genuinely taken aback when I warned him that whatever this language might be, it most certainly was not Tibetan. It may have been a phoney concoction, like the bottles' contents.

At dusk the reclusive Olga (I had almost forgotten her existence) swung down from her bunk, ignored everybody, carefully made up her face in the door mirror and ate a small supper before settling to contemplate dozens of photographs which soon caused tears to flow. Then Alexei, looking sympathetic, moved to sit beside her and laid a hand on her forearm – which gesture burst the dam of reserve.

At the end of her sob-choked story, Alexei gave me a résumé. Olga and a female friend had won a Moscow women's magazine prize, a week in Egypt. On their second day in Cairo she had fallen in love with an Egyptian of her own age: twenty. He was a medical student, she a hairdresser. For the following five days (and nights) they were together. They were not only body but soul mates, she could never love anyone else. They wanted to marry, but his family would reject him if he married a non–Muslim; her family would reject her if she married a Muslim. He had promised to find a holiday job in Moscow during the summer but she didn't believe he could afford to travel . . .

The thirty-five-year-old Alexei commented, 'This is a sad thing for a small time, it happens when people are young. Next month Olga will love a Russian. Her family is right. To marry a Muslim is stupid,

stupid! They are bad people, hating women. A Russian woman in Egypt would be unhappy, unfree – here women are the same as men.'

The team presented me with samples in bulk. 'Take them to Ireland,' urged Alexei, giving me his card. 'Tell if Irish people like them, then we could expand that way.'

At Ekaterinburg, two neatly uniformed junior officers, going all the way to Tynda, took over the vacant bunks. They were perfunctorily polite to the babushka, appreciatively attentive to the beautiful Olga. Very soon she had put away her handkerchief.

As the sun rose through a golden glow of cloud I sipped my tea standing alone in the corridor. No one else was awake, not even Maria. Beneath a clear sky the marshy West Siberian Plain stretched brilliant and limitless, its whiteness modified at intervals by miles of tall russet reeds. The tracks of snowshoes, skis and sledges were somehow startling as evidence of human activity. Only occasionally did a distant black dot appear, someone going – apparently – from nowhere to nowhere. Mobility is of course easier in winter over West Siberia's countless square miles of marshland – treacherous terrain during the short hot summers.

Omsk's nearness was signalled by a drab band of pollution lying above the horizon, long and menacing. By this stage both forest (the taiga) and marshes had been left behind. Less than 100 miles to the south was the border with Kazakhstan and beneath the snow lay those grassy steppes which for so many non-colonized, pre-industrial centuries supported the enormous herds of horses and cattle of several nomadic tribes.

Omsk is a dreary city of 1.3 million, 560 miles east of Ekaterinburg, overlooking the confluence of the Om and Irtysh rivers. Founded in 1716 as a Cossack fort – the origin of most Siberian settlements – it became in 1824 the Siberian governor-general's administrative centre. During Russia's Civil War the ferocious Admiral Kolchak made it his anti-Bolshevik headquarters and the local Cossacks, who owned 70 per cent of the province's arable land, fought with him. In November 1919, when 'White' French and British troops marched into Omsk, a ludicrous ceremony took place proclaiming Kolchak 'Supreme Ruler of Russia'. As James Forsyth records in *A History of the Peoples of Siberia* (1992):

Kolchak devoted himself with zeal to the task of defeating the Red Army, while in rural areas his men resorted to violent means to extract grain for the towns and to conscript peasants for service in the White Army, terrorizing the population and burning villages as mercilessly as the Japanese and Cossack atamans were doing in the Far East. As a result, the Siberian peasants, who until the summer of 1918 had been largely passive towards the revolution, were now forced to protect themselves against the Whites by organizing guerrilla bands.

After the Red Army's victory Kolchak fled east, only to be captured in Irkutsk by the Mensheviks from whom the Bolsheviks seized him. On 7 February 1920 he was shot and his corpse pushed through a hole in the river ice.

On Omsk's platforms railway staff of both sexes were using pick-axes to shatter the grey-brown ice, then shovelling huge thick slabs onto already existing hillocks. Here the 'industrial hawkers' were selling television sets and transistor radios. Unlike the glass workers they came on board (this is a long stop) and the dealing was not frenzied, perhaps because so brisk. Some traders sold out and urgently yelled to their comrades for replenishments. The young officers each bought a transistor to be sold on in Tynda, a town neither of them knew. I hoped they wouldn't be disappointed; Tynda is sufficiently far east to be offered such goods at bargain prices by the Chinese.

At long stops most passengers wrap up and get off, seeking sustenance: fresh bread, dried fish, hot potato cakes and roast chickens, salami, pickled cucumbers, ice creams, fizzy drinks, soup refills for giant thermos flasks, *pivo* (beer) in two-litre plastic bottles. These are jolly interludes, the passengers happy to have fresh air and exercise, the vendors happy to have customers – no haggling, bonhomie all round. The fresh air comes as a bit of a shock: from one's tropical coupé to −20°C or so. Several passengers and food-sellers were concerned about my clothing, fingered my expensive jacket and slacks and voiced alarm. Siberians scorn our synthetic hi-tech, high-altitude garments. When the cold gets real you wear *fur* – fur on the outside and wool on the inside. Here those fur coats ostracized in temperate climes are not ostentatious luxuries.

Before the arrival of the Trans-Siberian an earth road, the *trakt* – the 'Great Moscow Trakt' – formed the first continuous land route to the

Chinese border. Begun in 1763 and famous in its day, it seems scarcely less of an achievement than the railway, given the available technology. But the felling of wide swathes of taiga and the provision of a surface smooth enough for sledges – and, in summer, wheeled vehicles – had dire consequences. As Russian posts and villages proliferated, the nearby terrain became accessible to corrupt government officials, slash-and-burn peasant settlers, proselytizing priests and predatory traders. Also, the eastward flow of political prisoners and convicted criminals increased with the length of the *trakt*. In James Forsyth's words, 'As the frontier of settlement . . . moved steadily forward at the expense of the forest, the animal and human life it sustained was killed or driven farther to the east and north.'

In the sixteenth and seventeenth centuries Siberia's innumerable rivers had made possible Russia's exploration and annexation of northern Asia. But ice limited river traffic and maintaining fleets of barges and boats was costly. From the 1790s many of these were replaced by caravans of sledges or carts – though to this day the remoter regions depend on rivers, as I saw for myself in 2002 on a 1,300-mile paddle-steamer trip down the Lena.

However, the changes initiated by the *trakt* were fairly gradual, unlike those experienced a century or so later when the Trans-Siberian caused social upheavals similar to those suffered by many in our own day as motor roads abruptly expose remote regions to 'development'. Onto the train leaped itinerant merchants and resourceful kulaks (prosperous peasant farmers) from overcrowded European Russia, rich Austrian bankers, poor but daring cosmopolitan chancers, skilled mining engineers from South Africa and the United States, theory-ridden Swedish agronomists, versatile German speculators alert to any gainful opportunity, shrewd Danish butter merchants – all ambitious, all heading east. Russia's recent influx of greedy foreigners is not without precedent.

Investors talked excitedly about Siberia's immeasurable hidden wealth (gold, coal, tin, iron, lead), about its unimaginable, inexhaustible store of timber, about south-west Siberia's wheat-growing potential – soon it could beat the US and Canada on the world market! As yet oil had not been discovered, though it was already very Big Biz around Baku. There twenty refineries, owned by John D. Rockefeller's Standard Oil Company, had been in action since 1873 –

Azerbaijan's oil having been discovered soon after Russia grabbed the territory from the Ottomans in the early nineteenth century.

All this entrepreneurial enthusiasm delighted the czar's government. In European Russia the political pot was simmering ever faster; Siberia's development, it was thought, might solve some problems. At about the same time Peter Stolypin, Nicholas II's prime minister, was funding the transplantation to Central Asia of millions of Russian peasants, their mission to grow cotton. Wheat-growing on the southern steppes particularly appealed to his administration; they eagerly imported the latest agricultural machinery from the US – heavy, soil-damaging machinery.

The Omsk-centred export of butter to England began in 1896 when a Dane, resident in St Petersburg, chanced to notice the excellent quality of Siberian butter. Only four years later 30,000 buckets of butter, each containing thirty-six pounds, were being regularly despatched to England during the summer. Every week five trains, the wagons specially refrigerated and painted white, left Omsk for Riga. That Dane had launched a commercial rocket. Soon fourteen butter-exporting firms were competing in Omsk, thirteen run by Danes, the biggest owned by a Russian Jew. At every little railway halt butter was bought from peasants, who might have transported their suddenly valuable produce twenty or thirty miles on a horse-cart.

Initially these foreign developers, rapidly pushing modernization to increase output, came up against various prejudices and superstitions. The replacement of hand churns by steam-driven separators outraged many dairy farmers who asserted that no machine could possibly make butter. When the separators did just that, a minority of hardliners protested that the devil must be involved and wrecked the machines. Scythes also had to be discarded in favour of reaping machines to save more hay to feed more cows to produce more milk. This change quickly became acceptable; government loans and grants were available. The US manufacturers of such machines already had eight American salesmen based in summertime Omsk, a prompt reaction to the government's new agricultural policy. Their influence partly explained why the 1900 sugar beet crop showed a tenfold increase on that of 1899.

During the late afternoon I perched on one of the corridor's little pull-down seats to enjoy the prolonged sunset – prolonged because we were going due east. (Going west at BAM-speed is an even odder experience, when the dawn is equally prolonged.) Several other passengers soon joined me. It had been a blizzard-free day and now, below a milky blue meridian, slim dove-grey clouds trailed across the southern sky. To the north, beyond gleaming white flatness, miles of coniferous forest stood out blackly against a curtain of molten gold. For an hour or more, while the slim clouds turned rosy, a weirdly static crimson orb remained poised above the trees, not sinking perceptibly. Then very, very slowly it disappeared – and a wondrously lingering red-gold suffusion tinged the whole landscape until even the dark taiga glowed. When at last the dusk came we all silently exchanged smiles; words would only have been banal.

Next morning, seen through Krasnoyarsk's penumbra of pollution, the rising sun had a jaundiced look. This city, another Cossack foundation, has been dangerously polluted since the Second World War when Stalin moved most factories to Siberia. Its major industries being war-related, no foreigners were allowed to leave the railway station in the pre-Gorbachev era.

Here a spectacular bridge spans the Yenisey river, more than a mile wide and not, to my surprise, iced over. Perhaps because of the colossal Divnogorsk hydroelectric dam twenty miles upstream? Or because (so everyone told me) Siberia was having a mild winter? This river flows across the whole of Siberia on its way to the Arctic Ocean from the Sayan mountains on the Mongolian frontier. It separates Western and Eastern Siberia and to me feels much more emotionally significant than the Urals – mere mini-mountains forming an unexciting boundary between Russia-in-Europe and Siberia's most developed region. East of the Yenisey the landscape becomes increasingly unpredictable: sometimes mountainous, always austerely beautiful. What are confusingly known as the Central Siberian Uplands (average altitude 2,000 feet) have for aeons been in the grip of permafrost. This makes the construction of railways, roads and bridges extraordinarily dangerous and difficult – and uneconomic, unless a very big pot of gold lies at the terminus. In most regions food production (as we understand the term) is impossible, elsewhere it is difficult. Hence Eastern Siberia remains to this day largely undeveloped and sparsely populated. In 1710, when Western Siberia had 247,000 Russian settlers, only 66,000 were braving the lands beyond the Yenisey. Over the next two centuries the total population gradually increased, to 9.4 million (89 per cent Slav) in 1911; but the West–East proportions hardly changed.

Around Krasnoyarsk the snow was a thin, soiled, threadbare sheet. Then, as we climbed laboriously into the partially forested uplands, it became a thick, spotless blanket. Our coupé was mid-train and where the track curved sharply I delighted in gazing out from a corridor window, able to see both our gallant red engine, far away to the left, and our final green freight wagon far away to the right. There is something disarmingly romantic about these long BAM trains – seeming toylike amidst the vastness – chugging slowly through the unpeopled stillness of Eastern Siberia.

This was Day Four and Maria (a kindly soul, despite first impressions) had begun to worry about me; I wasn't eating enough, only fistfuls of nuts and raisins now and again. Dictionary in hand, I tried to explain that unexercised babushkas need minimal sustenance. But my message didn't get through and at noon Maria firmly escorted me to the restaurant car, sensibly eschewed by 99 per cent of passengers; its meals are meagre, insipid and expensive – even more expensive, I now saw, than in 2002, keeping pace with the rising train fares. When Maria had hastened away (*provodniki* feel uneasy about leaving their charges unsupervised) I ordered a *pivo* for three times the normal price from one of two underworked waitresses sitting behind the bar doing crossword puzzles. At the other occupied table sat a balding, pot-bellied railway security officer enjoying free *pivos* and breaking the law by smoking. That vice is permitted only in cramped, seatless vestibules, unventilated and in winter refrigerated. The nicotine-enslaved may often be seen passing along the corridors wearing outdoor garb.

Happily the restaurant advertisements displayed in every coupé – vividly coloured photographs of heaped plates, an innovation since 2002 – had not yet weaned passengers off their home-cooked picnics, augmented by platform vendors' dishes. These gross pictures are said to be extremely effective in our world, artificially stimulating the appetites of passers-by who have not even begun to think about their next meal. Everywhere one notices them becoming bigger, brighter and more numerous – while government departments and health experts and Special Commissions increasingly agitate about obesity. How topsy-turvy can the free market get?

From Krasnoyarsk to Taishet is a ten-hour meander, 245 miles through low, irregularly shaped rock mountains, their taiga cover mainly larch: west of the Yenisey, fir and spruce predominate. Sometimes the track ran level along ridge-tops, and much higher mountains — smooth-crested ranges — were visible far away to the north beyond narrow ravines, shallow bowl-valleys, bare boulder-strewn slopes and free-standing, densely forested conical hills as yet unmolested by loggers. In the crystal air these distant ranges seemed quite close. Above their radiant whiteness the clear noon sky was tinted an exquisite pale green — a colour surely unique to the region, nowhere else have I seen anything comparable. Overhead floated cotton wool cloudlets, round and fluffy and stationary: one half-expected to glimpse lyre-holding cherubs peeping around their edges. During the afternoon these were replaced by grey moving masses and the sun had to struggle to shine.

Apart from the railway, humankind has made no mark in this area. But other creatures, both furred and feathered, make many marks and at BAM's speed their numerous footprints, weaving patterns in the snow, were easily identified by Viktor, a Krasnoyarsk mining engineer who had grown up in a village and knew its wildlife. As we stood at a corridor window he would exclaim at intervals: 'Chipmunk!' — 'Polecat!' — 'Fox!' — 'Squirrel!' — 'Eagle!' — 'Wolf!' Sometimes elk hoof-prints crossed the track and continued in a purposeful straight line into the taiga. In summer, Viktor said, brown bears are also common but hereabouts sable are seen no more — though they do survive elsewhere in Siberia. He explained the prevalence of the larch: shallow roots give it an advantage in permafrost territory and by shedding its leaves it reduces water loss.

An hour short of Taishet we crossed the wide Tagut river — one of several tributaries of the Biryusa which is one of several tributaries of the Taseyva which is one of innumerable tributaries of the Angara which is the main tributary of the Yenisey. From the bridge we could see twelve men busy on the thick ice, pulling their supper out of holes bored that morning. 'Hard work,' observed Viktor. 'You have family needs food, you don't stop fishing when ice comes.'

During our descent to Taishet the south-western sky staged a muted sunset, all pale pink. We arrived at 6.0 p.m. local time, 1.0 p.m. Moscow time, exactly four days since pulling out of Kazan station.

Here the BAM line diverges from the Trans-Siberian and goes its own way to Vanino on the Pacific coast, 560 miles north of Vladivostok.

Viktor invited me to his coupé and offered vodka. Admitting to a preference for *pivo*, I fetched a bottle from my own carriage. Viktor looked puzzled. 'Why you like *pivo*? I think in Ireland everyone drinks much whiskey, mixing with coffee – yes?'

'Not really,' I said. 'Even if they wanted to they couldn't afford it at the equivalent of 750 roubles a bottle.'

Viktor yelped with horrified astonishment, then caressed his half-litre bottle. 'For this *fifty* roubles! In your country how much?'

'Same as whiskey,' I replied. 'Yet somehow our youngsters – too young to drink any alcohol – seem able to afford it. It's their favourite drink, they imagine its fumes are not detectable.'

Viktor looked gloomy, poured himself a second vodka and declared, 'Vodka is bad, it makes much big trouble for Russia. I have sorry for Ireland if vodka goes there.'

My biological clock had me up long before dawn and I sat entranced in the corridor. Given a snowy landscape and a clear sky there can be no darkness; by starlight all the world is quietly luminous, the details obscure but the outlines distinct. Having gained altitude during the night – up to 4,500 feet – we were now in that sternly magnificent range forming the western shore of Lake Baikal and extending for hundreds of miles to the north. Here lay an abundance of new snow and every tree held gleaming, grotesquely shaped burdens, balanced improbably on fragile branches, defying gravity. Close to the track, on both sides, rose chunky rough-hewn peaks 6,000 foot high linked by serrated ridges. Dramatic U-bends are frequent and, where the jostling mountains allowed no way through, BAM-builders completed a four-mile tunnel in three years and eight months. The Baikal Mountain Tunnel is thus known as the 'easiest' of all the BAM's many tunnels.

Towards nine o'clock a splendour of redness spread quickly across the eastern sky, then was reflected by peaks and escarpments to the north. But the mountain walls ahead concealed the sun until a final U-turn marked the beginning of our three-hour descent to Severobaikalsk, via the narrow Tyya valley.

When I began to pack up, the young officers pooled their strength to manoeuvre the Dog down from my upper storage space – a hazardous operation, that load of books having concussion potential. They then discreetly withdrew while I exchanged my T-shirt for a Damart vest and longjohns and two woolly sweaters. The Damart underwear, bought in 1978 for an Andean trek, was still effective. (N.B. – Damart do not sponsor me, nor does anyone else, but in our throwaway society goods of such remarkable quality and durability deserve praise.)

On this approach to Severobaikalsk Lake Baikal is invisible and while I gazed with affection at familiar landmarks my companions gazed with indifference at the town's unlovely suburbs. Too visible are huge trackside dumps of BAM-construction leftovers: rusty lengths of metal, stacks of rotting wood, long-since-cannibalized machinery, skeletal passenger wagons. When work was completed, a quarter of a century ago, someone calculated that it would be uneconomic to tidy up. Then there's the Old Town, a sprawl of wooden shacks with tin roofs and crooked stove-chimneys – the homes of the original BAM-builders. These were meant to be temporary dwellings; soon everyone would be housed in fine apartment blocks. But another Plan went wrong; not enough blocks were built and the shacks remain occupied to this day – some by good friends of mine.

From afar we could also see a high pedestrian bridge spanning multiple tracks where several freight trains, at least one hundred wagons long, were loaded with snow-lidded cargoes of timber or coal. Near the main platform a conspicuous six-storey building stood alone: the BAM Workers' Polyclinic, its external decor red, yellow and white. Beyond it rose Severobaikalsk's pride and joy, the cream-painted railway station, best described as a cross between the QE II and a Corbusier theatre. Allegedly its architect was a closet dissident influenced by the design of a 1960s Texan Christian Zionist church. But this allegation strains credulity, sounding like another of those fantastical rumours so keenly relished by Russians. Did Christian Zionists exist in the 1960s?

Our pace had now become funereal and I looked suspiciously at my watch. Sure enough it was only 1.57 and by continuing at 10 m.p.h. we would have arrived early – not at 2.05, as the Moscow time-table stated. That's centralization, that is.

3

The Free Market Comes to Severobaikalsk

IN 2002 SEVEROBAIKALSK became my refuge when two minor but disabling accidents frustrated a plan to cycle around the Russian Far East. In the August heat Lake Baikal provided aqua-therapy (four swims a day) and the BAM-builder population provided a host of kind friends who cared for me until I was fit enough to travel around Eastern Siberia by BAM and paddle-steamer. I then decided to leave Pushkin, my Moscow-bought bicycle, in Severobaikalsk and return there in July the following year: but for family reasons already explained my return had to be postponed. So now Plan C was in place and at the beginning of March, when I had been to the Pacific coast, Pushkin and I would set off from Severobaikalsk by BAM – and eventually by faster trains – to Rostov-on-Don, in southern European Russia, where the spring thaw would have rendered the roads bicycle-friendly.

I had left Severobaikalsk in mid-October when the thermometers outside living-room windows hovered around zero and the first tentative snowfalls quickly melted – to be replaced overnight. On nearby hills the taiga remained colourful, and Lake Baikal moved restlessly under a sombre sky. Fifteen months later I stepped off the train into brilliant sunshine – almost warm – and a bracing temperature of −15°C. This region is of course atypical; the lake acts as a storage heater, even when its frozen surface can bear the weight of motor vehicles.

It has to be admitted that the BAM Zone town of Severobaikalsk, built in the early 1970s, is not beautiful. From the station a wide street, Leningradski Prospekt, slopes gently up to the central square between stark rows of six-storey apartment blocks. In summer grassy embankments and gay flowerbeds separate the Prospekt from raised footpaths. In mid-winter everything lies under old, discoloured snow. January's low temperatures halt the blizzards; in February they start again and continue, on and off, into April.

My two-roomed, town-centre flat, unchanged since last I rented it, seemed oven-like. Unless crippled by 'economic reforms', Siberia's municipal central heating plants provide tropical temperatures throughout every elaborately insulated apartment block. Only summer garments are worn indoors, then it takes ten minutes to dress warmly enough to cross the road to a shop. Luckily each window has a ventilation pane, some six inches square and normally opened infrequently and briefly. By leaving these permanently ajar I achieved a personally comfortable temperature, not appreciated by my visitors.

The first visitor brought worrying news about a mutual friend, Larisa, who had attended university in one of Western Siberia's most polluted cities. After graduation, in 2002, all the women in her class were formally warned to avoid pregnancy for at least three years – preferably four. When first we had met, Larisa was suffering from chronic respiratory problems and a recurring facial rash. That September she started her teaching career and six months later developed a puzzling heart malfunction, quite frightening though not severe enough to be incapacitating. Severobaikalsk's doctors – a depleted corps, handicapped by a 90 per cent cut in their funding since 1992 – failed to make a diagnosis. Larisa's mother then borrowed roubles to pay for investigations in Irkutsk. There, too, the doctors were baffled; they recommended Moscow's leading cardiology clinic. Fifteen years earlier, Larisa would have received free health care; now she was expected to pay all her medical expenses on a junior teacher's annual salary of $360. Reluctantly she moved to Moscow, which she hates, and found work as an interpreter – her English is excellent. Friends urged her to borrow, arguing bluntly that given a dicky vital organ she might well be dead before she could earn the necessary fees. But borrowing is not easy for the poor. When Larisa made enquiries, 25 per cent interest was the minimum demanded – and who wants to become indefinitely embroiled with mafia-flavoured moneylenders?

In IMF terms, this is 'Health Reform'. As Paul Farmer has noted in *Pathologies of Power* (2003): 'The steady dismantling of the Soviet-era health infrastructure occurred at the same time as the social safety net was ripped apart.'

On my way to visit friends in the Old Town I approached the central square after dark and saw something utterly astonishing – an enormous glittering fortification. Momentarily I mistook it for a glass construction, so clear and sparkling were those massive ice blocks hewn from Lake Baikal, then cut with a stonemason's skill. Thick eight-foot-high walls, 200 yards in circumference, incorporated soaring towers, pointed pillars, arched entrances. Small electric bulbs embedded in the ice illuminated the entire edifice so discreetly that one registered only a magical silver effulgence, not its source. From within this fort at 7.0 p.m. on a Sunday (temperature −19°C) came sounds of excited merriment; dozens of children, and not a few adults, were having fun on slides sculpted from high hills of frozen snow. Some slides had challenging S-bends demanding strong nerves and sound judgement, others were suited to the three- and four-year-olds who zoomed down on tiny plastic tray-like seats, squealing with glee. In the centre of this 'fort' stood a thirty-foot New Year tree, lavishly decorated, from which hung a giant Father North (only a name change, he wears Santa's gear). I was to discover that most Siberian municipalities are equally ingenious in their use of natural resources to provide the public with three months of free enjoyment. But will the spreading 'compensation culture' end all such limb-threatening activities?

Next morning I set out by starlight on what used to be a fifteen-minute walk to Lake Baikal – across BAM's pedestrian bridge, through a thin strip of taiga. Now the underfoot ice slowed me, a nasal icicle soon formed and my breath produced a hoar-frost cravat. As I stood on the high cliff above the lake, a greyness tinged with saffron spread above the unbroken line of mighty mountains overlooking the eastern shore. Below me lay an almost eerie scene: Baikal's silent immobility, colourless in the dawn light, extending south for 400 frozen miles. On calm summer days the intensely blue lake is still, serene – yet liquidly alive, subtly responding to sunlight and air currents. In mid-winter it is unresponsive to everything, has become introverted, oblivious to sun or wind, seemingly lifeless. But of course only seemingly – beneath the ice life goes on as usual and by noon fishermen are busy around their drilled holes.

On my way down to the shore the sun rose, half-veiled by wisps of copper-tinted vapour. Walking on Baikal gave me a childish thrill; I was juvenile enough to photograph my footprints in the snow. A few hundred yards offshore a long ridge of angular ice-boulders puzzled me; later, my friend Rashit Yasin explained them. Violent equinoctial gales, common as the freeze begins, shatter the new ice and fling it about – while simultaneously the temperature is dropping fast, causing those broken chunks to form ridges.

A tiresome bureaucratic problem abbreviated this reunion with Lake Baikal. The Belarus hiatus had left me no time in Moscow for visa-registration, compulsory within forty-eight hours of entering the Federation. My 2004 'business class' version of The Great Russian Visa Scam had involved an £84 fee to a London agent who organized a phoney 'letter of invitation' which, when passed to the Russian Embassy in Dublin, entitled me to a €65 three-month visa. Then I should have paid a $15 registration fee in an indeterminate Moscow office where state bureaucracy and private enterprise seem to mingle. Once you've found the office, that procedure takes mere minutes – not so, however, in Severobaikalsk.

When my hostess of 2002, Raia Yasin, volunteered to help me I demurred; she is a busy elderly woman with a semi-invalid husband. Luckily my gesture of independence was ignored; I couldn't possibly have coped alone. We had to queue in seven offices, scattered throughout four separate buildings, for hours on end – six and a half hours, to be exact. Like most Siberians Raia speaks no English so couldn't explain why – for what – we were queuing. In fact my presence was superfluous: no one wanted to see me, I had to sign nothing, produce no roubles. Next day, to my great embarrassment, our marathon was resumed and we ended up queuing for fifty minutes at a specific counter in a specific bank to pay the registration fee of twenty-five roubles – less than a dollar, compared with $15 in Moscow. By then I reckoned I knew what was going on: Severobaikalsk's army of bureaucrats was having its first ever engagement with a 'business' visa. The town is visited annually by about 250 foreigners and any businessmen among them would have been through the Moscow hoop.

Raia's calm acceptance of this preposterous charade didn't surprise me. Such craziness is often mocked as a leftover from Soviet times though really it's an endemic disease. In the early eighteenth century Peter the Great's attempted reforms of the bureaucracy themselves created red-tape factories. And when the American journalist, George Kennan, had completed his pioneering tour of Siberia's prison camps, in 1886, he faced exit visa problems in St Petersburg:

I could not see how a formal letter from the diplomatic representative of the United States could cure the defects in a Russian document duly issued by authority of the Tsar, and properly stamped, signed and sealed by the East Siberian authorities; but I was not in the habit of raising unnecessary questions in my dealings with the Russian police . . . I obtained the 'formal letter' from Mr Wurts [the US chargé d'affaires], brought it to the passport bureau, declared that I was not a Jew, signed my name at the bottom of sundry blanks, disbursed various small sums for stamps, sealing wax and paper, paid an official for showing me what to do, received a document which I was directed to take to the police-station of the precinct in which I resided, brought back from there another document addressed to the passport bureau, and finally, after four days of going back and forth from one circumlocution office to another, received a little book, about as big as a religious tract, which certified that there was no objection, on the part of anybody, to my leaving the Empire.

Fifteen years later, when John Foster Fraser was halfway through his Siberian journey he observed:

The number of officials met with is simply amazing to the man from Western Europe . . . What must be the cost of this army of government employees, notwithstanding their poor pay? Every man in government service wears uniform, and as it takes at least four Russians to do in a post office what a girl of eighteen will do at home, some idea may be obtained of their number. In a small town through which pass four passenger trains a day and, say, eight goods trains, you will find two, or maybe three, great buildings. They belong to the Railway Administration, and eighty or a hundred men will be employed.

I, too, gaped at the number and size of Railway Administration buildings, even in the new BAM towns and cities where nothing approaching the Trans-Siberian volume of traffic is ever likely to be seen.

While Raia and I were touring offices it became alarmingly obvious that my footwear was unsuitable; repeatedly I skidded and twice I fell on the glacial packed snow. Those sturdy boots which had served me so well in the muddy mountains of Laos, and over the rough rocky tracks of northern Albania, were n.b.g. on iced footpaths. Cautiously I minced to the supermarket (septuagenarians become very cautious after two heavy falls) and for $60 (in roubles) bought appropriately soled fur-lined boots – made in Turkey, to my irritation.

Both the market and the palace of culture overlooked the Ice Fort – no less magical by day, with all its angles coruscating under a brilliant sun. I paused to watch small children on their mothers' laps hurtling down S-bend slides, the women's ankle-length fur coats held tightly between their feet. Then I continued to the glass-domed Winter Garden, an annexe of the palace, where my friend Tina cherishes an abundance of tropical plants.

Instead of another joyful reunion, my unexpected arrival caused Tina to burst into tears. Leonid, her nineteen-year-old son, a cadet stationed at Severobaikalsk's vestigial naval base, had befriended me in 2002 and been looking forward to my return. But now he was dead. A summer wedding party – fourteen merry guests crowding onto a boat only big enough for six – a group photograph, all lining up on one side . . . The nine capsize victims included the bride and groom. The survivors were those sober enough to swim to the nearby shore where Tina was watching as her only child drowned. She and her husband had tried to talk sense to the fourteen but 'vodka talked louder'. Guilt therefore augmented grief; if they had restrained Leonid physically he would still be alive . . . But teenagers resent being bossed in public and parents hesitate to antagonize teenagers . . . At this point Yuri's appearance lowered the tension. He came pacing out from behind a banana plant, curving his neck prettily before extending it, then standing on tiptoe and flapping his wide wings three times, allowing a glimpse of faint pinkness on their undersides.

Yuri was a mystery. Nobody could work out how a young flamingo came to be wandering alone by the Lena river in October, lost and enfeebled. Some freakish wind current must have swept him there – but from where? He was duly put on the BAM from Ust'-Kut, in a crateful of hay, destined for the Tropical Garden at Severobaikalsk, where he became Tina's responsibility. Being so debilitated, he needed constant t.l.c. and stayed in her home for three months. To everyone's relieved delight, her Peke and Persian soon accepted him and photographs showed dog, cat and bird sharing the warmest corner by the tiled stove. (Tina lived in a cosy 1970s *izby* built of irregularly shaped pine trunks discarded by loggers.) But Yuri grew fast, began to feel cramped in the *izby* and a week previously had moved to the tropics where he revelled in the 'water feature', a foot-deep pool complete with mini-fountain.

Towards his foster-mother Yuri showed a proper degree of grateful devotion – came when called and, if Tina hunkered down, affectionately preened her hair with his fearsome-looking beak. She had been disappointed to learn that he would retain his present colouring: body cream, wings various shades of brown. The flamingos' natural diet tints them pink and Yuri lived on a fawn mush of grain served in a red plastic bucket. A self-possessed young bird, he strolled unfazed through the groups of excited schoolchildren who came to admire him, photograph him, draw him, paint him, model him in clay and write poems about him. As I had observed in 2002, Siberian teachers are quick to avail themselves of any novelty likely to stimulate their pupils' creativity.

Among Severobaikalsk's attractions in 2002 had been a dearth of motor traffic, partly explained by a regional dearth of roads – no more than forty-five miles, twenty-five to the west and twenty to the east. However, despite this constraint the car population (according to official figures) had trebled in the past fifteen months. One friend suggested a startling and possibly apocryphal explanation. Allegedly, over-producing Japanese car manufacturers had circulated a rumour that another rouble crash was imminent – savings would again evaporate – cars were being offered at bargain prices and would prove more durable than cash. Now traffic lights were in place, though not yet really necessary, and a vulgarly decorated petrol station had just been opened on the town's edge. An absurd rash of traffic signs disfigured the aforementioned forty-five miles. One indicated a junction where a rough half-mile track – ending in the taiga, usable only by walkers – joined the Severobaikalsk–Nizhneangarsk 'highway'. It grieved me to see this blight on Baikal's shores.

Brand promotion had also arrived, though in a small way; the locals' purchasing power couldn't justify any great investment in logos and slogans. It has to be admitted that some logos, scattered among the Cyrillic lettering on business premises' façades, simplified my life; now I could buy a film unaided. The two gigantic hoardings advertised Japanese cars.

It dismayed me to hear of the closure of an excellent primary school with which I had formed a special bond on my previous visit. 'Lack of pupils,' explained a redundant teacher. During the 1990s life became so grim and uncertain that the birth rate dropped dramatically while the abortion rate soared. An alternative explanation mentioned 'Education Reform', IMF-speak for destructive cost-cutting. A school's excellence was not reason enough to keep it open once numbers had dwindled – though the evidence was all around, in buggies and cradles, that soon its intake would be back to normal.

The Buryat Centre had also closed, for lack of municipal funding. (The Buryats are this territory's most numerous indigenous people.) Yet the Centre's language and art classes, part of an effort to keep Buryat children linked to their own culture, had been well attended.

A large new restaurant near the market, on the ground floor of an apartment block, sported two McDonald's-type psychedelic illustrations over the entrance. As a sociological research project, I spent an evening diary-writing there, with an overpriced *pivo* (only one, as is not my wont, because of the price).

Part of the gloomy hallway had been partitioned off as a cloakroom and its morose male attendant looked snootily at my rabbit-fur *shapka* – bought in Yakutsk in '02 – before offering me his own much superior headgear for $100. The restaurant retained its New Year decorations, including a tree overloaded with bedraggled tinsel and plastic gimmicks. From the high ceiling depended a dozen revolving globes striped like beach balls. Around the walls snaked strings of multi-coloured, on-and-off lights; their pulsing, combined with the mobile globes, made me feel queasy whenever I raised my eyes from the page. Twenty-four tables were laid for dinner; on their fake grey marble tops shocking-pink paper napkins sprouted from tumblers, each accompanied by a tiny vodka glass – those glasses kept permanently aquiver by the reverberation from heavy-metal tapes. No diners appeared, nor were there any aromas suggesting earlier customers. And the long bar, displaying a wide variety of imported drinks, was deserted.

The two waitresses, slim and fair-haired, wore tight miniskirts, low-cut blouses, perilously high heels and long, dagger-shaped nails painted black to match long, dagger-shaped earrings. If relieved of their burdens of cosmetics they might have been good-looking. Both seemed half-afraid of me. As I cleared a space for writing at a corner table they exchanged alarmed whispers, then together responded to my beckoning and giggled uncertainly when I ordered a Russian *pivo*; it is commonly assumed that foreigners prefer imported brews.

I wondered if a menu would appear. But this restaurant wasn't into menus, unless one counted the depiction of hamburgers and frank-furters outside.

My sign-language request to lower the decibels flummoxed both girls; clearly their only customer was dissatisfied about something – but what? Most Siberians are poor sign-linguists, unused to commu-nicating with foreigners. So I personally confronted the offending 'music' centre, found the relevant knob and almost achieved silence.

Soon the girls withdrew to the hallway to smoke (forbidden in the restaurant) and get on with their crossword puzzles. An hour or so later they reappeared, accompanied by four teenage soldiers – under-sized youths with shabby uniforms, worn boots, bad teeth and sore-looking acne. These were friends, not customers; they had no roubles to spare for *pivo*. Immediately one of them turned up the decibels, causing the girls to glance apprehensively in my direction, but I smiled and said 'OK.' Those unfortunate youths needed their heavy-metal fix. It seemed rather touching that the waitresses – all geared up to be 'sophisticated' units in the new Russia, yet disquieted by the foreigner – were so happily relaxed with the conscripts. When I left, all six had settled down to a jolly card game.

Walking home, I thought about the future of that restaurant and the Federation's countless other small private enterprises. In a society dazzled by but not fully comprehending the workings of capitalism, many are likely to come to economic grief – especially those trying to operate honestly, without a mafia safety-net.

Amongst friends of my own generation in Severobaikalsk I detected an ambivalence about the borrowing habit developing among some of their children and many of their grandchildren. (Most septuagenarians had adult grandchildren; in the BAM settlements, especially, couples married young.) It half-pleased them to see the younger generations buying computers, new furniture, cars, the latest in electronic equipment – perhaps moving to bigger flats or even building a small house. But it worried them to see so much being bor-rowed from banks at high interest rates.

'It frightens me,' admitted one babushka, her granddaughter our interpreter. 'How can young people pay all these roubles back when they earn so little? What if banks get angry when they're too slow paying back?'

'They won't get angry,' I assured her. 'The slower they are the more the bank profits. For decades they'll be working hard to make the bank richer. Much harder than if they didn't buy all those things they don't need.'

The granddaughter (too poor to be a borrower) exclaimed, 'You're right! If husband and wife both have steady jobs our bank offers loans – you don't have to ask!'

'Quite so,' said I. 'Our capitalist controllers know all about luring people into debt – and keeping them there with endless urgings to use credit cards to buy this and that.' I had seen Visa card signs all over the town where in 2002 nobody had ever heard of them. Later I was pleased to discover that though the signs were displayed the system wasn't yet working.

In fact comparatively few of Russia's 1,300 (or so) private banks offer loans or hold deposits; their activities are less mundane. According to the English-language *Moscow Times*, Moscow's Interior Ministry believes that 85 per cent are mafia-run; Washington's FBI puts the figure at a more charitable 50 per cent. Either way, 103 bankers were murdered between 1998 and 2004. President Putin has so far proved unable to reform the Federation's banking and financial services.

Siberia's rulers, rather than its climate, were to blame for those extremities of suffering long associated with the land beyond the Urals. In fact, given enough food and clothing, inhabited Siberia's winters are fun and so regarded by the average citizen. Only when the wind blows do they complain of the cold. Sunshine all day almost every day fosters cheerfulness, while snow and ice generate enjoyable activities as rain and mud do not. People can skate, cross-country ski, roll around naked in the snow after a *banya* (sauna), then cook multi-course picnics over bonfires. However, in mid-winter the fine, dry snow resembles caster sugar and children must wait until the thaw is imminent to make snowballs and snowmen. Then every public space becomes a battlefield and snowpersons breed fast.

This atmospheric dryness also has drawbacks. Within days my maps and paperbacks had become wrinkled and brittle and my Rymans notebook was shedding its leaves – an inconvenience to this day, as I work with it on my desk. Then the leather jacket of a hip flask disintegrated, which rather upset me; it was a cherished mascot, presented

to me in November 1974 by my publisher, Jock Murray, on the eve
of my departure for the snowy Karakoram.

From Severobaikalsk's taiga-fringed clifftop a wide, steep track leads
to Baikal's narrow shore, sandy in summertime and blissfully free of
notices, advertisements, seats, kiosks or any other 'amenities'. Here
the autumn blizzards pile up broken ice, then smother it in snow.
Before that fall has time to freeze solid, youngsters dig caves and
mould embrasures, creating a winter-long play area – also enjoyed by
grown-ups who may be seen posing for photographs as they peer out
of caves, holding aloft gigantic slabs of ice.

Every Severobaikalsk home is within walking distance of the lake
and at weekends Baikal attracts many family groups and their dogs.
Yet the area never feels crowded; people soon become distant dots –
young trotting couples pulling babies on mini-sledges, solo skiers
swooping gracefully to and fro, older couples strolling sedately, small
boys duelling with long ice-swords, fishermen carrying hand-drills on
the way to reopen their holes.

On the last Sunday in January Baikal wore a sparkling new blanket
and at noon I was walking over the lake as briskly as is possible through
nine inches of 'caster sugar'. To east and west rose the formidable
magnificence of the Barguzinskiy and Baikalskiy ranges and yet again
I marked the special quality of Siberia's silence.

An hour later I was in a state of shock – perhaps an over-reaction
to the arrival of three cars. Rage succeeded shock as they parked on
the ice – engines left running, stereos blaring. From one emerged my
friends Tatiana and Lev, their small son Ivan and their Alsatian-
Labrador cross (acquired as a pup during my earlier visit and named
'Bertie' in honour of Ireland's prime minister). I'd planned to take
Ivan sledging but now, staring in horrified disbelief, I saw this traditional pastime being motorized. As the three young fathers proudly
towed their offspring over the ice those unfortunate children were
inhaling foul exhaust fumes while the fond mothers – awaiting their
own 'towing experience' – stood around videoing and/or photo-
graphing this lamentable scene. Thus was car ownership reshaping
those families' lives, parents and children no longer taking healthy
exercise together. Doubtless it will soon be seen as a mark of social
inferiority to pull your child's sledge instead of towing it while your
stereo violates Lake Baikal's tranquillity. In 2002 I had feared that

'developers' might wreck this region. In 2004 I realized that the locals can do it themselves.

One of the towing fathers was Lev's best friend, Andrei; together they had travelled to Vladivostok to buy their Japanese cars and load them on a freight train. Lev then taught Andrei how to drive, he himself having learned a month previously. And now, on the lake, Andrei was teaching his sons, aged nine and five. For the five-year-old this was a game, though one he took seriously. For his big brother, just tall enough to cope, it was a real challenge and his mother protested when his father permitted a solo run. However, if nine-year-olds must be let loose behind the wheel there can be no safer site than Lake Baikal.

As the towing continued – the children of carless friends also being given a turn – I steeled myself to offer unsolicited advice, a commodity normally reserved for my nearest and dearest. Tatiana translated for the other mothers and all three laughed indulgently at this babushka-ish fussing about fumes that couldn't possibly be harmful in the open air. But next day, when photographs showed Ivan on his sledge as a mere blur, Tatiana – though not Lev – did look slightly uneasy.

In 2002 Tatiana had been anti-car, mainly for economic reasons; now she condoned Lev's bank loan – 60,000 roubles at 18 per cent interest. All the usual specious excuses for car ownership were recited, plus a few shamelessly frivolous ones like taking sunset photographs at beauty spots and giving treats to grandparents by driving them out of town for shashlik picnics – the Siberian barbecues. To me that Sunday afternoon tableau on Lake Baikal seemed like a laboratory model demonstrating the universal qualities of a given element.

The motor industry battens on human weaknesses: physical and mental laziness, competitiveness, vanity, aggression, selfishness. And it encourages other forms of consumerism, making unnecessary expenditure seem easy, desirable and inevitable. ('Have vehicle, must use it!') In Ireland as elsewhere thousands of solo commuters take off daily from small towns, leaving almost at the same time, for jobs forty, sixty or even eighty miles away. They argue, 'I have to be at (or leave) Point A at 9.0!' Not 8.50 or 9.10 as might be the case were public transport or car-sharing involved. Notoriously, car ownership fosters 'instant gratification', one of our growth society's keystones.

The availability of a motor vehicle seems to banish common sense. Where I live children can learn to swim in an unpolluted river, being taught by older siblings, friends or parents. Yet many mothers drive them thirty or more miles to a chlorine-contaminated swimming-pool and pay for lessons.

While cycling around West Waterford's country roads I often over-take farmers driving behind their ambling cows on the 100-yard journey from pasture to milking-shed. (Or should I write 'milking-parlour'? Presumably this bizarre term was invented to soothe urban consumers who might otherwise visualize shit-splattered sheds.) Again, when I take my terriers for their morning run I regularly see a strapping young man jolting across a field in a Land Rover, herding cows from their pasture adjoining the milking-shed.

On that same dog-run I also observe two mothers, living fifty yards apart, getting into their cars and driving their children (one each) to a school fifteen minutes' walk away. These young women are not going to work; each returns home quite soon. Nor are they embroiled in any family or neighbourhood feuding, they're just addicted to 'freedom of movement' – independent movement in their own vehicle.

Then, as I lead the terriers home, I'm likely to pass one or two gigantic pantechnicons blocking the main street while delivering such items as potatoes from Spain, lettuces from Holland, celery from Israel, onions from Morocco – imported at a huge cost in pollution to a fertile island well able to grow all the vegetables it needs.

Do I sound cranky? Only to those who can't or won't accept that every needless food-mile, every farmer driving behind his cows, every mother avoiding a short walk, every commuter overvaluing 'independence' is contributing his or her mite to climate change. Admittedly it's hard to appreciate the importance of one's own mite, whether in relation to motoring or energy-saving in the home – espe-cially as the relevant industries do all they can to bamboozle us.

I'm not far enough out of my tree to advocate the elimination of motor vehicles, much as I detest them. But the case for an interna-tionally uniform tax on motor and aircraft fuel – a tax high enough to curb the irresponsible use of vehicles both personal and commer-cial – is irrefutable. However, such a revolutionary planet-protecting tax would be detrimental to a multitude of converging vested inter-ests: the oil industry, the motor industry, the road construction indus-try, the haulage industry, the food industry. This menacing coalition guarantees big bucks for the few (in global terms very few) at the cost of imminent catastrophe for the planet. And present catastrophe for those millions afflicted by asthma and other diseases caused or worsened by air pollution.

To be anti-car at the beginning of the twenty-first century is generally seen as irrational, unrealistic – yet what could be more irrational than promoting the unnecessary use of motor vehicles when ample evidence exists that already their emissions have done immense damage? A risk is something one can disregard; with luck all will be well. A certain future disaster, as a result of an avoidable present course of action, can only be disregarded by those whose logical faculties are paralysed.

Can it be that as a species we're on the way to mass-suicide, driven by a combination of unregulated greed and arrogant technological-scientific ingenuity? Our failure to take adequate measures to slow (or halt) climate change suggests that eventually we may become extinct because we're so stupid. A melodramatic scenario, yet not implausible. For pre-human aeons there was life on Earth and perhaps there will be for post-human aeons. *Homo sapiens* is an interesting evolutionary development, as were numerous other creatures no longer with us. Are human beings really necessary? Is there any reason to suppose our planet will sustain for much longer a species that has proved so lethal to most other species?

Before the BAM line was even a gleam in Stalin's eye, Nizhneangarsk existed. Then it was an isolated fishermen's settlement, eighteen miles east of the future Severobaikalsk, its 2,000 inhabitants having only the lake as their highway (small boats in summer, horse-drawn sledges in winter).

My Severobaikalsk friends, who relish apartment blocks, couldn't understand my enthusiasm for this impoverished 'village' – as they insisted on calling Nizhneangarsk, despite its present population of 10,000 and its status as seat of the regional government and headquarters of the BAM Tunnel Construction Organization. It grew suddenly after a 1972 decision to build a city here, an industrial centre of 75,000. According to that Plan, Severobaikalsk was intended to be no more than a smallish settlement of railway workers' shacks. However, like many another ill-researched Soviet Plan, this one fell apart when Nizhneangarsk's first few large buildings did likewise. None was above four storeys yet the marshy ground could not support them.

Two storeys is the limit on this narrow, twelve-mile strip of level land between Lake Baikal and a steep range of semi-forested mountains plundered by BAM. The apartment blocks and celebratory railway station and unsuccessful factories went up instead at Severobaikalsk, where the population never exceeded 30,000. And Nizhneangarsk remains an agreeable elongated town of (mainly) one-storey wooden dwellings, no two alike and many made beautiful by the elaborate fretwork of their façades, doors, windows, fences. The town looks its best in winter when snow and ice sculptures obscure the unsightly port, constructed at vast expense to receive BAM building materials ferried from Irkutsk. Its delayed completion coincided with the pre-punctual completion of the Taishet–Nizhneangarsk stretch of track, which made it redundant.

Early one morning I set off to lake-walk to Nizhneangarsk – a six-hour trek, I reckoned; at sunset I would return by bus. But I had chosen the wrong day. Suddenly a wind swept over Baikal, heralding the February snowfalls – not by Irish standards a strong wind, yet peculiarly piercing. Garments adequate for a windless temperature of −28°C were now frighteningly inadequate and within ten minutes hypothermia loomed. The phrase 'frozen to the marrow' seemed literally to apply to the state of my body as I scrambled up to the road, hoping to be rescued by one of those motor vehicles I so detest. Two cars sped past, ignoring my frantic thumbing. Then came a private enterprise minibus and within it I quickly thawed. After this chastening experience I always carried a knapsack of extra garments when going walkabout.

Back in Severobaikalsk, I chanced to call on my friends Anna and Ivan – who were about to leave for Nizhneangarsk, to visit Anna's eighty-four-year-old Buryat great-aunt, her paternal grandfather's sister. Nizhneangarsk's original Buryat population has been heavily diluted yet its influence is plain to be seen in many features (including Anna's) and in the most popular local footwear – individually designed and crafted knee-boots, made in the home of sealskin and dogskin.

As we drove along the shore the wind was playing with Baikal's carpet, in places creating miniature dancing dervishes of snow. 'You were lucky,' commented Anna. 'You are crazy to walk so much on Baikal. For us it's OK, we know the moods.'

Then Great-Aunt Tasha's biography was outlined. In 1970 her coal-miner husband died of a heart attack, aged fifty-one; later the second of her three sons suffered the same fate aged forty-one. The other sons and their sister all found BAM-related jobs far from Nizhneangarsk. Aunt Tasha herself had always worked around coal mines, mostly loading freight wagons. Now she was getting very stiff and the previous autumn her sixty-four-year-old son Sergei, recently widowed, had returned from Chita in Transbaikalia to care for her.

We stopped at Nizhneangarsk's oddly named fish factory to buy smoked omul for Aunt Tasha. (Omul is a salmon-like fish found only in Lake Baikal.) This, the town's only industry, employed sixty-two men and women in a semi-derelict scatter of sheds. Its compound was littered with old machinery, boat corpses and wheel-less BAM wagons. Built to employ four hundred, who would regularly despatch tons of salted or smoked omul to points east, it never employed more than a hundred.

'Here are no jobs for young people,' said Anna. 'The village will soon be smaller again, our age people won't come back, when they retire, like Aunt Tasha did.'

Unusually, Aunt Tasha's *izby* had a high picket fence, concealing it from the street. Built by her father a year before the Revolution, its three rooms (four if one includes a large porch) were low-ceilinged and ill-lit but kept cosy by a giant wood-stove. We sat in the cramped, drab kitchen – cracked linoleum on the floor, two benches draped with ancient bearskins, a photograph of Lenin in uniform facing the small window, a dented electric kettle instead of a samovar, a 1970s transistor radio instead of a TV. As though feeling this last 'deprivation' needed explaining, Anna said, 'Sergei wanted to bring his own set but his mother doesn't like to have it.'

Aunt Tasha was shabbily dressed, small and bent, arthritic and tremulous, obviously half-blind – at first glance a pathetic worn-out peasant. In 1985 she was awarded an 'Outstanding Worker' medal, later proudly displayed to me. In 1990 she retired and soon that medal became of only emotional significance. Decades of exposure to coal dust had caused a rare eye disease which needed three treatments a year, in distant Irkutsk, to avert total blindness. Her monthly pension was 2,000 roubles (about €80) but in the new Russia each treatment cost 400 roubles and she had to pay her full rail fare – no more pensioners' concessions.

We were offered nothing to eat or drink – given Siberian standards of hospitality, a poignant measure of Aunt Tasha's material poverty. Otherwise, she was not poor – or worn-out; that first glance misled me. She had a lot to say to the first European foreigner she had ever met socially and she said it with spirit. Anna, faithfully interpreting, sometimes looked uncomfortable. Her generation has accepted capitalism – not uncritically, but as Russia's only way forward. Aunt Tasha stood up for Communism. Even as a life-long heaver of coal onto freight wagons the system had offered her benefits she valued. In her spare time, before her sight failed, she enjoyed reading and the State provided well-stocked public libraries. She also enjoyed making music and in the mining town's palace of culture she had as a young woman learned how to play the violin, then gained a place in the local orchestra. Tentatively I asked about the secret police, their ruthless dissident-hunting, using neighbours as informers. But that was not a problem in Aunt Tasha's world. Maybe it was in Moscow, she conceded, where politics impinged more – but not in an Eastern Siberian coal-mining town. Anna then added, 'Aunt says "Moscow" when she means anywhere west of the Yenisey! She's never been past Taishet.'

Before we left, Anna showed me the other rooms. A curtain separated the kitchen from the living-room, very much a 'Sunday parlour' with frayed and faded rugs scattered on the pine floor. A low corner cabinet contained a meagre collection of cut glass and china. On one wall hung a superb old Buryat carpet – finely woven, subtly coloured – some four feet by six, almost covering the wall. 'Natural dyes,' said Anna dismissively. 'They give no nice bright colours.' On another wall a sepia studio photograph of Tasha, aged eighteen, was flanked by two of those garish landscapes sold in every market from Tirana to Vladivostok. A blanket hanging from the rafters concealed Sergei's cupboard-bed; his mother slept in the third room, scarcely bigger than a BAM coupé.

Sergei arrived then; his pension was little better than his mother's but through a family connection he had found a part-time job as a minibus driver – thus there was some capitalist trickle-down to this household. For him, too, a foreign visitor was a novelty and he urged us to stay longer. But we couldn't; Anna had to take the children to the Polyclinic at 4.30 that afternoon.

Our hostess insisted on seeing us out to the car, hobbling over the ice with the aid of two sticks. From the porch I noticed an ice-free duck-walk – made by Sergei on his return from Chita – leading to the earth-closet at the end of a quarter-acre garden. 'He's a good son,' said Anna. He had also built a new kennel for the watchdog Vlad, a shaggy mongrel permanently chained within his six-foot-square enclosure and seriously xenophobic – he almost cleared his fence as the foreigner arrived and departed.

Outside the gate Aunt Tasha posed beside me for a photograph and had remembered to wear her medal – large and shiny, hanging from a multicoloured ribbon. This award system used to prompt unkind jests in the sophisticated West yet it seems to have been genuine; subservience to the Party earned rewards more substantial than medals. On occasions, both the Yasins had vigorously opposed Party policy, in relation to BAM-builders' welfare, yet each had won two medals – also proudly displayed.

On the way home we saw a few cars driving short distances across the lake: newly motorized fishermen contributing their mite to climate change. Portable kennel-like wooden shelters marked some holes.

This 'Holy Sea' doesn't lie still beneath the ice and on every walk I spent fascinated minutes peering into holes, watching the dark water rising and falling with the silent regularity of a sleeper's chest. There was something pleasurably uncanny about witnessing those hidden rhythms of the deepest lake in the world. One morning I borrowed a ruler to measure Baikal's lid: approximately three feet thick, less than the January average.

Ivan had invited me to inspect the BAM Polyclinic so I waited in the car while the children were collected from their maternal babushka; conveniently, both babushkas lived in adjacent blocks. Maria, now aged two and a quarter, was an old friend of mine. Her brother, Ilya, had been conceived – so his mother told me – on the very day of my departure in 2002 when Ivan returned home after completing his training as a BAM engine driver. The plan had been to have a second baby in 2007 – 'Another failed Plan!' chuckled Anna. This failure was a source of much joy to four generations, a great-grandmother being also on the scene.

The Polyclinic (immune to 'Health Reform' cutbacks because subsidized by the railway authorities) was basic but impressive, unlike those Siberian municipal hospitals I had had occasion to sample in 2002. Each of the five floors – all freshly painted, neat, Swiss-clean – was dedicated to a separate department and the staff wore crisp, stylish uniforms. Anna praised the efficient administration but complained of a shortage of certain drugs, no longer affordable because no longer manufactured in Russia.

Punctually at 4.30 p.m. Ilya was summoned to have his booster jab and be weighed and measured – a monthly routine, during the first year. Maria then had her quarterly check-up – mandatory for the first three years – while Ivan was rebundling Ilya, a procedure of daunting complexity. His headgear alone comprised a woolly balaclava under a fur *shapka* under a long scarf. Finally came the swaddling: four soft blankets, each firmly bound, cocoonwise, with hide thongs. Thus protected, Siberian babies are parked on outside balconies or veran-dahs for three or four hours in temperatures as low as −25°C; they sleep longer and more soundly in the open air than in hot, poorly ven-tilated flats. When awake Ilya was stripped naked and turned loose to enjoy perpetual motion – apart from sessions on the breast, and deter-mined one-toothed assaults on slices of apple or crusts of bread. He achieved Olympic crawling speeds and at frequent intervals was held over the loo – which sensible nappy-conserving technique produced fewer pools than one might expect.

That evening, while recording Aunt Tasha's attitudes, I remembered Gaia Servadio's *A Siberian Encounter* (1971). A former member of the Italian Communist Party, then married to an Englishman, Gaia toured the Soviet Union in 1970 under Intourist supervision but spoke enough Russian frequently to elude her not very vigilant minders. Comparing this leisurely springtime journey with a shorter visit in 1960 she observed:

> Most people seem quite happy today, I thought. Whatever 'happy' means, this is the only way of judging a country; comparisons with other countries don't have much meaning. People now ate, even too much. They had clothes, they had a sense of purpose. For writers – good writers – and scientists, things were different, but their values were also different and they are a minority anyway. Freedom? What is it? They have never had it, Russians don't know what it is. People do not trust each other: radios are switched on to cover up conversa-

tions just in case. I found this horrifying but to the Russians it seemed quite natural.

Gaia viewed the post-Stalin Soviet Union as a valid experiment rather than a fearsome threat to Western civilization and one wonders how the critics reacted, in 1971, to her unfashionable stance. In 2005 a reviewer, Damian Thompson, diagnosed me as 'a typical old Irish Leftie [who] cannot disguise her sneaking regard for the Soviet Union'. Not quite a bull's-eye but Mr Thompson didn't entirely miss the target. However, there's nothing specifically Irish about recognizing that beyond its borders 'the evil empire' caused much less suffering than Western developers cause. Third World citizens who attempt to oppose First World commercial interests are repressed as ruthlessly as ever the Soviets repressed their dissidents. Democracy, so loudly lauded, is undermined whenever a democratically elected Third World government seeks to control its national economy for the electors' benefit. In the Soviet Union many 'human rights', as futilely defined in the UN Charter, were routinely trampled on; yet most citizens enjoyed certain fundamental rights denied to victims of the capitalist alliance (trans-national corporations, corrupt post-colonial governments, international financial institutions). In their fatally muddled way Soviet economists did put people before profits and, given the opportunity, millions on three continents would have opted for a local adaptation of Communism, such as the Kerala model. A full belly (however monotonous the diet), a weather-proof home (however cramped), adequate clothing (however drab), free education and medication – those 'rights' come first for most people. But while corporate capitalism Rules OK, billions throughout the Third World ain't gonna get 'em.

On 1 February, when the dawn temperature was −29°C, masses of pale grey cloud hid both the mountains and the sunrise. Then snow began to fall – an insidious sort, so fine and so gentle that one marvelled at the speed with which Severobaikalsk acquired a thick new blanket. It was time to buy a ticket for Tynda, but happily this wasn't a final parting from my favourite Siberian town. Pushkin remained hanging from the ceiling of the Yasins' garden shed and in early March I would be back to collect him before going south-west to Rostov-on-Don.

4

Evenk, Ewenki or Tungus?

I HAD FOUND a good home for the Dog, having already distributed more than half its contents. The remainder fitted into my rucksack because several bulky woollen garments were being discarded; I had miscalculated the layers needed under a fur-lined jacket, kindly lent by Ivan. It sported BAM's conspicuous logo on the left sleeve, a source of much amusement during the month ahead. So now my luggage was back to normal: one item easily carried.

Because it took the *provodniki* so long to hack frozen snow off the wheels we left Severobaikalsk four minutes late, at 2.49 p.m., my first and only experience of BAM unpunctuality. This was a vintage BAM (by now I rather fancied myself as a connoisseur) which uttered long loud groans and pathetic squeals, like a large animal in pain, as it jerked and swayed along the lake shore. Everything looked threadbare or scratched or in need of paint; the smallish windows were uncurtained, the old-style bunks wide, the washbasin lacked water – but the loo did flush. I had a coupé to myself, just vacated by a family of four, and the *provodnitsa* was doing her house-proud thing with broom, mop and duster.

Moving to the corridor, I almost trod on a pure white kitten, snub-nosed and long-haired, seven weeks old and about six inches long but already a dominant personality. He regularly perambulated the corridor, looking proprietorial, and even our stern *provodnitsa* deferred to him, serving milk and omul on demand. His name was Shenko; he had come all the way from Moscow and was continuing to Komsomolsk-na-Amure – where I was invited to call on his newly married owners, Vera and Igor, when eventually I got that far.

Initially, this journey's timing seemed unfortunate; we would be crossing the awesome North Muya range after sunset, via the ten-mile Severomuisk tunnel, begun in 1978 and opened at last on 5 December

2003. This event inspired a whole week of parties and general rejoicing in Severobaikalsk and Nizhneangarsk, the towns most intimately involved in those twenty-five years of tragedy and triumph. This is said to be the world's fourth longest railway tunnel – perhaps an idle boast of BAM buffs?

In the event, our timing could not have been more fortunate. In darkness I sat transfixed by my window as an almost full moon, sailing high in a clear sky, shone upon those aloof, angular mountains – bare silver rock peaks soaring above a radiance of soft, snow-smoothed slopes, all their boulders and dwarf pines obliterated by the latest blizzard. Up and up we chugged at 10 m.p.h. – here the official speed limit – until suddenly the luminous purity of this other world was violated by harsh beams from the tunnel's watchtower.

I wondered if my friend Boris, one of BAM's many security guards, was on duty. He had told me that Severomuisk is officially regarded as a prime target for Chechnyan terrorists, and is therefore protected not only by the military but by the very latest in electronic devices. At this altitude (about 4,000 feet) the mid-winter daytime temperature stays around $-46°C$, dropping to $-51°$ or $-52°$ at night, which means the devices must have special skilled attention – provided by Boris.

Whether because of terrorist fears, or because the tunnel is perceived (with some reason) to be inherently dangerous, a slight tension built up as we sped through at 20 m.p.h. Vera and Igor appeared in my doorway, imagining the babushka might be feeling twitchy, needing company. Said Vera, the English-speaker, 'Don't have worries! Soon we get out!'

When I assured her that I never have worries about remote contingencies she half-smiled uneasily, then forgot her soothing mission. 'Here in this mountains are many – ah, the word I forget! What is your word when everything moves a little?'

'Earth tremor,' I said, inwardly recalling the experts' advice that no tunnel should be built in this seismically hyper-active area which experiences an average of four hundred tremors a year.

Then we were out and glimpsed an enormous flood-lit monument to the tunnel-builders' heroism, sacrifices, determination. That brief glimpse doesn't entitle me to pronounce on the statue's aesthetic quality.

*

When I woke at 5.15 the next morning it was 6.15 local time; the time zone changes where three borders meet: the Republic of Sakha (previously Yakutia), Chitinskaya Oblast and Amurskaya Oblast. Leaving the light off, I gazed into ebbing darkness as we descended steeply and cautiously to the Khani river's wide valley. The sun rose as a globe of old gold, inflated by the suffusion of its light through long thin clouds. Already I had thrice travelled this route, in summer, autumn and early winter (October 2002). But now, in mid-winter, its features seemed dramatically unfamiliar.

Beyond the small town of Khani something odd appeared above the stillness of the distant frozen river – a serpentine swathe of mobile mist, perhaps 300 yards long, curling upwards like steam. Which is what it was: not really odd in this region of extinct volcanoes, daily earth tremors and numerous hot springs. As BAM ran closer to those springs, and slanting sun rays touched the scene, we were in a magic silverland. For brilliant miles, every hoar-frosted tree, bush and reed glittered and shimmered, their embellishment – never normally seen in Siberia's extremity of dryness – seeming the creation of some tutelary spirit. Twice during the next few hours this phenomenon was repeated.

Briefly we halted at the little settlement of Olekma, named after the Olekma river, more than twenty miles away. (But what is twenty miles in Siberia?) I remembered watching that river joining the Lena as I paddle-steamed to Yakutsk. During the last stages of BAM-building barges were towed 900 miles upstream from the Lena to a purpose-built wharf and their cargoes horse-carted overland to the railway line – which gives some faint notion of the Herculean nature of BAM-building.

Beyond Olekma one sees the confluence of that river and the Imangra; an hour later the Tas-Yuryakh joins the Olekma; ten miles further on the Yuktali does likewise. All these are mighty rivers in their own right, up to 500 yards wide, and each has a myriad tributaries which in Western Europe would themselves be seen as 'mighty'. Foreign geographers have not yet named all of Siberia's tens of thousands of rivers and lakes.

Beyond the Yuktali I lost my grip on the situation – we seemed to cross the same river twice (but which one was it?) before accompanying the Nyukzha up a wide flat valley between 5,000-foot ridges, some of naked serrated rock, others level and snow-clothed. Here the landscape did not correspond to our image of Siberia in winter. Only the rivers were flawless white expanses; the valley floor had a mere dusting of snow, not disguising its arid stoniness. The widely dispersed birches, puny and leafless, and the solitary sombre dwarf pines gave a melancholy tinge to the terrain, emphasizing rather than relieving its bleakness.

No doubt the hot springs' vapour explains a unique – in my experience – noon vision. In a cloudless deep blue sky two curved fragments of rainbow gradually appeared, becoming more and more vivid, poised on either side of the low sun, equidistant from it and midway between horizon and meridian. They remained visible for an hour or so, people crowding to the corridor windows to wonder at their eccentric loveliness.

Beside me in the corridor stood a middle-aged couple, Khabarovsk paediatricians returning from a conference in St Petersburg and travelling by train because they distrusted Aeroflot in its free-market reincarnation. Mr Zhdanov spoke English with an effort, his wife only Russian. It seemed they had been pitying me, a foreign babushka sitting alone in her coupé. When rainbow-gazing was over Mrs Zhdanov visited me with two fat photograph albums, one of family occasions, the other of professional trips abroad. This kindly gesture, typical of Siberians, was also, in the circumstances, rather unimaginative. By then it should have been obvious to all that the landscape enthralled me, that I wouldn't want to view instead weddings and New Year parties and international medical conferences in Helsinki, London, Tokyo and Mexico City. For half an hour I struggled successfully to be polite, then took advantage of our arrival at Taluma to return to the corridor – and stay there. Remorse followed when the Zhdanovs gave me their card and pressed me to visit them in Khabarovsk. Their son, studying English at the university, wanted to write TV film scripts and would be excited to meet an Irish author.

By 3.0 p.m. we were again taiga-surrounded, in an area rumoured to be coveted by foreign loggers. The timber town of Lopcha (one assumes no pun intended) is the site of an ageing North Korean sawmill, fed only from the nearby taiga, and certain 'developers' yearn to build roads where at present not even paths exist – apart from those made by foxes, wolves, elk, reindeer and bear. I wish I could share the optimism of a Tynda friend who believes the precipitous foothills of the

470-mile-long Stanovoy range – visible all day in the distance – will defeat even the most advanced technology of the richest corporations.

Deep snow lay on the next high undulating plateau, part of the Lena–Amur watershed, and here again, beside the track, many criss-crossing animal prints formed intricate patterns. Soon a prolonged red sunset had begun to inflame the treeless slopes to the north, making them glow like the sort of Christmas card one doesn't send. As we slowly descended to the complex Getcan creek a pink dusk lingered – until at 5.20 the full moon rose above Tynda's ridge and the narrow Tynda river glimmered between larches on our right. Soon, looking upstream from the lowish bridge near the town, I could see a tributary's whiteness emerging from black taiga, marking the spot where in August 2002 my friend Pavel laid on a memorable picnic – the sunshine hot until 9.30 p.m.

My disconcerting reception on Platform No. 1 was all the fault of whoever invented e-mail. Under pressure from the benignly authoritarian Rashit Yasin, I had e-mailed Pavel (a performance set up by Rashit since I can't cope with IT) and announced my arrival 'sometime soon'. Subsequently, unbeknown to me, Rashit and Pavel communicated directly. Siberian e-mails are unpredictable, they may or may not get through; unluckily all these did and my Tynda friends knew not only the date and time of my arrival but from which coupé I would emerge. As I stepped off the train I realized that I was being televised by a young man while a young woman hovered nearby with notebook and pencil at the ready. 'Return to Mid-winter Tynda of Famous Irish Travel Writer'– a disagreeable experience, but for Pavel's sake I made the best of it, uttering inanities about Siberia in general and Tynda in particular. As it was −29°C on the platform most of our long interview took place within the palatial station building where the cameraman requested me to remove my outdoor gear and unpack my rucksack to let his viewers see what clothing an Irish traveller judged essential for mid-winter Tynda. He and his colleague seemed rather taken aback by the fewness of those garments.

To my further discomfiture, Pavel then escorted me to a large black car complete with driver. When we first met he had walked about his business, hiring the cheapest possible taxi if motor transport was unavoidable. However, in the interval he had been deservedly promoted, was now Director of Tynda's branch college of Khabarovsk

University – and this thirteen-year-old Lada went with the job. Its use to collect me was, Pavel argued, justified by the duties he had arranged for me: three-hour-long talks, on Eng.Lit., on world geography, on European politics. He dismissed my protest that I'm unqualified to talk on any of these subjects to anyone over the age of ten. The Tynda college of Khabarovsk University is more than 2,000 largely uninhabited miles from its mother institution, is accessible only by rail and so can't be too choosy about guest lecturers.

I had planned to stay in the no-star Hotel Yunost, still run by Tynda's efficient municipality; in 2002 it earned my loyalty. But Pavel had other plans: his friends the Dzerzhinskys had invited me to stay. And at 9.0 a.m. on the morrow his colleague Ghantimur, an ethnologist and historian of the Ewenki tribe, would escort me to a nearby Ewenki resettlement village where he wished me to talk to the boarding-school pupils.

The Dzerzhinskys lived in an estate of redbrick-faced, and thus unusual, eight-storey blocks on the southern edge of this little city (population 70,000 but dwindling). Their first-floor flat was uncommonly spacious – large living-room, sizeable hallway and kitchen, three biggish bedrooms – though by our standards a little cramped for a family of five plus an in-law.

My host, Viktor, a forty-eight-year-old red-haired Moldovan, had been made redundant in 1995 when Tynda's always insecure 'industrial base' wobbled disastrously. Now he drove oil-company trucks on Sakhalin Island every other month, an odd work pattern explained by distance; you don't rejoin your Tynda family at weekends if you're employed as far away as Sakhalin Island. So Viktor, devoted to his family, clocked up twelve or fourteen hours a day, seven days a week, for a month – then took a month off. His always cheerful wife Oksana, a biology teacher, was – like an alarming number of middle-aged Siberian women – very overweight but indefatigable in the kitchen. At dawn she cooked the day's meals and baked in bulk, bread so delicious that most of it was eaten while still warm. She and her three slim, good-looking daughters made a happy quartet: much joking and teasing and hugging, no perceptible inter-generational friction. Natalya, aged twenty-four, was married to her father's nephew, Lev, another redhead who disconcertingly resembled his uncle/father-in-law. They hoped to be in their own flat by July, when the first baby arrived. Twenty-year-old Olesja, studying computer programming, was much diverted to hear that the Irish writer hadn't a notion what this means. Lest she might get a distorted picture of my native land (monks still using quill pens to copy the gospels) I assured her that most, if not all other Irish writers are computerized.

Seventeen-year-old Eva, in her last year at school, had sacrificed her room to the guest. Its walls were covered by posters and postcards of pop groups, their expressions peculiarly unpleasant – sullen, aggressive, discontented, defiant, some trying so hard to look nasty they seemed to be in pain. With such creatures as models, it's surprising there are any normal youngsters still around.

The Dzerzhinskys – none of whom spoke English – represented what I had come to think of on my last visit as a typical Siberian family: spontaneously and affectionately welcoming, lavishly generous in relation to their means, informally relaxed in their hospitality, feeling no need to 'put on a show' for the foreigner – and all subservient to their cat Misha, a long-haired brindle with basilisk eyes who had been exploiting them for nine years. I thought I'd already seen the full range of spoiled Siberian cats, but not so. For breakfast Misha had salami, cheese (very expensive in Siberia) and chocolates which she ritually chased around the floor before unwrapping them herself. At every meal titbits were placed near the edge of the table and everyone watched admiringly as she stretched up and dexterously transferred them from paw to mouth. In common with many feline residents of ground- and first-floor flats, Misha had her own narrow ladder leading from the kitchen window to the snow – and of course a tray in the loo, which had a cat flap, because she wasn't allowed out at night. Bono, the not quite pure-bred young Alsatian, with a half-pink nose and a diffident manner, was remarkably tolerant of all this preferential treatment, looking humbly grateful for any leftovers disregarded by Misha.

Tungus or Ewenki or Evenk? 'Tungus' was used by all pre-Soviet writers, Russian and foreign, but here we have a slight nomenclature problem, pointed out by James Forsyth in his *History*:

> The name by which the Siberian Tungus call themselves is Ewenki west and south-east of the Lena, and Ewen to the east, and these terms are now used as official designations in Soviet Russian writings, in the

forms *Evenk* and *Even*. However, the old and etymologically unex-
plained name Tungus has much to commend it as a unifying term for
the widely distributed groups belonging to this nation.

Having taken advice from Ghantimur, my choice is 'Ewenki'.

Out of Siberia's present total population of 32 million only 1.6
million are indigenous. In 1979 about 28,000 registered as Ewenki;
another 15,000 or so live in north-eastern China. It is estimated (but
how reliably?) that when the Russians began their annexation of
Eastern Siberia in the seventeenth century there were some 36,000
Ewenki scattered over two million square miles. With their reindeer
herds they roamed over all of south-eastern Siberia, from the Yenisey
to the Pacific, and into northern Mongolia and Manchuria. The
Buryats around – and east of – Lake Baikal, and the Yakuts along the
Lena, were larger and more advanced tribes but they roamed much less
widely. The three languages are unrelated; Yakut is a Turkic language,
Buryat Mongolian, Ewenki one of a group including Manchurian and
other languages of the Amur region. The Ewenki, being so dispersed,
had many dialects not always mutually comprehensible.

As nomadic hunters this tribe moved through the taiga winter and
summer, living in portable tents (about fifteen feet in diameter) made of
larch poles covered with sheets of birch bark or reindeer skins. They
depended on domesticated reindeer for transport and much of their
clothing. Between camps, reindeer carried small or sickly children,
women in the later months of pregnancy and the families' few possessions. The Ewenki themselves had devised appropriate saddles and
bridles. Because of the taiga's density, riding-sledges were of no use,
except for the type drawn by a human wearing snowshoes – still to be
seen in many villages. Unlike most Siberian tribes they milked their
does, but only in emergencies would they kill a domesticated reindeer
for food. The taiga's numerous wild herds of reindeer and elk provided
ample meat, supplemented by fish and, in season, nuts, berries and fungi.

Like their equivalents elsewhere, the Ewenki never thought in
terms of owning territory; the land and its resources were common
property. Their infrequent conflicts were usually provoked by the
abduction of women and children, or the conviction that another
clan's magic spells had caused a death. Then a group of warriors would
be organized (rarely more than half a dozen), wearing bone or wood

armour and wielding bows and arrows and improvised spears – knife-blades embedded in long branches. Sometimes the enemy's hunting parties were ambushed in the taiga, or the enemy camp was raided with much bloodshed. More often, as in many parts of pre-colonial Africa, each side was prudently content to be represented by one pre-eminent warrior, thus minimizing bloodshed. Occasionally jaw-jaw prevailed – prolonged negotiations between the clans' hereditary chiefs and shamans, the latter by far the more influential.

In winter the Ewenki lived in small groups of two or three families. In summer a score or so of families camped together, partly to enjoy a wider social scene and arrange marriages, partly to create a defensive barrier of smoky green-wood fires to protect their herds from Siberia's incomparable plague of summer insects. These are capable of driving reindeer to frenzied non-stop galloping and even to death by suffocation, when inhaled. The suffocation is obviously peculiar to Siberia but the frenzied galloping awakens memories. I have never forgotten one evening in August 1976, camping in Derek Hill's midge-infested field in Co. Donegal with my small daughter and her pony Scamp. Scamp went berserk – as did Rachel and I when the midges broke into our tent. Eventually Derek rescued us: a stable for Scamp, a bedroom for the humans. But it took poor Scamp a few days to recover from the trauma.

All Siberia's tribes suffered when the Russians arrived with guns, vodka and hitherto unknown diseases – a familiar story. The few Ewenki, scattered in the remotest recesses of the taiga, self-reliant and economically unimportant, were not too devastated during the seventeenth and eighteenth centuries – apart from those clans completely wiped out by epidemics. Then they became increasingly involved in the fur trade, exchanging pelts for manufactured goods, including vodka – despite the law against selling alcohol to natives. Also, their more accessible clans were forced to try to satisfy the colonists' insatiable demand for reindeer transport.

Tragically, the Communists' tunnel vision prevented them from seeing that the Ewenki, like all Siberia's hunting tribes, were already communists (with a small 'c'), living according to their traditional law of *nimat*. *Nimat* decreed that hunters' spoils must be shared equally with all in the clan and sometimes with those in nearby camps. It also ensured communal care for orphans, the aged and the unfortunate;

families who lost their reindeer were clothed, fed and sheltered by other clan members. Here was a genuinely classless society, kept that way for millennia by the rigours of life; with no surplus to be hoarded, a privileged class can't emerge.

In 1929 the Ewenki were first exposed to the unrestrained brutalities of Sovietization. Party officials abruptly told them that they now belonged to collectives and forcibly marched them from their taiga camps to settlements provided with unwanted houses, schools and clinics. In these 'communes' they must remain for ever – no more roaming – and they were compelled to overwork their commandeered herds as transport animals. Many however slaughtered their reindeer before the Russians could confiscate them, just as thousands of peasants slaughtered their cattle in European Russia. Many others fled back to the taiga – often to die there, for they could not escape if carrying possessions. Quite soon the Party had to admit tacitly the failure of Ewenki collectivization. From on high came an order to form no more communes; instead the Ewenki and other small tribes would be allowed to use their pastures and hunting grounds under Party supervision. But already the whole delicately constructed social framework of the tribe had been irreparably damaged and when next the Russians attempted Sovietization the Ewenki put up little resistance. Yet even in the 1980s a few clans remained free, remote from 'civilization'.

When the College Lada arrived twenty minutes early the driver was offered tea while I dressed for the Great Outdoors. 'Minus twenty-nine,' warned my hostess. Then she insisted on lending me an extra pair of socks which subsequently became a farewell gift.

Ghantimur, aged forty-ish, was small and compact, quiet-spoken and rather sad-looking – not surprisingly, after twenty years of researching Ewenki traditions and misfortunes. Brown-haired and brown-eyed, he had a high forehead, thick spectacles and a bookworm's pallor; in summer, he explained, Siberia's flying plagues confined him to the university libraries of Khabarovsk, Irkutsk and Novosibirsk. I wouldn't have identified him as an Ewenki had we met in the street; during the past half-century there has been much intermarriage between settlers and natives.

Because double-interpreting would have overtaxed Ghantimur's English – adequate for our one-to-one conversations – Pavel had provided Maria, a skinny young woman with large dark eyes in a pale neatly featured face. At first I mistook her for a not very successful student of English; in fact she had started her first job, as a lecturer in English, the previous September. This would have shocked me before my discovery in 2002 that the compulsory learning of English is, for 90 per cent of Siberian pupils, a mere sham. The territory's isolation partly explains this; typically, I was the first native English-speaker Maria had ever met.

We crossed the Getcan river on its 'winter road', the ice thick enough to bear Zarya's twice-daily No. 105 bus service. A rough road took us past Tynda's near-derelict industrial zone, scattered through clearings in dense taiga. Its dead or dying factories, surrounded by hunks of abandoned machinery, looked no less dismal for being brightly snow-wrapped.

As we drove slowly over humpy packed ice, Ghantimur talked of his maternal grandparents. Their clan – all nomadic hunters, not fur traders – had roamed for centuries on either side of the river Bureya, a tributary of the Amur. Then in the 1930s they were forced to join a short-lived agricultural collective set up in a permafrost area where agriculture is impractical – and anyway nomads know nothing about cultivating crops. Ghantimur quoted his grandparents' collective ordeal as a classic example of that notorious Soviet mix, zealotry and incompetence. The young Russian officials responsible for 'collect-ivizing' Siberia's tribes were few and untrained – newcomers from Europe, hated and feared. They could recruit no native collaborators or advisers and stumbled through a fog of ignorance from one expensive debacle to the next, shattering cultures as they went.

One had to look twice to see Zarya's scattering of little dwellings in the deep drifted snow below the road – which ends here, at the broken gateway to a former reindeer farm. This village, established as an Ewenki settlement in 1960, is older than Tynda, a 1970s BAM Zone city. Its two hundred or so families live in wretched-looking *izbi* and are distressingly dependent on their 'Minority Peoples' subsidies, now shrinking rapidly. The New Moscow isn't terribly interested in Minority Peoples, unless they can be induced to congregate in some tourist-luring theme park.

The coeducational boarding-school for a thousand pupils gives Zarya its local importance. Originally based in Tyndinsky, the village around which Tynda city was built, it moved to Zarya when Ghantimur was a pupil. In its spacious grounds, sloping up from the road, clever planners took care to preserve numerous magnificent trees and at intervals one glimpses, between the trees, wooden summer-houses covered with enchanting carvings of birds and beasts. The girls' and boys' houses – their entrances fiercely guarded day and night – stand far apart, separated by the academic block and the arts and sports departments. Several recreation spaces are well equipped, for juniors and seniors; many English fee-paying schools have less salubrious surroundings.

On our arrival, even before we had disrobed, I was presented with a book of photographs commemorating the seventieth anniversary of the school's foundation. Inwardly I flinched on seeing the dates: 1933–2003. In 1933 Ewenki children were being kidnapped by the State, forcibly dragged away from parents who had been directed to resume their nomadic way of life under Party supervision. And now this school, established to replace Ewenki shamanism with Communist dogma, has turned full circle and is encouraging Ewenki children to feel proud of their culture and revive some of their skills – especially the marketable ones, like boot-making.

In the headmaster's spartan office I was introduced to Mr A., middle-aged, nine years in his job and at first glance the epitome of the third-grade 'Party man': close-cropped hair, square jaw, expressionless eyes, wide thin compressed mouth, broad shoulders, quasi-military bearing. Later, I chanced to notice him talking with three girls in a corridor and got quite a different impression. Those four were having a friendly argument, the pupils being vigorously vocal, their headmaster listening attentively and no longer expressionless – seeming concerned and affectionate. Hastily I took out my camera but was then spotted by Mr A., who resumed the persona he deemed appropriate in the presence of a foreigner.

My tour of the senior classrooms disappointed Ghantimur who had evidently expected the pupils to question me about my travels and seek my view of important international events. Instead, they showed an interest only in the humdrum details of Irish life. Do people live in flats or houses? What do people eat? Are there dachas in Ireland? Are there *banyas*? Do people have cats and dogs? Does everybody have a job? Are there churches in Ireland? How is winter in Ireland?

To that last I replied, 'Damp and chilly. Much grey sky, limited sunshine, almost no snow. In general only a little colder than summer.' Everyone exclaimed incredulously on hearing that a wood-stove heats my home, that every winter morning I chop kindling and split logs – the way the poor live in Siberia, people like Aunt Tasha. I explained that that's my choice, that most Irish homes now have oil central heating, not provided by a central municipal heating plant but paid for by each householder. More bewilderment then – and some worry. If this is how capitalism works, would they soon be expected to pay the full cost of home heating? Now we were touching on a sensitive spot and the pupils became quite animated as I tried to simplify Mr Putin's major problem with the World Trade Organization (WTO). Ghantimur seemed relieved by this shift to a higher gear.

A less simple version goes as follows. President Putin yearns for WTO membership, seen by him as a guarantee, to the free-marketeering world, of Russia's respectability. At one stage he spoke confidently of acceptance by December 2003, then came postponement – for at least a year, maybe longer . . . Russia's lack of international accounting standards (for what those are worth), and the generally dodgy banking and financial sectors, constituted serious obstacles. But the most serious was Moscow's reluctance to free energy prices – or, more accurately, Moscow's inability to do so, for the stark reason indicated by those Zarya pupils.

Russia's dual-pricing system for oil, gas and electricity means its individual consumers and national industries are being cross-subsidized at the expense of foreign purchasers of those commodities. This the EU and WTO do not like, the former loudly insisting that Russians must pay higher prices. However, in October 2003, at a meeting between President Putin, the German Chancellor Gerhard Schroeder and big businessmen from both their countries Mr Putin was decisive. 'It is impossible', he said, 'that Russia should raise gas and electricity prices to world levels. We would cause the whole Russian economy to collapse.' His argument was irrefutable. Russia's economy depends on low energy costs, its finances depend on selling its exports at high world prices. With every $1 increase in the world market price of a barrel of oil, $1.5 billion flows into the Federation's coffers.

Most important of all, if the EU and WTO had their way, and what they define as 'the real economic cost for energy' were charged throughout the Federation, millions of Russians would die. It is as simple as that – especially in Siberia, where the cost of living is four times higher than in European Russia and the average worker earns one-twelfth of the average Muscovite's wage. In 2003 the Federal government paid $700 million in subsidies for fuel deliveries to Siberia – an unsurprising figure, given the distances involved. Yet many families and small businesses couldn't pay their utility bills, as I was told repeatedly wherever I went. The Russian Federation boasts the world's nine coldest cities with populations over one million. More than forty million Russians live most of the year in temperatures between $-15°C$ and $-45°C$ – dropping to $-50°C$ during a cold snap. Plainly the EU's demand could only be satisfied by the mass-extermination of Siberians – and Vladimir Putin, though a hard man, is not Joseph Stalin.

Before lunch Ghantimur showed me over the whole school, as impressive as every other Siberian school I had visited: spacious, clean, bright, with all the essential facilities but no frills – unless one counts the splendid wood carvings decorating doorways, galleries, banisters and cupboards, executed by past pupils and usually with a reindeer motif. Was the spaciousness of Soviet public buildings, in such contrast to cramped homes, intended to emphasize the power of the State?

Mr A. was justifiably proud of his pupils: healthy, cheerful, well-dressed, well-mannered. At least half looked decidedly Russian – not at all Ewenki – and Ghantimur, when questioned about this, became oddly evasive. 'Minority' youngsters still receive a free university education, as everyone did in the good old days; Russians have to pay for it. Maybe Russian genes tend to dominate in mixed offspring, but a doubt hovered . . . The new Russia, no less than the old, activates suspicion.

The teaching staff (only nine Ewenki) were as usual all female and mostly middle-aged. They looked less happy than the children, possibly because they hadn't been paid for two months. Did this, I wondered, presage the decline and fall of Zarya College? Ghantimur shrugged and said, 'Now about everything all is not sure.'

We lunched with Mr A. in the refectory's staff annexe where another artistic past pupil had covered two walls with life-size murals of Ewenki riding reindeer – in winter and summer. Here the juniors eat in two cohorts at tables for four; the seniors eat in their respective houses. We were served our portions of the day's lunch; nothing special was laid on for the visitors apart from a pink nylon tablecloth. First course, big bowls of reindeer broth thickened with slivers of meat, cabbage and onion; second course, herb-flavoured pasta with tender reindeer steaks and pickled cucumber; third course, a taiga-berry pie, the pork-lard pastry substantial and flavoursome. High piles of bread, baked in the adjacent kitchen, were swiftly demolished and promptly replaced by smiling cooks-cum-waitresses, wearing crimson uniforms and white chef's headgear. Instead of water we drank warm prune juice; the pupils had had prunes for breakfast. Lucky pupils! Let us pray the food industry never takes control of Zarya College's cater-ing department.

During the first course Mr A. tried to do his P.R. thing, claiming that all Zarya pupils go on to university and then get good jobs. Having seen the 'real' Mr A. with those girls in the corridor, I felt free to chal-lenge him – how could Zarya pupils be sure of getting even not-so-good jobs when millions of Siberians are unemployed and destitute? He relaxed then – he'd done his propaganda bit and it hadn't worked. By the third course he was admitting, with tears in his voice, that many pupils – jobless, bored and despairing – become vodka addicts within a year of leaving school.

As Ghantimur, Maria and I set out to tour the village Ghantimur glanced at the thermometer by the school door and exclaimed, 'It gets warm! Now minus twenty-eight!' Siberia's exhilarating dry cold acts on me like one of those drugs athletes take and soon my companions were objecting to my pace. 'Go slow!' urged Ghantimur. 'You have too much of speed! We have no hurry need!' Maria added, 'I say you are an old people that is strong, not same like Russian babushkas what is weak.'

Zarya is formless – groups of *izbi* here and there, each in its fenced vegetable garden, a few with inhabited chicken huts or cowsheds and haycocks in a corner. We followed narrow zig-zagging paths trodden through deep snow; it was impossible to guess what lay below the drifts – a track? a garden? a stream? a field? – and I found it hard to imagine the place in July. No Siberian (or Russian) village presents a bustling aspect in mid-winter but Zarya felt worse than dormant and Ghantimur confirmed my misgivings. For a decade it had been stag-nant: first the co-operative reindeer farm closed, then the clinic, then those few local industries which traditionally employed Ewenki. Only the tiny museum remained open, an uncomfortable irony not lost on

Ghantimur. In summer tourists arrive at the rate of about two a month and my arrival in February caused the curator great joy.

Mr Z., a half-Ewenki, was tall and lean with a short neat beard and a boundless enthusiasm for his main job as the school's teacher of traditional crafts. For twenty-five of his fifty years he had been trying to transmit to seriously deracinated pupils his own dedication to the 'Ewenki cultural revival'.

We disrobed in the vestibule under the sightless gaze of a gigantic Arctic owl; the several other stuffed birds, native to Siberia, couldn't compete with him – but were much more important, Ghantimur pointed out, as food. The museum occupies only one room where the exhibits – mainly garments and fashion accessories – are carefully labelled in Russian. I particularly liked a long, wide woman's girdle made a century ago of reindeer hide, studded with seed pearls and glass beads. 'Not very *traditional*,' commented Ghantimur. 'It is from the Lower Tunguska Basin where we had too much contact with trading Russians.' Most exhibits were similarly 'contaminated'; when the Russians broke up camps and dragged families away to communes no one preserved authentic Ewenki possessions. A man's knee-length horse-hide tunic, dating from the 1890s, was elaborately decorated with reindeer hair and glass beads sewn on linen. A reindeer-skin haversack cover, some four feet by three, had an intricate border of cotton velvet, linen and multicoloured glass beads. 'That was a big load,' Ghantimur remarked. 'Nomads must carry much.' Women's outfits of reindeer-hide knee-length dresses, and tunics and boots, were trimmed with reindeer hair, ground squirrel fur or sealskin from Lake Baikal and worn with helmet-like hats, the reindeer hair inside. Most conspicuous was a nineteenth-century shaman's ceremonial costume of interwoven bear-skin, deerskin, sealskin and felt. This was gorgeously decorated – every detail of profound symbolic significance – and bedecked with dozens of metallic objects including copper discs of varying sizes and tiny bells; from the high crown-like headpiece hung strips of pearl-studded velvet.

What Ghantimur described as 'a typical pictographic letter' intrigued me. (The Ewenki had no written language.) Drawn with charcoal on a two-foot-long cedarwood slab, it depicts four triangles, their bases joined, and three figures dancing within circles. 'We don't get the message,' said Ghantimur. 'It is from a very past date, we can't find who knows, all who knew are dead.'

Mr Z. was obviously impatient to show me around the bigger room, the workshop, where impressive achievements were on display and one could also admire work in progress. The pupils' raw materials were wood, bone, stone, hides, antlers, pelts, birch bark, fish skins. First they found and made their own ancestral implements: fishbone needles, grass thread, sinew string, rock hammers, hardwood nails, and so on. Ghantimur's later comment, that only a minority of pupils attend Mr Z.'s classes, did not surprise me. I felt rather sad for him as we said goodbye, which was a bit silly; he may live in cloud-cuckooland but his enthusiasm sustains him.

Ghantimur wanted me to meet two of his babushka friends – Mrs Rassokha, aged seventy-five, and Mrs Beryozov, aged eighty-six. 'They can tell you of past things,' he said. 'They are the most old people in Zarya, vodka makes it most people don't get old.'

A short walk took us to Mrs Rassokha's three-roomed *izby*, shared with a fifty-year-old daughter-in-law (a school cook) whose husband had died in 2000. Soon after, the two teenage grandsons went to seek work in some city and haven't been heard of since.

We disrobed in an unheated outer room now used for chopping logs and curing reindeer hides: three were nailed to the walls. Mrs Rassokha made knee-boots for sale in Tynda but the fashion favours synthetic soles so they had to be finished by a city cobbler who – Ghantimur complained – took most of the profit. In a poky kitchen-cum-living-room we sat around a tar-barrel wood-stove with a cat on each side. Mrs Rassokha looked bewildered at first, needing time to adjust to her foreign visitor. That adjustment made, she waxed eloquent about BAM. Pre-BAM, her clan had been exceptional, had eluded Sovietization (an ugly word for an ugly process) as they roamed through the otherwise uninhabited Stanovoy mountains. Then in 1971 geologists and civil engineers arrived, desperate for reindeer transport, for guidance through treacherous terrain, for local knowledge of the region's geological idiosyncrasies. Very quickly the few remaining free clans, scattered along BAM's route, were 'settled' and made to serve BAM's needs.

After a pause Mrs Rassokha looked directly at me and added something with passionate vehemence. Ghantimur translated. 'It is impossible her people have compensation for territory BAM spoiled. Ewenki are people of the taiga and reindeer. They are not money people, they had no roubles, for themselves they made everything.

Staying in one same place, having no reindeer, they are not Ewenki. They cannot be well and themselves in cities and towns. They drink and die. She wants you say all this in your book.'

I promised that I would – and impulsively I reached forward to clasp both her hands.

As we went on our way, towards the edge of the village, I found myself experiencing an absurd emotional reaction – absurd because of course I'd always been aware of my beloved BAM as a ravager of precious places. But that awareness had somehow been suppressed, until Mrs Rassokha spoke.

Mrs Beryozov lived alone with three cats and a dog of strangely vulpine appearance – even to his white-tipped tail. Her *izby* stood a little apart from the village, near the surrounding taiga, and had no fenced garden; she could no longer cultivate it and last winter the fence had gone into the stove. But she was a stayer and continued to make quite beautiful reindeer-skin wall hangings and table mats for Tynda's market: I remembered noticing them there in 2002. Although this work involved much close stitching she needed no spectacles. A tiny bright-eyed woman of great dignity, she had come far down in the world. Her father's clan herded a thousand reindeer in Khabarovsk province and their tents would have been both more comfortable and more prestigious (in Ewenki terms) than her present cramped home.

Some years ago a Boston anthropologist had interviewed Mrs Beryozov and when we arrived she mistook me for an American. Other foreigners she was vague about and Ghantimur didn't even try to locate 'Ireland'. Born in 1918, she had never been to school, was illiterate, spoke only a few phrases of Russian – which accentuated her isolation. Now Ewenki schoolchildren are learning their own language, as a separate subject, but amongst earlier state-reared generations many have lost it. In 1979, said Ghantimur, only 43 per cent registered themselves as Ewenki-speakers and that percentage would now be much lower. For this he didn't entirely blame the Soviets. The lack of a written language, and the multitude of very different dialects, required the first literate generation to use Russian. In 1931, just before the Party hardliners decided on the complete Sovietization of Siberia's natives, a standard Latin-based alphabet was devised for all the indigenous languages. But this impractical project never got far beyond the desks of comparative philologists and in 1937 it collapsed.

Then the Party decreed that all Soviet citizens must use Cyrillic and all children from the age of seven must learn Russian.

Mrs Beryozov had the first of her five children at the age of eighteen in the customary circumstances – isolated for several days in a temporary and not cosy birch-bark teepee at some distance from the camp, attended by one suitably experienced elder. Her other children were born in a commune clinic. According to Ghantimur, some indigenous women regarded their 'liberation' by the Russians as adequate compensation for separation from children, though these separations often meant life-long alienation. The Soviet insistence on 'equality of rights' led to more women than men supporting Sovietization, even to the extent of playing an active part in political life as clan soviets were set up throughout Siberia. In most tribes, women were excluded from clan councils.

However, according to S. M. Shirokogorov – a pioneering ethnologist and an anti-Bolshevik, writing in 1929 – Ewenki women always enjoyed 'equality of rights', were acceptable as shamans (the touchstone: women cannot be Roman Catholic priests), acted as decision-makers in their hunting husbands' frequent absences and were excluded from clan councils only because of certain taboos linked to female sexuality. Professor Shirokogorov was interestingly ahead of his time. He argued that the Bolsheviks' condemnation of bride-price, polygamy, levirate and childhood betrothals merely revealed their extreme ethnocentrism and total ignorance of how the Ewenki lived.

Since the steep rise in railway fares Mrs Beryozov's sixty-two-year-old daughter, who worked in an Irkutsk hotel, had been unable to visit her. All her four sons were dead – two killed in a coal mine disaster, two poisoned by alcohol. Most Ewenki can afford only gut-rotting illegal distillations. Ghantimur quoted an Ewenki researcher who had in 1988 found that 40 per cent of Ewenki schoolchildren were vodka orphans.

I longed to buy table mats from Mrs Beryozov, whose poverty was so evident. But Ghantimur said 'No'; if I tried to buy she would present me with a set – which in any case she did, as we were leaving.

Our final call was to Mrs Ogryzko, an Ewenki science teacher who spoke a little English and had invited us to tea. Her comparatively luxurious five-roomed home, built by the school authorities in 1973, seemed more bungalow than *izby*. Yet it, too, had an enormous barrel of melting snow near the stove. Zarya enjoys subsidized (previously free) electricity but has no central heating, indoor sanitation or piped water. Therefore everyone tips buckets of snow into kitchen barrels and in due course households have water. There was something surreal about the juxtaposition of that barrel and the video camera being compulsively wielded by Mrs Ogryzko's sixteen-year-old daughter, Garpalak – so excited by a foreign presence that my every move had to be filmed. Garpalak was an only child who looked pure Ewenki though her mother didn't (of Mr Ogryzko there was no mention). She wanted me to know that her name meant 'sun ray' and marked a reassertion of Ewenki identity after decades of adopting Russian names.

When Garpalak went out to fetch stroganina from the eaves I felt flattered. Stroganina is a delicacy, a fish caught in mid-winter, allowed to freeze the moment it leaves the water, then stored hanging from the eaves and eaten raw on special occasions, thinly sliced. Its slicing roused Yuyu, a sleekly elegant all-black cat, from his slumbers on a cushion by the stove. The Dzerzhinskys would undoubtedly have given in, but the more rational Ogryzkos propitiated him with scraps of reindeer meat.

As we savoured this treat, our hostess's younger half-sister joined us – Varya, more Ewenki-looking than Mrs Ogryzko but less so than Garpalak. Later, Ghantimur told me that she was a 'BAM baby'. When the Ewenki men and their reindeer were away on long treks, transporting loads for railway-builders (which was most of the time), many of those builders were fathering little 'Ewenkis', as other Russians were doing in other tribal contexts all over 'developing' Siberia. In the worst-hit settlements, the numbers of half-breed children reached 70 per cent. They were always registered as 'Ewenki' – or whatever – to enable mothers to collect the special 'Minority' children's allowance. Some of these brief liaisons appeared in the official statistics as 'mixed marriages' but they seem to have been more like 'provisional concubinage', the main source of India's Anglo-Indian tribe.

Mrs Ogryzko shared Mr A.'s worry about the Ewenkis' future. 'There is nothing to make the young have hope. Communists hated people who were different, all everywhere must be the same. That way they killed our culture, same way they killed their own. I have been once in Moscow, last year, and there is not *Russia*. It is America, like what we see on TV.' This plain speaking surprised me;

for whatever reason, I had never heard a Slav Siberian so openly condemning Communism.

Varya also worked at the school – 'in a non-academic way', as Ghantimur delicately put it – and she walked back with us to do her evening shift. We returned to Tynda in the school's brand-new twenty-seater minibus, taking pupils to special classes in the College of Music. This minibus – a gift from abroad, Ghantimur didn't know where – was by far the smartest vehicle to be seen on the city's streets.

Pavel awaited us at the Dzerzhinskys, nursing a heavy cold and coughing ominously but prepared to take my education a stage further during supper. Later I wrote in my diary:

Pavel says Zarya museum's opening in 1975 marked a Soviet mood change. There was then a revival of interest amongst the intelligentsia, all over the Soviet Union, in national cultural traditions. By 1980 the newly emerging native intelligentsia were free to show loyalty to their own heritage, so disparaged for the previous sixty years, not only by Russians but by most products of the internaty (boarding-schools for Minority children). In 1986 Yu. Rytkheu, an elderly Ewenki writer, boldly regretted, in print, the Party's ruthless destruction of shamanism – which sentiment would once have earned a single ticket to the Gulag. He admitted to feeling some sympathy with his ancestral religion, chiefly because it had fostered such a harmonious relationship with nature. As for the shamans themselves – derided by the Party as ignorant greedy frauds – he had come to realize that many were skilled healers, wise mentors and 'with the spiritual elevation of a poet'. Pavel smiled. 'I like that phrase!'

I didn't admit to my friends that I can't see the point of Zarya school and village. The Ewenki have long since been obliterated as a cultural entity – gradually and incidentally under the czars, quickly and deliberately under the Soviets. There is no place for Ewenki as Ewenki in twenty-first-century Siberia. When all the many extraordinary skills that maintained their way of being have been lost, why put them on this futile life-support machine? Why not let them merge in to Siberia's majority population as a minority neither discriminated against nor favoured? (Biologically they seem to be half-merged already.) As life gets tougher for Slav Siberians, favouring the natives will increasingly provoke hostility. The Dzerzhinskys were wondering at supper time why Ewenki should have free university education when the new Russia demands fees from their daughters.

★

Next day a bronchitis epidemic let me off the lecturing hook; Pavel, and most of his colleagues and students, were in their beds. I hadn't expected such bugs to operate during Siberia's winter. In Baltistan, my only other experience of very low temperatures, everyone remained healthy until the thaw began. Obviously overheated and poorly ventilated homes and offices are to blame. In 1975 Baltistan had no flats, no central heating, no extreme difference between inside and outside. Inside was only marginally less cold; one kept wrapped-up, discarding at most the outer layer, and the nocturnal pee-bucket was iced over by dawn.

The Dzerzhinskys were a gregarious family and everyone's numerous friends wandered in and out; at any time of day some caller might be sitting in the kitchen drinking tea, guzzling one of Oksana's confections and conceding to Misha's demand for yet another chocolate. Misha demolished my theory that all cats, unlike dogs, are sensible enough not to overeat.

That afternoon Olesja's friend Andrei dropped in, his visit coinciding with Anna's. Anna was Eva's twenty-five-year-old English teacher, keen to practise with a native speaker, so I heard something about Andrei's exploits as a junior army officer in Chechnya in the mid-1990s. He himself had killed twenty-seven 'terrorists' – or so he claimed – and his unit had lost only two men. He had had 'a good war'. Now he wished he could be back on the scene of action but his mother had bribed both himself and his senior officer to keep him safe in Tynda. Thousands of terrorists, he assured me, had come to Chechnya from all over the Middle East, from Afghanistan and Turkish Kurdistan 'and other Mussulman places' – all armed with 'the best weapons', all carrying 'sacks of dollars', all intent on destabilizing Russia and 'fighting the Orthodox Church'. Observing Andrei's expression as he recalled his personal bag of twenty-seven, it was too easy to imagine him gleefully participating in violence – as it seems the majority of young males will do, almost anywhere, if misinformed and roused to anger. Meanwhile Olesja sat gazing at him adoringly but her mother, who had just come in, caught my eye and made an eloquent moue. I said nothing. Had Andrei spoken English I would have challenged him (sensing Oksana on my side) about the barbarous destruction of Grozny and Moscow's real motives for its barbarities in that region. Unfortunately such matters can't constructively be debated through an interpreter.

When Olesja and Andrei had gone to a film at the Palace of Culture, and Oksana had gone to her second – menial – job at Tynda hospital (ill-paid teachers need second jobs), Anna made another pot of tea and talked about herself. An only child, she couldn't remember her father, killed in Afghanistan when she was a toddler. She never got on with her mother, a captain in the militia whose military mindset led her to discipline her small daughter as though she were a raw recruit. Aged twenty she married a BAM engineer and now he was getting restless because the baby he longed for wasn't forthcoming. On the morrow they were going to a specialist for advice. They knew all about the latest hi-tech baby-making procedures but those were unaffordable – happened in Moscow and they couldn't even pay the train fare, never mind the fees at the American Clinic.

I was making comforting noises when Eva and twenty-year-old Sergei arrived, the latter wearing an improvised surgeon's mask over his nose and mouth by way of not infecting others with what sounded like a very sore throat. He had been on the Dzerzhinsky scene when I first arrived – in fact was rarely off it, unless he and Eva were in his mother's flat. An endearing young man, tall, handsome and loose-limbed with a wide happy smile, he spoke only a few phrases of English but, unlike the average young Siberian, was not shy about using them. In July 2006, when he had qualified as an electrical engineer, he and Eva would marry and move to Novosibirsk where his father lived and where Eva hoped to study medicine. His mother, an electrical engineer, would also move; she had a relevant contact, manager of a US-owned company recently set up in Novosibirsk.

Eva and Sergei – 'in love for two years', explained Anna – seemed content to do their courting in their respective homes. They were not publicly demonstrative, except in their exchanged glances, but as the days passed I noticed that in both flats they withdrew from the company at intervals, to be on their own for a little time, and this was taken for granted – no parental nods and winks, far less sibling snig-gers. Both were already being treated as established and loved in-laws. There was something curiously mature about this case of young love, a touching calmness and certainty.

At 6.0 p.m. and −29°C, Anna, Olesja and I set off to walk across the city by moonlight; Mrs V., director of the municipal art school, had telephoned to invite me to admire her pupils' work. During winter Tynda enjoys a blissful absence of motor traffic after dark and the over-heard conversations of our few fellow-pedestrians sounded oddly distinct in the still air.

Anna and Olesja, both alumnae of this art school, proudly showed me round. The municipality provides three hundred children, aged five to seventeen, with excellent tuition at an annual cost to parents of R150 (about $5) for materials. Other materials come free: scraps of velvet, fragments of gnarled wood, corks, plastic yoghurt lids, dried ferns, bits of copper wire and broken glass (blunt), beer cans flattened and chopped up – 'rubbish' from which some extraordinarily imaginative collages had been created. We toured classrooms for painting, sculpting, weaving, ceramics (equipped with six ovens), metalwork, wood-carving. Several junior classes were in progress despite the late hour, seven- to ten-year-olds happily painting, carving or sculpting. They and their teachers seemed equally enthusiastic and again I noticed that relaxed – almost affectionate – relationship between Siberian teachers and pupils which had so impressed me on my earlier visit and seems all the more remarkable given the new Russia's educational 'reforms'. My Muscovite friends have told me this phenomenon is rare nowadays in European Russia.

We found Mrs V. still working in her frugally furnished office while two kittens played with the waste-paper basket. She spoke no English but was fluent in German, learned from a Volga German grand-mother. Stoutish and fiftyish, she had long fair hair, shrewd blue eyes, a strong face and strong views. In all countries, she pronounced, chil-dren's creativity should be encouraged, however slight their inborn talent might appear to be. Given patient and skilled tuition, most chil-dren's creativity blossomed. Cultivating it would do a lot to reduce drug addiction, alcoholism, vandalism and the sort of crime bred by drifting aimlessly around the streets. The graffiti urge could be directed towards brightening dreary blocks with all sorts of murals: comic, tragic, representational, abstract, historical, political – Mrs V.'s eyes shone as she looked towards that brighter future. Also, being creative would boost adolescent self-esteem, now threatened by consumerist pressures – so many things advertised and available but unaffordable. In the Soviet Union numerous activities organized for the young greatly boosted self-esteem, though the West had only seen

Communism suppressing individuality. The more Mrs V. talked, the more I warmed to her.

As we drank tea sweetened with blackcurrant jam, and the kittens shared a saucer of milk, Mrs V. spoke of her most immediate problem. Tynda's fifteen- to seventeen-year-olds had been invited to enter an international art competition and at present the best work was being done by youngsters whose parents couldn't possibly afford the fare to Paris. Yet for the honour of Tynda and the honour of Russia the school's most promising artists must compete and appear in person – surely some funding could be found! But if it were, those parents of the less talented who could afford the fares would resent their offspring being deprived of the kudos, not seeing the irrelevance of comparative wealth in a situation all to do with *talent*. We agreed that unequal wealth, though unavoidable, is divisive (unavoidable even under Communism, though I didn't make that point).

As we re-robed I observed above the cloakroom door a large coloured photograph of Mr Putin, unsmiling and stony-eyed as ever. 'Is he popular?' I asked. 'Will most vote for him next month? Do Tynda people like him?'

Anna looked shocked – then reproving, even indignant. 'Vladimir Putin is our President! We must like him, everyone likes him, he is a good leader for Russia, very powerful. He protects us from the Mussulmans in Chechnya, if we won't win there they are waiting to come to attack us from Central Asia. Have you forgotten what Andrei told you?'

On the way home we passed Tynda's small new private art school where, said Anna, the tuition is much inferior but its snob value appeals to parents with more roubles than artistic sensibility. Soon after, she and I quarrelled mildly, about flowers. A florist's kiosk was still open – improbably, at 9.0 p.m. and minus 30 – which provoked me to deplore that industry. It enrages me to see flowers grown in some African country, to the grievous detriment of its farmers, on sale in our world. 'But they all come from Holland,' said Anna, 'and that's a rich country in Europe!'

'They're only distributed from Holland,' I said testily. 'They're mostly grown in Africa – I've watched it happening, on huge commercial farms that poison the villagers' drinking water. I've seen them being sent to Holland, loaded into refrigerated cargo planes.'

Anna stood still, looked disbelieving, returned to the kiosk – then rejoined us saying, 'They *do* come from Holland! The woman showed me her documents! It doesn't matter – in winter we must have flowers to brighten our dark moods! It's not necessary to worry about Africans.'

While eating a three-course breakfast (bliny, fish stew and rice, buns hot from the oven stuffed with blackcurrant jam) I revealed my plan for the day: a long solitary walk in the hills around Tynda. Appalled, Oksana at once rang Pavel – still bed-ridden and coughing – then informed me that at 8.30 their friends Pyotr and Igor would arrive to escort me. Pyotr was a youngish college lecturer on Tourism Development, Igor an English language student who would interpret whatever advice I might have to offer Pyotr on Tynda's touristic future. Oksana assembled a generous picnic and at 8.25 (Siberians are sticklers for punctuality) a taxi, ordered and paid for by Pavel, took us to the foot of the hills.

My companions were agreeable young men but their presence modified my enjoyment of steep winding paths through thin taiga. I dislike being escorted; other people get between you and 'the spirit of place'. Yet I could understand Oksana's concern; a silly babushka, who left those paths, might get stuck in very deep snow.

Back on the road, at 3.15, it horrified me to hear that the taxi was due to collect us at 3.30, though a two-mile downhill walk would have taken us home. I suggested going to meet the taxi but Pyotr and Igor preferred to stand and wait while our breaths gave us moustaches of ice. Too easily human beings are made dependent on motor transport.

That evening Sergei's mother laid on a banquet for the Irish writer/babushka; four of her woman friends were eager to meet me. Writers have a high status in Siberia – in all of Russia – but the babushka as solo traveller was the main talking point, the puzzling part. Why was I not afraid to be alone? (I wish I had a euro for every time I've been asked that question!) How could I travel around not speaking Russian? Why had I abandoned my family for three months? Grandchildren need their babushkas nearby – two if possible. I tried to explain that Irish babushkas are less important, and anyway my family live in Italy which is far from Ireland – almost as far as Tynda from Severobaikalsk – therefore when writing my next book I wouldn't see my granddaughters for six months. At this point, lips were compressed.

Many Siberians don't see their grandchildren for six years or more because of travelling costs – but that's a cross to be borne. The notion of a rich babushka being so detached caused censorious ripples. Then we talked about books and editing, and everyone lamented the cost of new volumes since the end of subsidized publishing.

As we walked home the outsize illuminated municipal thermometer registered −31°C and Sergei remarked, 'Our most cold this year, for your memory souvenir!'

Next morning, going to buy my ticket for Komsomolsk-na-Amure, I got a nasty shock. Eighteen months previously this BAM booking-office on Tynda's main street was sensibly utilitarian, a large bare space with one wooden bench and minutely detailed but easy-to-read train timetables on greyish walls. Now the walls were apricot, variegated tiles hid the plain plank floor, a pink sofa and two armchairs replaced the bench, tall imitation Ming vases (good imitations) stood in the window embrasures, an all-glass kiosk opposite the entrance sold videos, crossword puzzles, chocolates, cigarettes, beer, soft drinks and soft porn – magazines depicting naked women half-covering their pubic parts with machine guns and masturbating with revolvers. The dowdy middle-aged clerk I well remembered was gone, replaced by a svelte young woman wearing a stylish uniform and a professionally pleasant smile, whose fingers flew swiftly over the computer keys. The timetables were also gone, replaced by enormous garish advertisements for Moscow and St Petersburg hotels. (The vast majority of Tynda residents have never been within two thousand miles of either city.) Reluctantly I paid fifteen roubles for a glossy train schedule pamphlet decorated with pretty pictures. And I thought of Mrs Beryozov's daughter in Irkutsk, who used to visit her mother regularly before the booking-office was refurbished but can no longer afford the fare. Here was the cruel face of capitalism.

For the 945-mile journey (thirty-seven hours) to Komsomolsk-na-Amure I booked into a *platskartny*, described in the *BAM Guide* as 'the most common type of carriage in Russia but not the most pleasant. It has two tiers of berths in open compartments on one side of the corridor with a row of berths arranged lengthways down the other side. It accommodates 58 passengers. Mattresses and pillows are supplied. By an ingenious mechanism, the aisle berths can be lifted up

and down to make aisle seats and tables.' *Platskartny* are more conducive than coupés to an active social life but have one disadvantage: the
berths lack individual reading lights. Conveniently, departure time was
5.30 p.m.; dawn is the best time to arrive in an unknown city.

Pyotr had urged me to visit Tynda's museum that forenoon;
he wanted my opinion of this tourist 'attraction'. Two of the
Dzerzhinsky sisters accompanied us; all my reactions to their home-
town fascinated them.

The museum fills an imposing three-storey neo-Georgian building
and its three sections – Tynda, Ewenki, BAM – are linked by long
high-ceilinged corridors and sweeping staircases. In the new Russia
some things changed quickly – like ownership of the main national
assets – and other things, like the running of provincial museums,
didn't change at all. In an overheated little office I paid fifty roubles
for my own ticket and forty roubles for the four Russians' tickets – a
fair disparity. Each ticket came in three parts, for the separate sections,
and the filling in of numerous duplicate dockets, and the transferring
of details (what details?) to a fat ledger, took nineteen minutes – I was
watching the wall clock. When I intimated to Pyotr that a party of
five foreign tourists would not take kindly to this procedure he looked
rather puzzled – it's how things *are*.

A guide and an interpreter then joined us, the former a plump
elderly woman who stood to attention beside each exhibit and
explained it at length, her spiel fluently translated in a toneless voice
by a thin pale woman with a slight limp. Later, I advised Pyotr that
explanatory legends in the main European languages would be more
tourist-friendly than a guide who dictates how much time may be
devoted to each exhibit. He looked worried and said, 'Then would
be two jobs lost!'

The Tynda and Ewenki sections were limited and trite, the BAM
section was excellent though not entirely honest. I attempted to abbre-
viate our guide's detailed yet censored history lesson by explaining that
I knew the story and only wanted to look at the many relief maps,
photographs, models and tools on display. The attempt failed. Finally,
in exasperation, I referred to the bitter controversies that for decades
surrounded the BAM project, and to the tens of thousands of German
and Japanese prisoners of war who died while BAM-building under
the most horrendous conditions. The interpreter then took umbrage

and my companions looked unhappy. Afterwards, I warned Pyotr that twenty-first-century tourists won't relish Soviet propaganda.

'But we don't know it's propaganda,' he protested. 'We think it's true, we don't get the information you have.'

'But now you can get it,' I reminded him. 'Now you have *glasnost*.' (Openness, free speech.)

A convalescent Pavel awaited us at the Dzerzhinskys and over a late lunch I mentioned my criticisms of the museum and wondered – had they been too harsh? Did Pyotr regret our expedition? Pavel laughed. 'If he did he shouldn't! He knows we must learn in isolated places like Tynda. For us, moving out of the Soviet way of doing things happens slowly, we need foreign thoughts to speed it up.'

I consulted Pavel about a suitable 'thank you' present for the Dzerzhinskys. Perhaps a concealed gift of dollars for each daughter, to be found after my departure? Pavel winced. Unless Siberians have formally set up 'homestays', cash is insulting – as in Muslim countries. Small gifts 'for the memory' would be greatly valued and luckily I had brought a supply from Ireland. I tried to tell Pavel how much my stay with his friends had meant to me. This family seemed to radiate affection not only for each other but for the world in general. And their home was so laughter-filled one felt they could only see the funny side of life.

Saying goodbye, a few hours later, involved much hugging. Oksana and Viktor wrapped up to see me out to the College Lada, the girls and Sergei somehow squeezed into it and at the station other Tynda friends from 2002, whom I'd also been visiting, were gathered to see me off, inevitably laden with farewell bags of food. As the *provodnitsa* checked my ticket Pavel's driver drew a bottle of vodka from his pocket, insisted on my having a quick swig, then handed me half a juicy pear. 'An old custom,' smiled Pavel. 'It means you must come back to Tynda to eat the other half.'

5

Stalin's One-Purpose City

A N ORANGE MOON was rising as train No. 964 moved off, very slowly, into the dusk. I had been allocated a lower bunk in a half-empty *platskartny*; above me lay an unsociable man with shoulder-length black hair who despite the dim light remained immersed, day and night, in a fat hardback science fiction volume. Two friendly young men occupied the opposite bunks and the lengthways bunks across the corridor were vacant. I immediately transformed the lower one into a writing-desk and two seats.

The crew-cut army lieutenant was returning to his Komsomolsk-na-Amure barracks from a fortnight's leave in Severobaikalsk. With an engaging sort of bravado, he drew my attention to the blood-group details emblazoned on his battledress tunic. His friend, tall and lanky, was going to Khabarovsk where an uncle, a mobile phone dealer/importer, had offered him a job. When a snack trolley came around (another manifestation of privatization) my companions bought me a little bar of chocolate and a little packet of biscuits – the sort of gesture one remembers after more important events have been forgotten.

In the distance some uncivic-minded person played loud rap on his or her transistor until 10.0 p.m. when Olga, our *provodnitsa*, took action. In general, *provodniki* are noted for efficiency rather than amiability but Olga combined both. Middle-aged and hefty, with arms suggesting much hard work at the dacha, she had short auburn-tinted hair, broad irregular features and a maternal attitude towards all passengers. She dressed casually – loose blue shirt, brown slacks – unlike the lissom *provodnitsa* pictured in that glossy train schedule who wore a trim bottle-green uniform with matching tie. Olga adopted me at first glance and, dismissing my cornucopia of food, insisted on cooking me a hot supper (noodles and minced reindeer) in the *provodniki's* private cabin.

Because No. 964 was experiencing a temporary coal shortage the insides of the windows were thinly iced and everyone retained their sweaters and jackets. Early next morning we paused for forty minutes at some little settlement where an antique coal lorry (*c.* 1970?) drove along the platform restocking each carriage.

For moments, as the sun rose, the whole sky became gloriously inflamed above level taiga – the tall bare birches no thicker than broomhandles. Away to the east, all along the horizon, stretched the gleaming symmetrical humps of the Turana range. Soon we were crossing a plain where golden-brown reeds, poking through the snow, indicated swamp land. Overhead flew a Tokyo–Moscow jet, its destructive trail very beautiful – flamingo-pink. I felt privileged, daw-dling along by BAM, *seeing* Siberia, not having to fly over it because time is money.

Siberians seem able to sleep for fifteen hours at a stretch and no one else was awake at 11.0 a.m. as we began to climb into the Turana – lowish mountains, nowhere above 4,500 feet, their contours smooth under snow, our rising track sometimes visible ahead, rounding a distant shoulder. As we gained altitude the snow deepened and each pine and larch bore improbable burdens as though nature were organ-izing a competition – which tree can sustain the heaviest load? Siberia's uninhabited vastness mesmerizes me; as I write these words I long to return. Yet this train ride was shadowed by what I had learned at Zarya. All day we were traversing traditional Ewenki territory and each little settlement marked another stage in that people's destruction.

Just below the pass, where all the world was white, something inex-plicable – not white – caught my eye. How to explain a series of pale green ponds and short snow-free sections of streams looking like slabs of green glass? In the absence of steam, warm springs couldn't be responsible – and the ice was solid, not cracked and shifting. I met no Siberian who could explain this oddity.

At 1.15, seven hours ahead of Moscow time, we entered Khabarovski Krai (province) where a colossal monument to BAM-builders marks the regional border – a concrete 'X'. Soon after, beyond the ugly would-be industrial town of Etyrken, the south-eastern sky became blizzard-hazy. In the shallow valley of the Bureya river, one of the Amur's major tributaries, we crossed a famous BAM bridge near the village of Bureinski. In appearance it is no more remarkable than hundreds of other metal BAM bridges spanning very wide rivers but its construction made extraordinary demands on the railway troops. (Soldiers built most of BAM's eastern section.) For an undisclosed reason, doubtless to do with some muddle in Moscow, there was an urgent need for this particular bridge to be completed by May 1975. Normally nobody is expected to work outside when the temperature drops to −45°C, or −35°C with a wind. In such conditions machinery often fails, axes shatter and human beings daren't expose their skin to metal. However, that winter the railway troops kept going and the bridge was opened on 22 April 1975. Who knows how many young men fell by the trackside.

As we rumbled over the Bureya I could see fishermen crouching around their ice-holes, collecting the family's supper. A narrow wooden road bridge was visible nearby, built in 1954 to serve the coal-mining settlement of Chegdomyn, ten miles away. Three months after the opening of the BAM bridge both structures were tested by a catastrophic flood. The *BAM Guide* records:

> All along the river, the torrent washed trees and houses away. While the road bridge could withstand the water, if trees got caught under it, the pressure behind would simply push the bridge over. As it was impossible to get within 2km of the bridge, troops were lowered by helicopter to string a safety line across the top of it. Soldiers then stood on top of the bridge working to free any trees or other obstacles that got caught under it. The troops stood for hours in the freezing water, constantly afraid that the bridge would give away. It didn't and many won bravery awards that day.

Towards sunset we came to Novy Urgal, the only big town between Tynda and Komsomolsk. (The Russian Federation has many Komsomolsks but for the rest of this chapter I shall drop the 'na-Amure'.) After so many hundreds of pristine miles, Novy Urgal's pollution hit hard – a grey-brown sky, brown-black snow. We halted for half an hour beside coal and timber trains so long I couldn't see their beginnings or ends. Here is that Siberian rarity, a railway junction. When the Chegdomyn mine opened, in the late 1940s, a rail track was essential to carry its output some 300 miles south to the Trans-Siberian. Both Chegdomyn town (its name means 'black stone' in Ewenki) and the track were built by Japanese prisoners of war and

Stalin's gulag victims. A generation later Novy Urgal was built by Ukrainian troops who set up their first camp in December 1974. Each BAM town had its sponsor from beyond Siberia and Ukraine sponsored Novy Urgal.

At 5.40 we went on our way, darkness concealing the Bureinskiy and Badzhalskiy ranges as No. 964 wriggled between them along the Amgun river valley.

On 10 May 1932 Komsomolsk was founded in the middle of nowhere. Its remote unpopulated site catered for the Soviet paranoia about military industries; the Trans-Siberian was 225 miles to the south, the Chinese border 250 miles, the Pacific Ocean 280 miles down the Amur, Khabarovsk 320 miles up the Amur. By 1939 this new city was the fourth largest in the Russian Far East yet it had never met its prescribed monthly targets. Everything had conspired to slow construction: exceptionally cold winters, poor leadership, ill-trained workers and inadequate supplies which had to come from Khabarovsk by sledge on the frozen Amur – or by boat, during the two and a half months when the river is navigable. Therefore on 10 May 1937 Komsomolsk was purged. (Stalin was then at his most purgatious, throughout the Soviet Union.)

Writing in *Komsomolskaya Pravda* a month later, the Director of the Amurstal steelworks declared, 'We are mercilessly rooting out this scum of wreckers.' Allegedly, 'agents of foreign intelligence services, bandits and diversionists' had infiltrated the various workforces; their leaders were accused of neglecting security and executed en masse. Because Komsomolsk's further development needed many thousands of labourers the city soon became known as 'the Gulag capital of the Russian Far East'. Its camps processed at least 900,000 purge victims and several enormous factories and a hospital have been built over mass graves.

For its first fifty-nine years Komsomolsk remained tightly closed to foreigners – and to Russians who had no business there. It is said (but who knows?) that during this political quarantine it prospered, once Stalin was out of the way. Many of its citizens earned fat salaries; they were the sort of narrowly clever scientists, technicians and managers who can run an efficient war industry, keeping their skilled workforces – also quite well paid – producing at speed to meet 'important deadlines'. But then came 1992 with its sudden drastic cutbacks on military expenditure. Massive unemployment followed in Komsomolsk – now open to the rest of the world, but that new freedom doesn't pay for bread and kolbasa. In 1993 the population was 312,000; it has since been dwindling fast.

The *BAM Guide* opines, 'Komsomolsk has a lot to offer travellers.' The relevant Lonely Planet Guide thinks otherwise: 'It's probably the most depressing city on the BAM.' I agree with the former.

When I woke at 5.45 we were stationary in Khalgaso, twenty miles short of Komsomolsk. Hereabouts was much snowier than Siberia, because of the nearness of the ocean. Nobody was moving, either on the train or on the platform, but No. 964 had to loiter; it wouldn't do to arrive early. Near this little station is a memorial built by the Japanese, as soon as the Soviet Union collapsed, to honour their thousands of prisoners who died building the BAM.

A few miles further on we stopped again, in Silinks, where again no passengers disembarked. Here (oddly, before sunrise on a Sunday morning) a long freight train was being loaded with tin concentrate from two nearby mines – to be smelted in China, which causes much anger. Why won't Moscow invest in a local smelter?

The eastern sky was only faintly grey when we pulled into Komsomolsk's almost deserted station. Seeing a queue-free ticket guichet open I booked a *platskartny* bunk for the next stage, three days hence, to Vanino on the coast. Disappointingly, this twelve-hour journey (my shortest ever Russian train ride) would have to be overnight; there is no day service either way.

The station thermometer read −32°C but the air was still. Leaving my rucksack by a tram stop I paced to and fro; there was no sign of life, not a person or a vehicle to be seen. Arriving BAM passengers meet Komsomolsk at its grimmest; nearby loomed several nine-storey blocks, urgently needing maintenance, and between them could be glimpsed – through a pall of pollution – the unlovely contours of the Amurstal steelworks. On two block gable ends the strengthening light revealed gigantic murals, faded but well executed: enthusiastic hard-hatted young men and women, flourishing shovels and pickaxes, seemed to be striding towards me.

A No. 2 tram took me across the city to the Amur – a half-hour ride, several early workers hopping on and off, the filthy windows hiding Komsomolsk. These battered trams, surely as old as myself, are hard to heat; their drivers sit in bearskin cocoons, their conductresses sip frequently from large thermoses of tea. The flat-rate fare is about fifteen US cents – four roubles.

My timing seemed stage-managed. This 'City of the Dawn' (Stalin's nickname) has as its emblem a stalwart Komsomol 'volunteer' silhouetted against the beams of a rising sun – and when first I saw the mile-wide Amur a pallid orb was rising above long smooth mountains on the far shore. The slanting rays gave a coppery sheen to one midstream patch of the river's colourless, corrugated surface. Just below me, two small barges and two trawlers were fixed fast in the ice. On the quayside behind me grey snow was piled high, decorated all over with dog poo and pee – long-lasting excretions in mid-winter.

When a wind suddenly rose I hastened towards the nearby bus station, large and grotty with an implacably unhelpful staff. Here began my steep learning curve: Komsomolsk people are *different*, have not yet overcome their city's congenital handicap. Belonging to an introverted community conditioned for generations to imprison or kill all intruders, how could they have become 'normal' a mere twelve years after being exposed to public view? As ordinary passers-by would have nothing to do with a foreigner I sought directions to Hotel Amur in the palace of culture where a grumpy concierge reluctantly drew a diagram. The hotel was ten minutes' walk away, on Prospekt Mira.

Since 2001 Komsomolsk had been enjoying a slow flow of inward investment, mainly from China and Japan, and Hotel Amur, 'downmarket' according to the *BAM Guide*, was now quite 'up-market'. Japanese prisoners of war designed and constructed this attractive four-storey corner building, newly painted ochre and pale gold. For $23 I luxuriated in a third-floor suite: hallway, bathroom, double bedroom, sitting-room with a four-person sofa and a giant TV – immediately switched on by Maria, the *deezhoornaya* (floor-manageress), as though it were a life-support machine. The temperature was rational – one didn't sweat – and for this Maria apologized. Here Intourist anachronisms survive; the receptionist gave me a card, Maria exchanged my key for that card and whenever I went out the key had to be locked in the *deezhoornaya*'s drawer and my card shown to a security guard.

Komsomolsk, underfoot, was uncommonly hazardous and falls attracted no attention; given so much padding, coming down on one's coccyx is a minor mishap. People stood up, ruefully rubbed their behinds, went on their way. Everybody, I noticed, skilfully fell backwards, not endangering heads or arms. I used my walking stick and wondered why other people didn't have them – especially the elderly.

Short careful steps insufficiently stimulate the circulation and when the dreaded wind came I needed to thaw out, every half hour or so, in whatever bus or tram chanced to be passing. One impromptu tram-ride took me to an enormous bustling open air market on the city's edge where most of the shoddy goods were, as usual, from China. Stallholders who had been standing around all forenoon – so wrapped-up they moved like cartoon figures – still seemed relaxed and cheerful. One could scarcely see their features but they sounded poly-glottal: from the Caucasus, Central Asia, India, Korea – the majority of course from China, which seriously worries some people.

Central Komsomolsk pleasantly surprised me. In a city founded to produce what a Communist army craved, there was something per-verse about those wide, tree-lined bourgeois boulevards where five-storey edifices of stucco and brick sported fanciful friezes, jolly cupolas, irrelevant turrets, over-elaborate balconies, pointless colon-nades and several busts of Lenin so placed in wreathed niches that he might be mistaken for a philosopher of antiquity.

Not far from the centre stand streets of solid two-storey wooden houses – the pioneers' dwellings – with first-floor French windows giving access to improvised plank balconies brightened by scarlet and turquoise blankets hung out to air. And just behind Hotel Amur, at the other extreme of the chronological scale, reared the frameworks for three nine-storey blocks, abruptly abandoned in 1992 – raw and bleak against the deep blue sky, like some magnified unfinished Meccano construct. Who was planning to live here? Are those people now in Khabarovsk or Vladivostok, job-seeking and hungry? Such abandoned projects are to be found in every Siberian city – 'talking skeletons', as one of my Tynda friends described them. Talking about failure.

Towards sunset a *pivo*-hunt proved arduous. For lack of explanatory shop windows, I pushed open numerous heavy double doors: to a florist's, a DIY store, a bookshop, a boutique, a white goods store, a shoe shop, a computer shop. All were doing business, at minus 33 late on

Sunday afternoon, so perhaps that inward investment had begun to trickle down. Then at last a door opened on a small supermarket where a scowling young security officer grabbed my plastic bag, thrust it into a locker and handed me the key. As I left he sneered at my purchases: *pivo*, black bread, kolbasa. (Kolbasa is a sort of salami, made from pork, which keeps indefinitely even in hot weather.)

That evening I rang Vera and Igor Khubov (owners of Shenko the white kitten) who had invited me to contact them. We arranged to meet for an early lunch with their friend Arsen, a fluent English-speaker. Vera would collect me from Hotel Amur.

In the public arena of a BAM corridor, with inquisitive fellow-passengers listening, both Khubovs had obviously felt inhibited by their limping English and I only knew that they had been honeymooning in Moscow, their first visit to their capital city. Now, as Vera and I walked down Prospekt Mira, I heard much more. Circumstances were making married life difficult. They couldn't yet afford a flat of their own and were living with Igor's parents. His mother had never really approved of their marriage, saying nothing but looking sour. Vera seemed admirably understanding about this, could see her mother-in-law's viewpoint. As an aspiring actress she spent a lot of time resting and during those intervals didn't look for work but wrote plays which never found a producer. Igor, a graphic designer, had hoped to find a job in Moscow where he believed his wife's talents would be more appreciated. But both had recoiled from the Moscow scene – too intimidating, without 'strong contacts' you couldn't get started.

Igor and Arsen were waiting for us, drinking *pivo* and nibbling fishy snacks. Komsomolsk's smart new restaurants, enjoyed by an expanding cohort of mafia comrades (not entirely dissociated from inward investors), opened only at sunset on weekdays. Arsen had therefore chosen a small would-be-smart L-shaped restaurant halfway down Prospekt Mira. A betrothal party had reserved the long part of the L where each table had its floral decoration – artificial, I was pleased to see, though convincing. The fat security man straddling a camp chair by the entrance wore no insignia but had a large revolver stuck casually in his belt. At the table beside ours, two worn-looking women were anxiously arguing over sheaves of documents with the aid of a calculator. 'Accounts people from the maternity hospital,' murmured Vera. 'They have problems without enough money.'

Igor, handsome though not attractive, looked a decade or so older than his round-faced, wide-eyed, twenty-year-old bride. She was, it now emerged, his second wife and he couldn't afford a flat because he already owned one – occupied by his semi-invalid ex-wife and their two children. As Igor explained all this, with Arsen's help, Vera looked rather put out – then wanted me to know that when she first met Igor he was free, a divorced man.

Arsen was a Muscovite businessman temporarily working in Komsomolsk on behalf of a Japanese corporation. An Armenian by origin, though Moscow-born, he had done time at the Harvard Business School and didn't temper his opinion of Komsomolsk in the presence of two Komsomolskians. 'Here is the most uncivilized city in our Russian Federation. These people, they are living somewhere else, they can't relate to reality. You try to help them, make jobs, they reckon you're trying to cheat them!'

I felt a surge of sympathy for all the uncouth, xenophobic Komsomolskians. 'Don't forget their background,' I said. 'Give them time to adjust!'

Angrily Arsen waved his napkin. 'Background! You know about our Armenian background? You've gotta forget background, move on, grab chances when they come. If folks here can't wake up fast the Chinese will have them for a snack. Leave a vacuum anywhere in this century, the Chinese will fill it!'

I remarked that my Siberian friends had been voicing much more unease about China than in 2002. According to Igor, in the Russian Far East people were not merely uneasy but afraid. Twenty million Chinese, he asserted, had either settled in the region or were toing and froing so often they controlled most business and development, were cleverly positioned for a takeover. And only four million Russians remained.

I said, 'Those figures sound incredible. Who counts the Chinese and how? Anyway, many must be fly-by-night speculators, taking advantage of the present legal and economic anarchy.'

'OK,' said Arsen. 'Some are like you say – but not so many. Most are here to stay, planning way ahead.'

Vera quoted her father, who blamed Moscow for allowing this scary demographic shift – even encouraging it by apparently losing interest in Eastern Siberia and the Far East, saying they couldn't afford to develop various mines.

A waitress interrupted ('Tea or coffee?') and Arsen, who had insisted on taking over the role of host, apologized for the limited menu. I made polite noises though that meal was the worst ever to come my way in the Russian Federation. Then our heavily chlorinated tea arrived, equally heavily sweetened; Russians find the notion of unsweetened tea disgusting. (On the train from Tynda, and in Hotel Amur, chlorination also overwhelmed the tea aroma.)

As the betrothal party arrived, we departed. The men were working, Vera had an audition for a part in Gorky's *The Lower Depths*. Why, I asked, was depressed Komsomolsk's theatre being so masochistic, staging such a play?

'For therapy?' suggested Arsen and Vera confirmed this. It could be cathartic, indirectly, for older people who had 'so many repressed childhood memories of bad things happening all around them'.

'And maybe they saw parents *doing* bad things,' said Arsen with a tinge of ghoulish relish.

I accompanied Vera to the imposing theatre, then walked on down to the Amur, passing the Great Patriotic War memorial, an assemblage of monumental sculptures making up in bulk what they lack in beauty. A decade after its foundation Komsomolsk was no more than a middle-sized town, yet almost 6,000 names are engraved here. These conspicuous war memorials, to be seen even in villages, always reminded me of that infamous assessment of the senator for Missouri, President-to-be Truman, reported in the *New York Times* on 24 June 1941 as Hitler's troops marched into the Soviet Union:

If we see that Germany is winning, we ought to help Russia, and if Russia is winning, we ought to help Germany, and that way let them kill as many as possible, although I don't want to see Hitler victorious in any circumstances.

Within the US and Britain, many people of influence preferred Fascism to Communism (or even socialism), as they had just proved in Spain. Hence their ignoring of Stalin's repeated pleas to Washington and London, from September 1939, to assist Moscow in a stand against Hitler. Silence enveloped this awkward fact until 1 January 1970 when the British Cabinet papers for 1939 were released. By then it was easy to minimize the revelation's significance; it never received much attention in the English-language media.

Another monument stands closer to the Amur, commemorating the arrival of Komsomolsk's founder group, intrepid pioneers who had to fell trees and drain swamps. Five muscular young men, three times life-size, are eagerly facing inland and carrying a nice mix of gear – shovel, gun, guitar, surveying instruments. Not far away, yet another monument is incomplete, an oblong stack of large stones some ten feet high and twenty feet long with short metal rods decorating the top like candles on a birthday cake. It honours the thousands of Soldier-Builders who, in 1934, marched down the frozen Amur from Khabarovsk, driving prisoners before them as ice-testers. No one counted the prisoners lost en route. One day soon, it is said, this monument will be completed. I rather liked it as it is, resembling some mysterious prehistoric burial mound.

Westerners tend to mock the Soviets' 'hypocritical' glorification of the common worker, to recall only Stalin's labour camp abominations and overlook later generations, people like Aunt Tasha in Nizhneangarsk, to whom her medal 'for good work' meant so much. And all my BAM-builder friends are gratified that numerous monuments honour them en masse – though they do resent the deletion from the record of those who died as victims of official brutality or stupidity. To have remembered them would have tarnished officialdom's share of the glory.

In the West we are more inclined to raise monuments to individual Fat Cats, many of whom were indifferent to their workers' welfare – hardly thought of them as human beings. Now, in a world where deregulation and privatization make a uniquely safe habitat for such felines, the Soviet recognition of ordinary workers' input looks positively humane.

To the amusement of three fishermen I slid down to river level on my bottom, using their steep, soap-slippy path. Then for a mile or so I walked downstream on an Amur bumpy with frozen wavelets, the afternoon sun brilliant though heatless. Along the left bank stretched low mountain ridges, looking uninhabited, desolate. The flat right bank was not enhanced by Komsomolsk's industrial core: all those aircraft and submarine factories, and their ancillary plants, outlined jaggedly against the horizon.

Paranoia prevailed for the sixty years of this city's isolation – but where did it start? When the Red Army was nearing victory over the

Whites and their capitalist allies, the normally staid *New York Times* ran numerous scare stories:

Reds Seek War With America *30 December 1919*

Allied officials and diplomats foresee possible invasion of Europe *11 January 1920*

Allied diplomatic circles fear an invasion of Persia *13 January 1920*

Well-informed diplomats expect military invasion of Europe and Soviet advance into Eastern and Southern Asia *16 January 1920*

No War With Russia: Allies to Trade with Her *17 January 1920*

Reds Raising Army to Attack India *7 February 1920*

Fear That Bolsheveki Will Now Invade Japanese Territory *11 February 1920*

For two years, from the summer of 1918, more than 13,000 US troops fought in Siberia and European Russia with British, French, Japanese, Czech and other Allies – all under orders, in Winston Churchill's words, 'to strangle the Bolshevik state at birth'. He himself, as Britain's Minister for War and Air, had organized this support for the White Army. A decade later he wrote:

Were they [the Allies] at war with Soviet Russia? Certainly not; but they shot Soviet Russians at sight. They stood as invaders on Russian soil. They armed the enemies of the Soviet Government. They block-aded its ports, and sunk its battleships. They earnestly desired and schemed its downfall. But war – shocking! Interference – shame! It was, they repeated, a matter of indifference to them how Russians settled their own internal affairs. They were impartial – Bang!

Thousands of young Americans died in that campaign, yet these heroic defenders of capitalism have no memorial. According to the American historian D. F. Fleming:

For the American people the cosmic tragedy of the interventions in Russia does not exist or it was an unimportant incident long forgot-ten. But for the Soviet people and their leaders the period was a time of endless killing, of looting and rapine, of measureless suffering for scores of millions . . . For many years the harsh Soviet regimentations could all be justified by fear that the capitalist powers would be back to finish the job.

The capitalist powers dared not ignore the Soviet experiment. Suppose it had succeeded, had not been handicapped by Western hostility in general and the arms race in particular? Suppose the newly freed colonies in Africa and Asia, and the Latin American countries long since annexed de facto by the US – suppose all those peoples had been shown that a non-capitalist system could benefit 'the masses' more than a capitalist system? It was unthinkable that such an experiment should be given any chance to succeed.

After 1945 the spy business boomed as obsessed governments wasted billions of dollars, pounds and roubles on the puerile pursuit of useless facts – or fancies, if an agent couldn't deliver enough facts to gain his reward. The CIA employed many hundreds of young émigré Russians to collect tons, literally, of detailed but valueless information to do with military and industrial installations, special attention being devoted to nuclear and missile matters. Tons more were collected by submarines, satellites, electronic listening-posts along the Turkish and Iranian borders (what if Soviet listening-posts had appeared along the Mexican border?) – and of course spy planes flying high from US bases in Norway, Greece, Turkey, Iran, Pakistan and Japan. As William Blum notes in *Killing Hope* (2003): 'There is no evidence that any of the information collected ever saved any lives, or served any other useful purpose for the world . . . Much of it has never been looked at, and never will be.'

The CIA's tame émigrés belonged to the National Union of Labor (NTS) which contained two groups – the sons of families who had fled the Revolution, and Soviet citizens who had chosen to settle in Western Europe as the Cold War began. The main NTS base, in West Germany, was funded throughout the 1950s by the CIA. Members were 'educated' at the CIA school, known as the Institute for the Study of the USSR. They then received special training in the US and UK, learning how to do terrorist tricks like derailing trains – tricks described as 'sabotage' if performed on behalf of 'democratic' governments. When parachuted onto Soviet territory their gear included sophisticated weapons, frogmen suits, collapsible bicycles and rubber mats to make possible the crossing of barbed wire electric fencing. (Miles of such discarded fencing lie around Komsomolsk's Lenin District and may now be snipped for free souvenirs – the only sort I acquire.)

The NTS spies' objectives were varied: info-collecting, gathering samples of up-to-date identity documents, assassinating key personalities, helping Western agents on their way home, derailing trains, blowing up bridges, power plants and arms factories. Thus we see that Komsomolsk, and the many other 'closed' cities, were closed against real threats. And we also see why such cities were closed to *Russian* non-residents.

The KGB found it easy enough to infiltrate the NTS in West Germany and they stymied scores of operations. In 1961 Moscow's English Language Press published *Caught in the Act* (CIA), giving the names and details of a few dozen spies captured almost as they touched the ground. Some were shot, others jailed. But CIA methods made the KGB's infiltration task unpopular. In Munich the CIA routinely tortured young NTS volunteers suspected of being KGB agents. Turpentine applied to the testicles worked well, as did Indonesian music played as loudly as possible in a small cell day and night.

When US soldiers were detected torturing Iraqi prisoners in 2004 the shock-horror reaction at once astonished and exasperated me. For half a century US military forces and 'intelligence' agencies have been amongst the world's most ingenious and enthusiastic torturers. Also, their School of the Americas (based in Georgia and formerly in Panama) ran torture classes for the Pentagon's Latin American military puppets. (Perhaps they still do.) In 1979, in a South American capital, the ambassador of a Western European country showed me a School of the Americas' textbook; the chapter on 'Sexual Humiliation' included clinical but explicit diagrams.

John Foster Dulles, a major influence on US foreign policy immediately after the Second World War, left no more space for non-aligned, independent-minded nations than do the twenty-first-century neocons. 'For us,' said Dulles, 'there are two sorts of people in the world. There are those who are Christians and support free enterprise and there are the others.' Subsequently 'the others' wonderfully loosened US Treasury purse-strings, deflecting billions from real human needs to 'defence'. Now the terrorist threat is serving the same arms industry purpose. And the Cold War fantasy about Soviet troops being poised to invade Western Europe had its echo when we were told that Saddam Hussein was another Hitler-figure, threatening the world with weapons of mass destruction.

Before dressing I checked the temperature: −34°C. By now I understood the omnipresence of thermometers; a few degrees up or down can mean a garment more or less. And one looks for arboreal guidance. That morning the birches and larches – almost touching my window – were motionless.

Outside Hotel Amur a woman wrapped in many ragged layers was using an odd implement, a heavy axe-head on a spade handle, to clear the pavement of rock-hard snow, a foot deep. Her chopping looked ineffectual – a straight up-and-down stroke, as though churning Tibetan tea – yet some ten yards had been cleared by sunset. Throughout the city centre similar endeavours were in progress, the choppers – mainly elderly women – looking bad-tempered and who can blame them? At first these clearances appeared to be random, then a pattern emerged. Since it seemed the municipality couldn't cope, hotels, banks and big stores hired choppers for their customers' benefit.

Komsomolsk's traffic seemed hectic compared with Siberia's; recently a 500-mile motor road to Khabarovsk had been built. Yet now, looking at my photographs, I see only one or two vehicles – or none – on each boulevard.

I spent a happy unguided forenoon in the excellent Regional Museum which devotes rooms to every aspect of local life from ornithology to aircraft design; clever models and dioramas inform the non-Russian speaker. I was the only visitor, apart from a group of schoolchildren who asked their teachers many questions and at intervals sat cross-legged on the floor to take notes.

In a small café near the museum I met my first outgoing Komsomolskian – Angelica, who proved to be not the real thing, having moved from Bratsk in 1988. She looked out of place wearing an overall behind a counter; tall and graceful, she had greying hair, fine features, dark deep-set eyes. As I paid for a *pivo* no words were exchanged but her friendly smile lifted my spirits. While diary-writing I was conscious of being observed. Then Angelica was replaced by a younger woman, obviously her daughter, and she came to my table to offer me a *pivo* 'on the house'. Twenty minutes later, after an arduous dictionary-led conversation, we were on a trolleybus together, going to a distant suburb. Angelica's youngest daughter, Nina, dreamed of talking to English-speakers . . .

From a bus stop amidst a grimness of factories we followed uneven paths between the many blocks of a residential district that might have been anywhere in the Federation. Angelica made apologetic gestures about the broken lift while we climbed an ill-lit stairway, strewn with cigarette butts, to a seventh-floor flat. As she peered at her multiple keys it astonished me to hear an English conversation within. Nina on the telephone? But no – she had been speaking English to a complacent tabby tom, Issayev, who lacked ears: one night he stayed out too long at −38°C and lost them to frostbite. At school Nina's teacher didn't herself speak English, could only read it and correct written work. Therefore this determined pupil, seeing English as her exit strategy from Komsomolsk, listened daily to the BBC World Service and talked to Issayev at length. She almost wept for joy when her mother presented me as a trophy – 'Look what I found in the café!'

Nina had inherited her mother's build but was blonde and blue-eyed. While Angelica prepared a meal we talked briefly about me, then came to the family history – a slow narrative, for this student wished all grammatical errors to be corrected.

Angelica was born in 1942 in Stalingrad (now Volgograd) during the Siege. Orphaned as a baby, she grew up in a children's home knowing nothing of her origins, nameless, registered simply as 'Angelica' by her carers – a common enough fate, in that time and place. At nineteen she married an engineering student from a similar background and Olga, their first child, was now thirty-nine, owned the café and had a daughter only a year younger than eighteen-year-old Nina. In between Nina and Olga came a thirty-five-year-old daughter (manageress of a Chinese-owned boutique) and a twenty-seven-year-old son who had just bought a second-hand truck and gone into the slowly expanding haulage business. 'I was a miscalculation,' said Nina. 'The most of Russian women would not have born me. I am so lucky my mother has a Baptist religion with feelings against that operation.'

Angelica called us to eat in the kitchen: potato soup, pelmeni, processed cheese. During the meal we talked grandchildren, then my hostess had to rush off to do a three-hour stint in the boutique which remained open until 10.0 p.m., by order of its Chinese owner, though customers were few on winter evenings. This seemed a united, hard-working family; Nina had done an early morning shift in the café.

During the next and more intimate chapter of family history Nina no longer craved grammar lessons, only wanted to unburden herself – as people sometimes do in conversation with a total stranger they will never meet again. In 1988 the family had moved from Bratsk when her father was appointed to a senior post in the Komsomolsk municipality. In 1994 'he walked away from us, got a divorce, married a young woman in his office. That's why here we have too much furniture, the new wife wanted everything new, we got everything old from the bigger flat.' Nina spoke of her father with resentful contempt. 'I was nine years, when children think father loves them. I thought he loved us all, then he was gone! He sent messages saying he wanted to see us every week but we didn't want seeing him! Except my brother, he meets him. I think men don't be able to feel so much what women feel when their man walks away.'

A year later Angelica met and married an impoverished aeronautical engineer who had been made redundant at the age of fifty, then lost his wife in an Aeroflot crash. He had no children, badly needed comforting. 'That made my mother happy again for two years until he got a big pain in his chest and died in the ambulance. He was fifty-five years old. Too many Russian men die at that kind of age.' I sensed that this bereavement had not greatly distressed Nina. The overfurnished flat must also have felt overpopulated when stepfather was in residence and she was sleeping on the living-room sofa – at just the age when we reckon each child needs his or her own space.

Nina had never been further than Vladivostok (twice) and felt trapped. 'The radio tells of all happenings around the world and I know I can't go on here. I must to get free, be living like you always in different places. How can I do this? Should I speak English good enough to be interpreting, can I earn jobs in London or New York? Making enough dollars to travel like you, then more jobs and more travel!'

By current Western standards, Nina's ambition was almost banal: jobs in 'glamorous' cities, saving enough to backpack around the world – to her capitalist contemporaries, a human right. But this Komsomolsk eighteen-year-old was in a position not unlike my own in 1950, trapped in a little Irish town, longing to be free. I was constrained by family responsibilities, she by her economic circumstances and other peoples' immigration laws. Roubles and a Russian passport don't take you far. As we considered her career prospects I recognized a true kindred spirit; Nina didn't want to migrate to get rich, her wanderlust was genuine. And she wished to travel alone, off the beaten track – not that the twenty-first century offers many unbeaten tracks to solitary travellers. It can be destructive to rouse false hopes but given Nina's doggedness, and the propellant power of her motives, it seemed reasonable to predict that she would soon be out of Komsomolsk, though perhaps not in London or New York.

As we waited for the bus I told Nina of my earliest memory – listening, entranced, to foreign languages on the wireless my parents had given themselves for Christmas in 1936. Perhaps the seeds of my own wanderlust were sown then. Vividly I remember the thrill of slowly turning those knobs, marvelling at the magic that enabled me to hear voices speaking or singing *now* (not on a record) from London, Rio de Janeiro, Bucharest, Tokyo, Helsinki, Rome, New Delhi, Leningrad. Aged five, I could read those station names, having no idea where any of them was, only knowing they were all very far away – and beckoning. I still have that wireless, made in Holland by Phillips, measuring eighteen inches by twenty-four – a handsome object, its solid walnut cabinet ensuring a mellow tone.

Nina accompanied me to the centre where she was meeting her Korean boyfriend of whom Angelica disapproved because he drank too much. As we parted she said, 'Thank you! I feel now not crazy, you show my dreams can be real life!'

Back at Hotel Amur, an aggressive young security guard challenged me as I crossed the foyer – roughly grabbed my arm, demanded to see my key chit. Tall and burly, he had a low forehead, thick lips, a ginger crew-cut and teeth already nicotine-stained. I looked towards the hall porter: pasty-faced, with sleek black hair, cold grey eyes and a stylish blue and gold uniform. He was lounging as usual on a black plastic settee and instead of intervening on my behalf he smirked and winked at his colleague.

Another unpleasantness marred my departure next morning when I was wearing a bulky rucksack and carrying a plastic bag of food in one hand and my walking stick in the other. For some reason the narrow swing door to the foyer was blocked – being held ajar – by two large chairs. Peering around them, I again looked towards the porter on his settee, three yards away. He responded with an insolent sneer which infuriated me though I'm not easily angered. As he watched me negotiating this obstacle an embarrassed-looking receptionist came hurrying to my assistance.

*

The Arts Museum's English-speaking curatrix, Svetlana, acted as my guide and what she had to say fascinated me – so much so that I forgot to jot down the name of the remarkable Japanese artist of whom she talked. His donated works laid the foundation for the museum's Foreign Art section, inspiring other artists – Chinese, Korean North and South, Thai, Indian – to contribute generously. As a young prisoner of war he spent four years in Komsomolsk and found his Russian captors so likeable that much of his life has been devoted to Russo-Japanese reconciliation. *Glasnost* allowed his book on that theme to be translated into Russian and it is still selling steadily. Returning to Komsomolsk in 1990, as an internationally renowned artist, he was able to contact three of the Russians with whom, as a helpless prisoner, he had formed friendships.

Amidst all the constantly reiterated accounts of brutality, hatred and prejudice, it's heartening to hear an occasional story with a happy ending. Then one wonders, how many other cases are there of civilized behaviour? In every conflict it suits the war-makers to propagate accounts of brutality, hatred and prejudice – even to invent atrocities. It is too easy to forget that down on the battleground are millions of ordinary human beings, all swept into wars not of their making, conditioned to hate the enemy, yet sometimes able to overcome that conditioning and treat their opponents as fellow-victims.

Svetlana was an unusually outgoing Komsomolskian whose Soldier-Builder father had marched down the Amur in 1934. Her doctor mother arrived two years later to find herself one of the few women on that pioneering scene. They soon married but judged conditions too tough for child bearing and rearing; Svetlana was postponed until 1948. Proudly she showed me around the museum's one-room Russian Art section, consisting mainly of folk art: carvings, tapestries, ceramics, paintings on wood – all displayed here to put Komsomolsk's settlers in touch with their ancestral skills. Neither the original builders nor the scientists, technicians and factory hands who later laboured to fulfil the city's purpose had the time or material to maintain such skills. Svetlana's way of explaining this, her facial expressions and gestures, emphasized Komsomolsk's peculiar emotional isolation which in the twentieth century needn't have been a result of geographical isolation – but was.

6

Pollution Over the Pacific

IN THE STATION waiting-room at 5.45 p.m. two figures rose to greet me – Angelica and Nina. Guiding me to my *platskartny*, they requested a steely-eyed, square-jawed *provodnitsa* to cherish the Irish babushka, presented me with a plastic bag of sustenance (bread, salami, chocolate, *pivo*), then vigorously hugged me before withdrawing to make way for a throng of heavily laden passengers. Nina and I are still corresponding.

This Komsomolsk–Vanino section of the BAM long pre-dates the rest; its completion during the Great Patriotic War enabled Soviet troops to take Sakhalin and the Kuril Islands soon after 8 August 1945, when Russia declared war on Japan. Ten miles south of Komsomolsk is the longest of BAM's 3,000 bridges: eight 159-metre spans, five 33-metre spans – in total more than a mile. It took ten years to build, partly because of the river's depth at this point and the ferocity of winter gales so near the coast. Trains are forbidden to halt on the bridge, nobody may walk over it and soldiers guard it at either end. As I peered through a blue-tinged dusk the pale expanses of the Amur seemed surprisingly close; here its banks are low.

By bedtime my *platskartny* was less crowded; at every little town people disembarked. These numerous towns surprised me, then the *BAM Guide* explained that this whole region was developed to serve military needs. As we began the long climb to a 2,700-foot pass I lay on my bunk feeling thwarted; everyone else wanted the window blinds pulled all the way down.

BAM takes thirteen and a half hours to cover those 300 miles and we were still in the Sikhote Alin range at 5.15 a.m. when I raised the nearest blind to see a world all silver and black in the light of a three-quarters moon. Some slopes were forested, others had been stripped bare and their wide smoothness seemed lit from within rather than above. Darkness possessed the valleys and ravines, their immeasurable depths full of ghosts. One cannot forget the human cost of this section of the BAM. Its builders lived in six camps – a total of 124,000 men, of whom 9,000 were free workers, 2,600 escort guards, 1,600 railway troops, the rest convicts and prisoners of war. Tens of thousands were overworked to death in the haste to complete this line to carry soldiers to Vanino for the invasion of Sakhalin.

Several of my companions got off at tiny stations: Tumnin, Ust-Orochi, Mongokhto. Others made tea, chatted cheerfully – but were wary of the foreigner. According to rumour (a well-founded rumour), Mongokhto stores many disasters waiting to happen, chemical weapons in fast-deteriorating containers. The army can't afford to destroy them and if/when the worst does happen few outsiders will worry much about a small poisoned town in the foothills of the Tumninskiy range.

I had been staring at the Pacific for several moments before identifying it. In a grey dawn the frozen ocean, scarcely 200 yards away, also looked grey. As did the flat shore; one couldn't see exactly where Eurasia ended and the Pacific began. Soon BAM left the shore to dawdle around a high headland, disfigured by oil refineries and other, anonymous, industrial installations. Then we were overlooking Vanino's small port – not a beautiful sight. Webs of thick electric cables, towering cranes and equally tall security-light pylons crowded the sky. A long, two-storey, pale green station – neo-Georgian, Vanino's most impressive building – stands beside the port's main gateway, still closely guarded. Only those with workers' passes or ferry tickets for Sakhalin may enter.

After Komsomolsk's minus 34 the air felt balmy at minus 18. Within that enormous station finding the unmarked Railway Lodge was impossible until a kindly elderly man guided me through the labyrinth of hallways and corridors to a narrow door that opened onto an unlit stairway that led to several dormitories opening off a large unfurnished space. Nobody was around at 7.40 in the morning. I sat on my rucksack and noticed unpleasant effluvia drifting from the adjacent loos – one of the few smelly loos in my Russian experience, though doubtless there are others.

Punctually at 8.0 a.m. two railway officers, Eva and Marina, came on duty and I paid $6.50 for thirty-six hours' lodging. To qualify, I had to show my ticket from Komsomolsk, then buy my ticket to Khabarovsk, after which both tickets and my passport were photocopied for the files. But alas! the Vanino ticket clerk got one digit of my passport number wrong, thus causing the two amiable women and another clerk half an hour of angst – real angst, for those three minor officials took that one digit error very seriously. Had communication been possible I would have argued that on a dark platform, with many passengers to be processed, no *provodnitsa* was likely to notice it. But of course someone else might, weeks hence, when checking the files – maybe 3,000 miles away, in Taishet.

Being as yet the only lodger I had a choice of seven beds in dormitory No. 3 – huge and high-ceilinged, its plank floor creaky, its furniture a shaky table, two camp chairs and a small wardrobe hammered together by someone unskilled. The three windows were thickly frosted over inside, and Marina fretted about the babushka feeling cold; to soothe her I had to unroll my flea-bag. These dormitories are public spaces, never locked; anyone could wander in from the waiting-room or platform by day or by night and lodgers' luggage is unguarded in their absence. Happily most people in most countries are honest, as fifty-five years of travelling have taught me.

Significantly, Vanino was not celebrating its sixtieth birthday though Russians relish such celebrations; in 2002 I had found Yakutsk en fête, all aflutter with banners proclaiming 'AET 370'. Vanino's founding in 1944 as a gulag transit camp cannot be remembered with pride. People destined to die in the northern goldfields of Magadan, Kolyma and Kamchatka spent a few days in this settlement of ten camps while mine managers chose their victims. One mine's yearly demand was for 12,000 prisoners, including women, adolescents and old men – all supplied by arrangement with the NKVD, sire of the KGB. Until the gulag system ended, soon after Stalin's death, no prisoner who passed through Vanino ever returned home.

Now this commercial port handles some five million tonnes of exports per annum: oil products, freight for the Sakhalin and Kuril islands, timber for Japan. The town, on its low ridge overlooking the Tatar Strait, is singularly ugly. Residential blocks with broken balconies wore frills of domestic refuse around their bases. The high snow-banks lining each steep street seemed leprous, were pollution-frayed – eroded by chemicals into ghastly shapes. Vanino is also in a formerly 'restricted zone' (much of it remains restricted) and here, too, the natives were unfriendly.

At 9.0 a.m. few were visible; in winter nothing opens until 10.0. But by 9.30, along the narrow main street at the foot of the ridge, several hardy pavement vendors were unpacking their limited wares: frozen hunks of green-tinged meat, kilo bags of offal, frozen fish (mainly mackerel), tubs of orange juice and forest berries (also frozen), jars of pickled cucumbers and onions, little pyramids of sunflower seeds and peanuts sold in twists of newspaper. There they sat until 3.30, presumably selling enough to make that endurance test worthwhile though each had so little to offer.

Topography (and security) frustrated my ambition to walk on the Pacific. The coast was nowhere accessible; in places security barriers blocked the way (high-voltage electric fences), elsewhere the cliffs were themselves inaccessible, cut off by expanses of deep snow.

In Tynda, Viktor had given me the name of another truck-driver who lived in Sovetskaya Gavan-Sortirovka, near Vanino, with his English-speaking teacher daughter. On the way, bus No. 5 passed a row of stacks exhaling lethal fumes, then turned off the main road towards a large village and put me down outside the sort of railway station you expect in a toddler's pop-up book – all phoney fretwork turrets. Sovetskaya Gavan-Sortirovka proved to be more than a village; ten low-rise blocks stood a little apart from its *izbi* and massive security fortifications surrounded a gigantic abandoned factory. As the primary school was closed I shoved a note under the door.

A six-mile, U-shaped walk took me back to Vanino: Sovetskaya Gavan-Sortirovka, on its ridge, tops one side of the U, Vanino the other. In between lies a long, wide, shallow valley bisected by a single railway track to the once-important naval base of Sovetskaya Gavan. High above sailed a few wispy white clouds – the first I'd seen since leaving Lake Baikal – and the broad band of pollution along the horizon varied from charcoal grey to dark brown. On wayside hedges the heaped snow was blackly pock-marked. From the road's highest point my binoculars showed a sparkling strip of unfrozen Pacific, a narrow channel through which ice-breaker tugs liberate ships – though liberation adds considerably to transport costs and is not routine.

On Vanino's main street, near the pedestrian bridge to my lodging, a new 'development' was conspicuous: 'Bar – Restwrong – Niteklub

– Discow'. The purple, white and orange decor was hard on the nerves and the staff viewed me with disdain; I fell far short of their image of a Western tourist. Four pairs of expensively dressed young Vanino women were chatting over coffees and pricey slices of vividly coloured cakes. Then I noticed a tall balding man in his fifties finishing a late lunch – another affluent native? No – the whole cut of his jib, and his interaction with the waitress, indicated 'outsider'. When our eyes met he addressed me in precise Muscovite English. 'You are touring this area at an unusual season! You are a biznizwoman?'

'Sort of,' I replied. 'Writing is my bizniz. And what are you doing so far from home?'

The Muscovite wiped his mouth with his napkin before moving to my table and offering me a *pivo*. Through him I complained to the waitress about the lack of Russian brews and he laughed. 'You must have noticed, Russians who can afford it will always drink foreign beers.'

I nodded gloomily. 'And eat foreign fast food and listen to foreign pop groups and drive foreign cars and wear foreign shoes. Don't you find that sad?'

My companion shrugged. 'It's human nature. When our Soviet Union fell apart everything Russian looked inferior – even when it was superior, like our chocolate. The free-market sales research people knew how to use that.'

Unusually, the Muscovite had not reciprocated when I introduced myself. Now I repeated, 'So what are you doing here?'

'I'm a medical man, here for a research year, looking at local health problems. An overseas agency funds the project.'

Grimly I observed, 'Your research must be depressing.'

Dr Anon hesitated, glanced down at my notebook, seemed to take a warning from it and replied, 'Most people do not have good health, that you can see for yourself. The causes can be complicated. Heredity, poverty – researchers cannot come to hasty conclusions.'

I gazed out of the wide window beside us at the layer of pollution poised above the port and thought of those chemically eroded snow-drifts and remembered the all-black contents of my handkerchief when I blew my nose in the restaurant cloakroom. Then I said, 'Seems to me you're quite brave, to spend a year in Vanino. Not being a researcher, I've felt free to come hastily to the conclusion that this region's industries render it unfit for human habitation.'

Dr Anon considered me impassively for a moment, then smiled a quick conciliatory smile, almost an apology for his caginess. Next he looked at his watch and exclaimed – 'Must go!' At 4.0 p.m. he held a clinic for juvenile asthmatics, at 5.0 for adult respiratory diseases. When we shook hands he momentarily extended that gesture and said, 'Happy writing!'

A few days later, in Khabarovsk, I heard that a recent survey (Dr Anon's?) had found 86 per cent of Vanino children under the age of fifteen suffering from chronic asthma and 82 per cent of the adult population diseased in one way or another – information conveyed to the casual observer by their appearance.

By nightfall two more beds had been taken in dormitory No. 3. On one lay a middle-aged sailor whose English (learned in Japan) might have been more comprehensible had he not been half-drunk and in the process of getting drunker. He took umbrage in a small way when I politely declined a swig from his litre bottle of gut-rot. An engineer on an ice-breaker, he had just come off duty, was on his way home to Tumnin. On the other bed sat Osip, doing an English-and-Commerce course at Khabarovsk University. His father's death had drawn him back to his birthplace, Sovetskaya Gavan, a town where he spent as little time as possible. He wanted to eat in the station restaurant and anxiously asked me to look after his knapsack and guitar, casting sideways glances at the gut-rot bottle.

Not long after, Eva arrived to berate the sailor. In Railway Lodgings nicotine and alcohol are strictly forbidden, he must either hand over his cigarettes and bottle (still half-full) or get out. As he got out, loudly abusing the railway's 'virtue police', I clapped Eva on the back.

Osip gradually became less shy as we talked. In his opinion, I should have gone on to Sovetskaya Gavan, not stayed in Vanino – 'a bad place'. 'Why bad?' I asked. Osip frowned, tugged at his hair, struggled for words. 'The people are not happy,' he said. 'The place has bad times but the people don't know that. In Sovetskaya Gavan we know our past – it is an old place, made in 1853. Vanino is a new place made only for bad things. In Khabarovsk an Englishman tells me how Vanino is made and then I see why these people are never happy. What is in my head is not easy to say. It is about feelings people have from where they live. Past times are not really past if a place was made only for bad reasons. I can't say good English, I have no practice. We have not many talking English with us.'

'A common complaint,' I said. 'But if I spoke Russian as you speak English, I'd be very proud of myself.'

At sunrise, still fixated on intimacy with the Pacific, I took a bus going north across the headland. Here industrial and domestic litter competed to disfigure the snowscape and this four-mile branch road ended in a supremely dreary townlet of dilapidated though inhabited six-storey blocks and a few defunct or dysfunctional oil-related plants.

Now I was tantalizingly close to the ocean, hidden by a cliff-top belt of taiga. Hope surged when I found a path through the snow – but then my way was blocked, at the edge of the wood, by another electric fence of military dimensions. And it was switched on; I could hear the menacing hum. What, I wondered, is it protecting from whom? Or did someone just forget to switch if off when the spy industry collapsed? Or has that industry not collapsed? Are CIA agents still lurking in the coastal taiga, diligently collecting facts ('Here the cliffs are 72.5m high') for their War On Terrorism?

I bussed back to the port; those four littered miles were not walker-friendly. Vanino's geriatric bus fleet had recently been augmented by a gift from Japan, two shiny state-of-the-art vehicles that looked like ladies of fashion lost in a slum. All the town's bus-drivers showed proper respect for underwheel conditions and thrice I saw enraged drivers shaking their fists at arrogantly speeding young men.

Walking away from the centre, uphill and inland, I came upon Old Vanino, a large village of substantial *izbi* lining long, straight, unpaved laneways. From here no high-risery was visible and often one glimpsed the Pacific beyond expansive snowfields occasionally broken by patches of taiga. A rickety mini-church recalled Stalin's wartime rapprochement with Orthodoxy and, at some little distance from the church, an elaborate new belfry with a gilded dome was near completion. It would have made more sense, I thought, to restore the church. And thereby hung a tale; that evening Osip gave me an unrepeatable account of the relevant mafia/clerical intrigues.

In Old Vanino I experimented by cheerfully greeting everyone: old men whose long sledges were loaded with firewood or jerrycans of kerosene – young mothers drawing infants on mini-sledges –

gum-chewing adolescents returning from school wearing popstar-decorated satchels – a babushka dragging a screaming small child to the clinic. All my greetings met with blank stares, or a few flickers of hostility. But the numerous independently strolling, well-fed mongrels were not hostile.

On the west slope of this ridge, below the village, I paused beside the skeleton of a tall wooden watchtower to try to photograph two magnificent ravens, perched on its rotting roof. Hereabouts, in summer, it is possible to see the remains of one prison camp and this may explain the behaviour of a bent babushka who was hauling a sledgeload of potatoes up the rough track. Pointing at my camera she yelled angrily, and the ravens flew away.

Walking on, overlooking an uninhabited sweep of whiteness, bounded by faraway hills, I found myself ruminating again about Stalin. The gulags were his remedy (perhaps inspired by Trotsky's advocacy of compulsory labour) for the State's destitution, caused by the Bolsheviks' repudiation of czarist Russia's foreign debt. After that, naturally enough, no more foreign loans of any size were available. Stalin therefore expended human lives, instead of capital, on his gigantic development projects. At its zenith the gulag system, begun in 1930, controlled twenty-one million prisoners and was administered by 800,000 officials. This slave-labour economy resembled that of the Southern States and Caribbean plantations but was even more brutal. The slaves were 'owned' by the State rather than by individuals or trading companies and this unique system, neither communist nor capitalist, quickly developed its own internal governmental structures. There were gulags for mining, forestry, nonferrous metals, roads, railways, hydroelectric dams and the building of such cities as Komsomolsk, Magadan, Norilsk. The section leaders – always powerful, not always professionally well-qualified – met regularly at 'cabinet' level. Did any of them remember Karl Marx's observation that a national economy seeking to develop must avoid forced labour – 'the slave has no interest in raising the productivity of labour'? If any did, quoting Marx to Stalin was a bad idea. During the Great Terror (1937–38) more than a million were executed and seven or eight million sent to camps. On 12 December 1937 – an ordinary morning – Stalin initialled 3,182 death warrants. As Robert Conquest has written in his book on *The Great Terror* (1990): 'Since every person arrested was forced to denounce dozens of accomplices, the tally of the condemned soon swelled to unmanageable proportions. The purpose was to destroy through fear not just the opposition, such as it was, but the very idea of dissent.' In contrast, between 1876 and 1904 the czar's regime imposed the death penalty on 486 criminals and terrorists, an annual average of seventeen.

Voluntary personal denunciation, an infamous tradition deeply rooted in czarist times, was invaluable to the Party and much encouraged; people informed against envied neighbours, technological or academic rivals, detested in-laws. Also, the more arrests a local official could organize, the brighter his career prospects. Soon the woodworm of distrust had caused society as we know it to crumble. Catherine Merridale describes the process in *Night of Stone* (2000):

> Sub-cultures, bureaucratic rules and social myths evolved to cope with fear. Methods were found to deal with the management of disappearing personnel, to live in the shadow of nightly arrests, the sound of gunfire. There was not one logic working in the terror, in other words, but many. Some people's contribution was no more than to ignore it all . . . Others swallowed any propaganda they were offered, thereby turning a blind eye to their neighbours' fear. It was a closed system; there was no outside criticism, no alternative.

Numerous Russian-speaking foreigners have remarked, in shocked tones, that even today millions of ageing 'onlooker' Russians firmly believe that all zeks (labour camp detainees) were guilty and deserved punishment; their crime doesn't even have to be labelled, far less proved. Is this how onlookers deal with their own and their parents' failures to oppose Stalin? Saddest of all, however, is Catherine Merridale's account of her meetings with 'so many people who still believe in their own guilt, cannot accept the meaning of repressive politics, the propaganda messages of torture, show trials and mass death'.

One has uncomfortable thoughts in places like Komsomolsk and Vanino. The behaviour of the two unpleasant young men in Hotel Amur had, more than any tables of statistics or gulag memoirs, brought Stalinism alive for me. They were more than 'unpleasant'; despite the brevity and triviality of our encounters their potential for cruelty was evident. And I have met others – happily not many – of similar calibre. They were very young; their grandfathers and great-grandfathers would have been of the gulag generations. But what exactly happens when such a regime ends? Most of those involved in that quarter-century of state terrorism, whether as victims, onlookers or collaborators, were in their different ways profoundly disturbed and damaged. The collaborators certainly didn't change overnight when Stalin was publicly denounced in 1961 and his body symbolically removed from the mausoleum it had shared with the mummified Lenin. One has to wonder what sort of parents they made – and what lingers on, beneath the surface, in communities partly composed of the descendants of those men and women.

On this journey, as in 2002, I met several Russians of all generations who openly admired Stalin or were ambivalent about him. This gave me an uneasy feeling, as though I were listening to someone talking in their sleep, communicating from another realm of consciousness. The Stalin they couldn't condemn had saved the Revolution from the bourgeois parliamentary-minded Mensheviks, had led their army to a glorious victory in the Great Patriotic War, had laid the foundations for the Soviet Union to win the space race and become a superpower. One twenty-eight-year-old woman said, 'Some tell us Stalin was bad, some tell us he was good. How can we know was he bad or good?' A middle-aged man asked, 'Have you in Ireland been told the truth about Stalin? Leaders in your countries like to make propaganda about us being cruel and not civilized like Europeans.' During such conversations an odd inhibition muzzled me; I could never bring myself to speak of the historical reality of Stalinism. That would have seemed wrong, unless I'd been much closer to the individuals concerned – rather as it seems unwise to waken sleepwalkers.

I thought then about Osip's struggle to explain why Vanino is 'a bad place', its residents 'not happy'. I intuited what he meant: the population had been soured by residual emanations from the transit camp era. And, Dr Anon might have added, by bad health. A debilitated population can't be expected to seem 'happy'.

On the northern edge of the village, where a tarred road descended a gentle slope to the port, Vanino's 'new elite' were creating a suburb of small two-storey multicoloured brick villas sporting a variety of twee trimmings and looking alien – though the watch-dog kennels by each front door were true to rural Russia. Several other sites had been marked out and stacks of bricks and timbers awaited the thaw. It may seem absurd to attribute this crop of modest dwellings to 'capitalism rampant', but in the Vanino context is it absurd? While the new elite can build villas, the vast majority of residents must endure rising levels of poverty.

At 6.0 p.m. the station's incongruously stately waiting-hall (no mere room this) was half-full of passengers for the twice-weekly Vanino–Vladivostok service. I asked a few student types, male and female, if they spoke English but got the by now familiar response – a vigorous 'Nyet!' or a silent turning away. Yet when I opened wide my large map of Russia one of the young men moved to sit beside me, signed his wish to borrow it, then was joined by a friend. After a few minutes I attempted to show them my route – whereupon they looked startled, hastily returned the map and withdrew.

Osip arrived as the train was announced; we were travelling in carriages far apart but he offered to meet me in Khabarovsk's station waiting-room and guide me to a suitable hotel.

My *platskartny* – at the end of a very long, very old train – was scarcely two-thirds full and women predominated. Judging by their attire and reading matter, several passengers would have been travelling coupé before privatization. My immediate companion was Julia, a frail sixty-five-year-old with an alarming breathing problem and a few words of English. Her South Russian parents had migrated to an embryonic Vanino when she was a small child. I watched her unpacking her medication: an inhaler, a bottle of embrocation, three sets of capsules – green, white and orange. I decided our sign-cum-dictionary language would be overtaxed by a chatty comment about those being the colours of Ireland's flag. When Julia remarked that many Vanino people need many pills I remembered the previous evening's talk with Osip; cheap medicines, he had complained, are imported from South Korea and most Russian doctors doubt their efficacy but patients can afford nothing else.

For once, I slept badly. Julia's audible distress worried me – our bunks were only a yard apart – and I made a few attempts to build her a bed-rest, using blankets from the empty upper bunks. But only after taking her white capsule at midnight did she get some sleep.

At 5.30 a.m. the half-moon was useful; given a snowy landscape, a little moonlight goes a long way. On this aged train our carriage's samovar was coal-fired, a red glow at the end of the corridor as I went to brew my first chai. When we halted for an hour at Komsomolsk Julia was comforted by a visit from her daughter and three teenage grandchildren who presented her with a selection of 'luxury' foods – biscuits from Germany, olives from Italy and more. As she pressed cash gifts into grandchildren's hands the fifteen-year-old grandson finally gave way to tears; his adored babushka, I then discovered, was about to have a lung cancer operation. At that stage I moved away, to view the bustling platform from another window.

This Komsomolsk–Khabarovsk service must surely hold the all-Russia non-speed record: eleven hours and forty minutes to cover 235 miles. The *BAM Guide* puts a 'dull' label on these miles but I disagree. Several series of curiously symmetrical conical hills rise out of the Amur flood plain and human interest is provided by short stops at many hamlets, and long stops at the little logging or railway towns of Elban, Bolon and Litovko. The region around Elban – forty miles from Komsomolsk – provides the city with many of its vegetables and dairy products. At Bolon, outside our window (noon temperature $-31°C$) a ragged grey-bearded drunk was frantically fumbling through layers of undergarments to free his willy. All passing eyes were discreetly averted as he peed copiously onto the platform's iron-grey snow – then wavered on, muttering to himself. Julia, looking out-raged, flicked her thumb against her throat and said, 'Vodka make man like dog!'

The Amur flows sixty or so miles east of this BAM offshoot and beyond the river is the newish motor road; all the towns and settlements we passed are accessible only by train or helicopter. The coastal range east of the flood plain is invisible and to the west the Kukanskiy and Vandan ranges are distant pale blurs. We met many half-mile-long, snail-paced freight trains en route to Vanino with their heart-breaking cargoes of timber.

During our halts, most of the men seen loading timber were North Koreans. In this area, in 1967, the first logging camps for these Soviet allies were opened; from 1975 the North Korean government was permitted to set up many more along the main BAM line. Loggers must spend three years in exile but are allowed home for a short annual holiday. To discourage absconding, their families receive their wages. In exchange for 70 per cent of the timber felled, the Russians supply machinery and fuel and leave the Koreans to run their own show. In Soviet times, when security forces caught fleeing Koreans – their sights unrealistically set on China or South Korea – they were handed over to the camp authorities who sent them home for punishment. Nowadays Russian police tend not to notice defectors. According to TASS, in 1997 some 20,000 North Koreans were employed in logging, agriculture, fishing and construction work (which indicates a considerable relaxation of the rules in Pyongyang) and many employers seek them out, praising their reliability and sound workmanship.

As we pulled into Volochaevka, five miles from the BAM–Trans-Siberian junction, Julia drew my attention to Hebrew station signs; we had entered the farcical Jewish Autonomous Oblast, established in 1934 as a homeland for Russian Jews. It soon became a notorious debacle. Those 23,000 square (and uncultivable) miles were inhabited only sporadically by nomads and no one wanted to settle there. Of the present population of 100,000, less than 15,000 are Jews.

Julia then smilingly caught my left hand, said, 'Blyukher! Blyukher!' and pointed to the date on my watch – 14 February, the eighty-second anniversary of the Red Army's victory in one of the Civil War's major battles. It was fought around this railway station from 5 to 14 February 1922 in an average temperature of −35°C which affected Commander Blyukher's men less than General Molchanov's White Guard. By then I had discovered that Julia was a retired history teacher.

Khabarovsk's station – rivalling Irkutsk's in grandeur – was being renovated and bewildering barriers of scaffolding, razor wire and skull-and-crossbones placards confronted arriving passengers. At 8.40 p.m. on the ill-lit platform three groups of rowdies were drunkenly arguing. Having seen two solicitous nephews meeting Julia, I found my way, with difficulty, to a subterranean waiting-room, a vast, shadowy cellar where monstrous heating-pipes writhed overhead and many hopeless, homeless aged men sat slumped on tin chairs while several young men cruised around looking predatory. In Komsomolsk Nina had warned me that muggers frequent this station, seeking foreign prey. Khabarovsk, being on the Trans-Siberian, is tourist territory – I was no longer in the almost crime-free BAM Zone. I had listened attentively to Nina, as one should to local advice, while reserving judgement; such advice can be alarmist. Now I reckoned Nina might have been understating matters.

Osip had explained that he couldn't meet me for an hour or so; he was responsible for delivering goods from Sovetskaya Gavan to a Khabarovsk merchant and would have to fill in many forms and sign many documents and then find the particular clerk authorized to counter-sign them.

Among the waiting passengers, flanked by mounds of unwieldy-looking luggage, Chinese and Koreans formed a large minority – reminding me of a strongly flavoured passage in *The Real Siberia*. A century ago, when this station was new and John Foster Fraser was waiting for his train to Vladivostok, the young Englishman noted:

> The entrance hall was packed with Chinamen shouting gutturally and bumping about with loads, while meek, white-robed, and quaint-featured Koreans squatted on their heels in corners. Russians, chiefly officials in their greys and blues, gilt epaulettes, white-peaked caps, and top boots of pliable leather, took possession of the buffet with their bundles . . . The scene was one that had a close comparison to that you see in India. Instead, however, of British officers walking up and down with the confident stride of superiority, while the Hindus and Mohammedans gave way acknowledging inferiority, there were Russian officers clean and smart promenading the platform while the slithering, cowering Chinese and the cringing frightened Koreans made room for them . . . There was little that was arrogant in the demeanour of the Russians, save the consciousness of importance that every man shows more or less when in uniform. But marked was the dominance of character displayed by the Russians and the recognition of it by the Chinese and Koreans.

During the twentieth century some things changed for the better.

When one of the prowling youths brazenly stole a holdall from a sleeping woman sitting opposite me, those around noticed the theft, nudged each other and muttered – but no action was taken. Soon after two early teenage prostitutes appeared, one too fat, the other too thin, both wearing tight miniskirts, spangled tights and diaphanous stoles which they hopefully stage-managed to reveal mini-breasts under transparent bras. The fat lass immediately found a customer, a stocky man of indeterminate race who took his luggage with him when they went – where? One doesn't fornicate alfresco at −32°C.

Osip arrived then; he had already secured a taxi and twenty minutes later I was settling into a simple $8 room, sans TV, telephone or fridge and not 'en suite'. Without Osip I could never have found such satis-factory city-centre accommodation; no legible (to me) sign marked this Hotel of the Regional Administration on the first floor of an old and not recently renovated building.

7

Of Troops and Terrorists

THE RUSSIANS DECIDED to take the Amur river seriously in 1854, after 165 years of indifference. British cruisers were then patrolling near the Tatar Strait (the Crimean War had broken out in October 1853) and it made sense to secure the Amur estuary, claimed for the czar in 1850. A year previously Captain Gennady Nevelskoy had discovered to his delighted astonishment that Sakhalin is an island, and seagoing ships could therefore sail up the Amur: suddenly that river was seen to have considerable geopolitical significance. So it came about that in the summer of 1854 Nikolay Muravyev, Governor-General of Eastern Siberia since 1847, led a mile-long flotilla down the Amur: seventy-five barges and rafts carrying one cavalry squadron, one division of mountain artillery, one infantry battalion. Muravyev himself sailed in the *Argun*, Eastern Siberia's first locally built steamer of which he was rather proud.

Just downstream from the awesome confluence of the Amur and Ussuri rivers Muravyev stood on the *Argun*'s deck, surveying a high wooded promontory. Then impulsively he decreed, 'Here there shall be a town.' And so was Khabarovsk conceived. Legend has it that Muravyev scooped a tumbler of water from the river and drank to the unborn settlement's prosperity. Those were the days! Now one is warned not to swim in the densely polluted Amur.

The fortified village built in 1858 was named after that vicious seventeenth-century explorer-entrepreneur, Yerofei Khabarov, who in 1651 led the first expedition down the Amur. The river had been 'discovered' by Poyarkov in 1644. I have written elsewhere of Khabarov; suffice it to say here that his cruelty equalled Stalin's.

For forty years Khabarovsk remained a rough and ready garrison town, only noted for its river port and fur traders' depot, yet by 1880 it had become the administrative centre for the whole vast Pri-Amursky region. Then the arrival of the Trans-Siberian transformed it into a multiracial trading emporium and the headquarters of the czar's Far Eastern Army. In 1902 C. H. Hawes, another itchy-footed young Englishman, estimated that at least a quarter of the population of 16,000 were Chinese or Korean.

The 1901 census revealed males outnumbering females by eleven to one. This continuing imbalance, throughout the Russian Far East, eventually gave rise to the Khetagurova Movement. In February 1937 Valentina Khetagurova-Zarubina (aged twenty-two, married to a Far Eastern Army major) wrote an open letter – probably not unprompted – to the maidens of the Soviet Union urging them to 'Go East, young women!' Her letter depicted a Paradise where instant husbands were guaranteed – maybe even a well-paid engineer or scientist or army officer. It was reprinted in various forms and so widely circulated that by the end of 1937 more than 70,000 of the nubility had volunteered to migrate. History does not record how many of the 5,000 chosen lived happily ever after; very likely the women had no alternative but to make the best of their exile.

Khabarovsk suffered greatly during Russia's Civil War. The Treaty of Brest-Litovsk, signed by the Germans and Bolsheviks in March 1918, had provided a shaky excuse for limited Allied intervention in that conflict. Before the Revolution, vast quantities of military matériel and other supplies, including vintage wines, had been stockpiled in Vladivostok, Murmansk and Archangel; post-Treaty, many feared the Germans might grab those goodies – by that date a very remote possibility.

In June 1918 President Wilson admitted to a friend, 'I've been sweating blood over what's right and feasible to do in Russia.' He then wrote his historic aide-memoire, for distribution by diplomatic pouch, calling upon all the Allied leaders to avoid 'any interference of any kind with the political sovereignty of Russia, any intervention in her internal affairs, or any impairment of her territorial integrity either now or hereafter'. He might as well have saved his typing-ribbon. On 2 August Japanese troops occupied Khabarovsk, cheered on by Winston Churchill, shortly to become Britain's War Secretary. Within the next three weeks Japan seized all of the strategically crucial Russian-owned Chinese Eastern Railway (through Manchuria), though the Allies' mandate sanctioned no such aggression and President Wilson had recommended that Japan deploy only 7,000 troops, the number Washington had committed 'to steady any efforts at self-government or self-defense in which the Russians may be willing to accept assistance'.

Blandly, the Japanese gave Wilson a geography lesson. Russia shares borders with Inner Mongolia and Manchuria, which are contiguous to Korea. Everyone must understand that all those territories were 'in very close and special relation to Japan's national defence and her economic existence'. By mid-October 75,000 Japanese troops were swarming through the Amur and Ussuri valleys and Transbaikalia. Fourteen other nations between them contributed an additional 50,000 men, variously armed, but several members of this 'coalition' were not really 'willing', having blundered into the Civil War almost by chance.

The US commander, Major-General William S. Graves, was feeling extremely confused and too worried to sleep. Before taking up his post he had read Wilson's aide-memoire and listened to a warning from Newton D. Baker, Secretary of War – 'Don't create situations demanding impossible military exertions on the part of Allies and particularly of the US, and involve our country in complications of the most unfortunate kind'. So why, Graves wondered, had US troops been brought from the Philippines in August? He didn't know what Washington wanted – and all the signs are that Washington didn't know, either.

By trying to 'play it neutral' Graves infuriated both the White army and the other Allied commanders. Soon the State Department, egged on by Churchill, was unsuccessfully seeking to have him replaced. Admiral Kolchak, the White commander-in-chief, sneered at Graves' troops as 'Jewish emigrants' and 'the offscourings of the American Army'. The last czarist government (notably Vyacheslav Plehve) had railed against 'the revolutionary Jew' and one of Hitler's favourite propaganda terms, 'Jewish Bolshevism', was coined by the Whites. As Benson Bobrick has pointed out in *East of the Sun* (1992), 'The entire White movement was rank with anti-Semitism, and pogroms, persecutions and other atrocities followed in the wake of all its armies. Some two thousand Jews were killed in Yekaterinburg, for example, in July 1919.'

The end of the 'Great War' – as it was known in my childhood – blew away the Allies' fig leaf; now their counter-revolutionary intervention stood naked. President Wilson, so recently busy lecturing his allies about not meddling in Russia, saw the continuing presence of US troops on the Civil War battlefields as a considerable embarrassment and offered to mediate a peace. But the British and French told him to get lost (using a few more syllables) and during the next year the Allies presented the Whites with approximately 97,000 tons of weaponry, thus prolonging the Civil War until October 1922 – and a year more, in isolated corners of Yakutsk and the Chukchi peninsula.

I like compact cities, explorable on foot, a category to which Khabarovsk does not belong. Its 250 square miles include satellite estates of workers' blocks separated from the centre by a mile or two of flat land (pasture? arable? market gardening?) bounded by stunted pines. I visited one of those in error, having taken the wrong tram, and it didn't tempt me to disembark. The red-cheeked conductress, wearing mittens and two scarves and made barrelesque by her padded layers, was puzzled to see me remaining in my seat while she and the driver snacked before the return trip. Then I was silently handed a mug of scalding sweet tea from their samovar-thermos and the driver offered squares of chocolate.

The right tram took me down to the Amur, even wider than at Komsomolsk as it curves around the promontory, its far bank disfigured by factory stacks at the base of low mountains. Muravyev's statue is back on the headland's highest point, having been ousted by Lenin for seventy years. From here I had hoped to gaze upon China; on a clear day one can see the hills of Manchuria some twenty-five miles to the south. But this day was not clear enough: overhead a blue sky, along the horizon snow clouds. The river-station was deserted; in summer it is a bustling place with cafés and kiosks along the nearby strip of beach and hydrofoils offering day trips to China (no visa required). Several ice-gripped barges were inhabited, their wood-stove smoke streaming horizontally in the menacing wind. The river surface was smooth to walk on but I didn't walk far; that wind, at $-37°C$, soon sent me back to the tram terminus.

I would have preferred Khabarovsk as Fraser described it in 1901: 'The town, divided by deep ravines, is connected with long rows of stairs, while on each ridge runs a main street, with the branch streets tumbling down the mounds, so that the place almost looks like three towns tacked together.' Now the stairs are gone and, between the world wars, two ravines acquired streets of steep unremarkably pleasant buildings. As in Komsomolsk, flourishes abound – pinnacles sprouting plaster fruits, medieval window-slits, purposeless domes and arches and niches. Now those shops, offices and flats are competing for space with boutiques, art galleries, discos, trendy Japanese restaurants and other symptoms of a growth society. The most startling symptoms dominate one slope: all its old buildings have been recently razed to make way for gigantic, violently colourful edifices (orange, harsh blue, scarlet, chemical green) taking innovative architecture beyond the absurd into the lunatic. For these, I was told later, Chinese and Japanese investors in Khabarovsk's 'leisure industry' are largely to blame.

Ulitsa Karla Marxa, on the central ridge, led me to ploshchad Lenina, where a winter-long exhibition of fragile ice sculptures covered the enormous square, glittering and twinkling in the noon sun. Here were reindeer, swans, ballerinas, trees, seals, squirrels, fish and a multitude of mythological figures and abstract creations – each artist's work in separate sections, their names discreetly displayed. As background to all this elegant frivolity loomed the czarist Town Hall: stolid red brick, four storeys high, thirty-seven windows long, austerely pedimented, asserting a dominance not to be questioned over the former empire's most distant territory.

In the mile-long public park, sloping down to the Amur, stood many groups of more substantial ice sculptures, some fifteen feet high, elaborate fantasies incorporating birds and beasts and fishes and foliage. On this bright Saturday afternoon parents were exercising children and dogs, the former skiing or tobogganing, the latter chasing balls or rubber bones. Everyone was muffled to the eyes, children wearing double or triple headgear with scarves tied at the back. Yet again I wondered why those living in the world's coldest inhabited region never wear balaclavas. Can it be because criminals and terrorists favour the balaclava for non-climatic reasons?

In summer this birch-rich park must be a gladsome sight; now all those thin tangled naked branches formed an untidy black pattern against the cobalt sky – a pattern matched by the disorganized toing and froing of glossy loquacious ravens. Here I found myself brooding again on the want of logic involved in the existence of the Russian Far East. It is *too* far east to make sense as an integral part of Russia.

By horse transport it took between two and four years, depending on the quality of your horses and the severity of the winter, to cover the 3,500 miles from Volga to Amur. Initially Muravyev had to use force to populate the Amur and Ussuri colonies; between 1851 and 1862 16,000 Cossacks (men and women) were compelled to move east from the Transbaikal. All settlements began as military posts, replicating the early settlement and exploration of Siberia. Then voluntary civilian migration was stimulated by exempting peasant settlers from the poll tax, military service and other quasi-feudal obligations. More than 100,000 had come from Siberia and European Russia by 1900: the pace quickened after 1882 when sea transport from Odessa started. By 1898, in the area around Vladivostok, over 96 per cent of the civilian population were Ukrainian and Fraser noted that between Khabarovsk and Vladivostok 'Not one in ten of the Russians had come here through Siberia. The great majority had travelled round from Odessa by sea.' If we accept that the indigenous tribes were not, as history unfolded, going to be left in possession of their territory, a Chinese or Japanese annexation would have made more geographical sense. At the beginning of the twenty-first century these provinces are largely dependent on Chinese, Japanese and Korean 'developers'.

The military motive for expansion was reinforced by gold fever after an exciting 1868 discovery in the Zeya river basin. Soon many other deposits came to light, on various tributaries of the Amur, and by 1910 thousands of workers were finding amounts second only to the Lena goldfields' yields. However, even this failed to make the colonization of the Far East economically worthwhile and Japan's humiliation of Russia in 1905 proved the region's militarization to have been a miscalculation. Even had the czar's admirals and generals been capable fighting commanders (they were only capable of fighting among themselves), distance would have defeated them, as Dominic Lieven makes plain in his authoritative history, *Nicholas II* (1993):

> When the war began, only two of Russia's twenty-nine army corps were in the Far East and it took months of effort to transfer sufficient troops to the theatre of operations. Supplying the field army along the single-track Trans-Siberian railway was a difficult task. The Russian navy could not bring its full strength to bear since the Black Sea squad-

ron, one-third of the fleet, was not allowed by international treaty to pass the Bosporus. The Baltic fleet needed to steam around the world before it could enter the fray; by the time it arrived off the coast of Japan, Russia's Far Eastern squadron had already been destroyed. Although on paper the latter had been a match for the Japanese fleet, its lack of bases and repair facilities was a major disadvantage.

As Dominic Lieven also points out, the last czar saw Russia's future prosperity and influence depending on her Asian possessions rather than on her troublesome and unrewarding links with the Balkan Slavs. His empire – in size only outdone by Britain's - mattered much more to him than the home patch. (Some patch! Its population far exceeded that of any other European state.) This 'facing East' bothered Nicholas's advisers, who by 1900 were tensely foreseeing the First World War. The Finance Ministry protested against the diversion of funds to the Pacific fleet. The Foreign Ministry protested that Russia would soon be too weak in Europe to hold the balance between Germany and France. The War Ministry protested against the diversion of roubles and troops to Manchuria and its Minister, Kuropatkin, warned: 'Never in the whole history of Russia has our western frontier been in such danger in the event of a European war as is true today.' But the czarina told him to stop fretting about Europe and concentrate on the real threat, the 'yellow peril'. Poor woman – for her and her family the real threat was on the doorstep.

The hotel receptionist – elderly, asthmatic, affable – allowed me to use his telephone. I had two contacts: Larisa, an ethnologist met in Tynda in 2002, and the Zhdanovs, the paediatricians met on the BAM who had an English-speaking son, Leo. Conveniently, Leo answered my call – and was a fluent English-speaker. At 3.0 p.m. he didn't consult me about my plans; within half an hour he would collect me from the hotel.

While waiting, I got through to Larisa and it transpired that she and the Zhdanovs were acquainted – not really an odd coincidence. As academics of the sort who go abroad to international conferences, they moved in the same social circle.

Leo was tall, dark and handsome, courtly and vivacious – the sort of person I needed after Komsomolsk and Vanino. During our short taxi-ride he presented himself as an idealist who could escape to a wider world, through his parents' connections, but who felt bound by loyalty to the Russian Far East. 'If people like me go, it makes it easier for the Chinese and Japanese and Koreans to take over.' Remembering Nina, desperate to escape from Komsomolsk but with no 'connections', I resolved to mention her predicament when the moment seemed right.

The Zhdanovs owned a top-floor flat in an imposing, well-maintained 1930s mansion block, very unlike the fast-built post-war prefab blocks. It overlooked the park and had recently been repainted old gold and white. Here I was not going to see how the average Khabarovskian lives.

The senior Zhdanovs welcomed me with a shy formality which didn't last. Evidently they had been intrigued by the solo Irish babushka and even before Leo had finished translating my potted biography his mother was inviting me to stay. In her view the Hotel of the Regional Administration did not provide suitable accommodation for a foreign writer – and there could be problems, most of my fellow-guests must be Chinese traders (they were) of uncertain respectability (I had no reason to think so) and the sooner I moved out the better.

Here was a dilemma with rather sharp horns. My hotel was congenial and Russian hosts do tend to organize their guests, to plan for them – in the kindest possible way, often at some inconvenience and expense to themselves, but I don't like being organized. (Presumably this is a Soviet hangover; people jib at the notion of an individual foreigner wandering alone through an unknown city.) Then I saw that my hesitation was causing disquiet – did I think the living-room sofa-bed inadequate? I could have a room, Leo would be happy on the sofa-bed. That left me with no option but to proclaim the sofa-bed's adequacy and promise to move in on the morrow.

Food emerged. Mere titbits to keep us going until supper time: cubes of cheese on rings of pickled cucumber, slices of hard-boiled egg on rings of salami, sun-dried sardines, biscuits and chocolate and toffees in gay wrappings, individual saucers of blackcurrant jam to be spooned into our tea. Then an embarrassment. Leo asked, 'Do you drink alcohol?' and I admitted to that weakness. 'You like vodka?' I said no, only *pivo* – whereupon Leo disappeared and twenty minutes later reappeared laden with enough *pivo* to content even me for at least two evenings. The Zhdanov household was teetotal but a guest craving alcohol must have it.

During supper (my biggest meal since Tynda) I remarked on the absence of election posters all along my route though the presidential election was less than a month away. At this stage in any Irish campaign, I explained, every lamp-post, telegraph pole and other public space would be festooned with party slogans and candidates' photographs – the latter counter-productive, I often think. Men and women in pursuit of political power do not smile winningly.

Leo gestured dismissively and said, 'Russia has no real contest, so how do posters make a difference? It's known who will win. But to make sure of all nationalistic and militaristic votes Putin now plays a war game – in the Barents Sea, Russia's first big strategic war game for twenty-two years. And we're laughing because it's gone wrong. While our President stood on one nuclear submarine, watching and waiting, two ballistic missiles just wouldn't take off. They say a satellite was blocking the launch command – maybe that's what happens when you don't play war games often enough?'

'And maybe someone was lucky,' I said. 'Suppose the satellite had otherwise affected the launch command? Maverick missiles wouldn't do much for international relations.'

At sunrise it was snowing gently, like a languid sprinkling of caster sugar, but after an all-night fall the silent city wore a new cloak and the temperature had risen to −31°C with no wind-chill. At 9.0 on a Sunday morning, as I walked to the Zhdanovs, my footprints were alone on the wide pavements. My hostess Zoya had been dissuaded, with difficulty, from sending a taxi to fetch me – how else could I carry my luggage? Khabarovsk's women have not yet discovered the liberating power of the rucksack.

After a slow-paced, three-course breakfast a tram took me to Hotel Turist to meet Larisa at noon. She had apologized for not inviting me to her nearby flat – 'My mother is eighty-two and a bit confused.'

From a corner of the foyer I watched a coachload of Japanese skiers assembling, most equipped with cinecameras as well as skis. Then three local youths lounging on a central sofa (pink plastic) noticed the European foreigner. They had spiky rainbow-striped hair and tattooed forearms and wore expensive watches, designer garments (Chinese counterfeits) and chunks of metal embedded in ears and noses. One of them approached me: if I spoke English they would like to practise theirs. I moved to sit with them and at once heard how well the invasion of Iraq suited Russia – Americans were learning what it's like to have your army attacked by terrorists, the fate of Russia's army in Chechnya. All three spoke eccentric but graphic English with American accents.

Larisa seemed slightly disconcerted by the company I was keeping. Three pert teenage girls had followed her through the revolving door, causing the youths to look proprietorial, and immediately all six hastened to the lifts. 'Group sex,' diagnosed Larisa. 'You've met specimens of our junior oligarchy.'

Larisa was in her early fifties, tall and thin, dark-eyed and sallow-skinned, childless and long since divorced. She looked even more tired now than when we first met in 2002; her mother's 'confusion' was rapidly worsening.

What would I like to do? Larisa could recommend the Regional Museum, founded in 1894 and proof that a Russian cultural institution could thrive throughout 110 politically stormy years. My heart sank a little – more dragooning by guides? But of course Larisa's status made a difference; in a largely ethnological museum, an eminent ethnologist could ward off even the most insistent guide.

Historically the tiny Amur–Ussuri tribes were less isolated than Siberia's natives; since the fourteenth century – possibly earlier – they had had trading links with China. Furs, ginseng roots (found in the damp coastal forests) and the antlers of the tufted deer (supposedly aphrodisiacal) were exchanged for tea, rice, cotton and silk materials, iron cooking-pots and, latterly, tobacco and guns. From China too came some basic knowledge of animal husbandry and agriculture and the novel notion of a heated house. These peoples were never completely subjugated but the Manchus did regard the Amur region as rightfully 'within their sphere of influence' and to emphasize that point nominated certain clan and village chiefs. Occasionally, despite the tribes' ranking as barbarians, marriages were arranged between Ainu, Nivkh and Nanai chiefs and Manchu nobles' daughters – who must have been prostrated by culture shock in their new homes.

As we admired tools, blankets, weapons, birch-bark containers and fish-skin garments, Larisa pointed out the Chinese influence on the tribes' decorative art – which indeed was evident even to my inexpert eye, comparing their craftwork with that of the Ewenki, Yakuts and

Buryats. In addition, the Amur–Ussuri shamanist beliefs had been slightly diluted by Chinese Buddhism, a few tribes even celebrating the Chinese New Year in a rather vague way.

'But in my student days', said Larisa, 'all this was officially hidden. Moscow then hated Peking and we were taught China never had any commercial power or cultural links with our Far East. Luckily that sort of censorship didn't always work. In the 1950s Russian scholars had done deep research and acknowledged the facts. My professor lent me such books from his own library, those banned in the university library. *Glasnost* didn't happen as suddenly as the West thinks. Gorbachev had a foundation to build on, laid by people like my professor.'

Having caught a note of admiration – even affection – in this reference to Gorbachev, I asked, on our tram-ride back to the centre, 'How is Mr Gorbachev spending his old age?' (He and I are exact contemporaries.)

'People don't mention him,' said Larisa. 'He's fallen off the stage since Raisa died. They married as students – she philosophy, he law – and were never apart. Some think she was the intellectual dynamo. As our leader, he was too mixed up, a kind man and honest, and wise in certain ways but naive in others – over-optimistic, only half-understanding the West. The military-industrial half he understood very well, the corporate grip on Third World economies he misjudged. He looked forward like an excited boy to making Communism, socialism, work properly for ordinary Russians. Then he upset too many by admitting how badly it worked in the past. He didn't spend enough time putting the case for *perestroika* (restructuring) convincingly. He said there was no time available and maybe he was right. I wish he'd been born twenty years earlier; *perestroika* could have worked in the mid-sixties.'

'Or twenty years later?' I suggested. 'With US militarism scaring more and more people, his thinking about peace-making might be taken more seriously now.'

Larisa looked surprised. 'You know a lot about Mikhail Sergeyevich!'

'Not really,' I said. 'I'm just a fan – have been since I first read his book in 1987.'

Larisa volunteered to accompany me to the railway station, our tram's terminus. I wanted a bunk on a BAM-speed train to Irkutsk, avoiding the Trans-Siberian *Rossiya* which races along at 60 m.p.h.

'That will be a problem,' said Larisa, 'if I don't interpret. The clerk won't believe a tourist wants a slow train.'

Train No. 537 would depart at 2.45 p.m. next day, arriving in Irkutsk sixty-two hours later.

Leo had invited three of his English-speaking fellow-students to supper and during a lively evening I sometimes felt like a spy. I was being hypocritical by omission, not fully revealing my own opinions to avoid damming the flow of others' opinions. Everyone except Leo seemed to agree with the junior oligarchs' skewed view of Iraq as a learning area for US troops. Konstantin and Zoya, in whose bedroom three icons were revered, heartily supported the 'War on Terror' – to them a war against 'the Mussulman'. Leo and his friends were more aware of the complexities, while agreeing that the bombing of dangerous Muslims – in Iraq, Afghanistan or wherever – was always a good idea.

Andrei, a medical student, said, 'Americans like to have a threat. Before it was us, now it's Islamic fundamentalism but they call it terrorism.'

Irina, a physics student, said, 'Iraq is all about oil. Chechnya the same. Russia doesn't need Chechnya for itself – what's Chechnya? Nothing but mountains and savage primitive people! Only its pipeline is important!'

Konstantin disagreed, deploring the younger generation's ignorance of history. Larisa, who had joined us after the meal, recalled Chechnya's strategic importance – 'Czars and Soviets have been trying to subdue those people for more that two centuries. They never will, the Chechnyans are not like anyone else. And I say that as an ethnologist.'

Zoya reckoned the Chechnyans should have been left in Kazakhstan, where Stalin had banished them in 1944 under conditions verging on the genocidal. Khrushchev had made a big mistake when he allowed the survivors back to their mountains in 1956.

When I came out of my hypocritical corner to condemn the blanket bombing of Grozny Leo retorted rather sharply – and inaccurately – 'It's what NATO did to Serbia!' We all agreed that terrorism is a global threat but since we hadn't gone down the rocky road of defining 'terrorism' our agreement may be considered somewhat spurious.

*

It is useful to compare attitudes to terrorism at different periods in different places. George Frost Kennan, in his Introduction to an abridged edition (1958) of George Kennan's *Siberia and the Exile System* (1891), refers to

> the terrorists, mostly young people who had turned in despair and impatience to organized assassination as a means of bringing home to the regime their bitter discontent and their insistence on change . . . Kennan himself had no sympathy for terrorism as a political method, and he could not remain wholly unaware of the particular responsibility borne by the terrorists for the violent methods of repression to which the regime resorted. But even to these young assassins, he could not deny his sympathy, nor could he refrain from attempting to tell the world their side of the story.

In his classic study of Siberia's exiles, George Kennan explained:

> It is not my purpose to justify the policy of the terrorists, nor to approve, even by implication, the resort to murder as a means of tempering despotism; but . . . circumstances seem to lay upon me the duty of saying to the world for the Russian revolutionists and terrorists all that they might fairly say for themselves . . . The Russian government has its own press and its own representatives abroad; it can explain, if it chooses, its methods and measures. The Russian revolutionists, buried alive in remote Siberian solitudes, can only tell their story to an occasional traveller from a freer country, and ask him to lay it before the world for judgement . . . In the years 1877, 1878, and 1879 . . . the whole system was a chaos of injustice, accident and caprice. The local authorities reversed the humane rule of Catherine II and acted, in political cases, upon the principle that it is better to punish ten innocent persons than to allow one criminal to escape. [Here Kennan gives several harrowing case histories.] In the light of such facts terrorism ceases to be an unnatural or inexplicable phenomenon. Wrong a man in that way, deny him all redress, exile him again if he complains, gag him if he cries out, strike him in the face if he struggles, and at last he will stab and throw bombs. It is useless to say that the Russian government does not exasperate men and women in this way . . . The so-called 'propagandists' of 1870–74 did not resort to violence in any form until after the government had begun to exile them to Siberia for life with ten or twelve years of penal servitude, for offenses that were being punished at the very same time in Austria with only a few days – or at most a few weeks – of personal detention. It was

not terrorism that necessitated administrative exile in Russia; it was merciless severity and banishment without due process of law that provoked terrorism.

Russia: Country of Extremes – one of my favourite books about the pre-Revolutionary decades – was published in 1914. Its author, Madame N. Jarintzoff, had then been living for some time in England as a voluntary exile and chapters of her book first appeared in such journals as the *Contemporary Review* and the *Fortnightly Review*, where they caused a few frissons of unease. Among this volume's illustrations is 'A Revolutionary Student who Perished in the Midst of his Chemical Work for Terroristic Purposes'. Madame Jarintzoff reports:

> From 1874 onwards, unrest at the universities became almost the normal state of things. In 1878 the disorders in Kharkov University acquired enormous dimensions; to check them, military force was for the first time openly used, and academical meetings developed into street fights . . . This was the year when Terror made its first appearance in Russia.

St Petersburg's Chief of Police, General Trepoff, provided the first target; his would-be assassin was a young woman named Vera Zassulitch whose bullet only wounded him as he entered his reception hall. When the jury acquitted her, in an open court, trial by jury was promptly abolished for all political offences.

Fifty members of the Will of the People Party – men and women – volunteered to throw the bomb that was to kill Alexander II on 1 March 1881. These were the suicide bombers of their day, knowing that they would be arrested on the spot and hanged soon after. For that murder six were tried, including twenty-five-year-old Sophia Perovskaya – 'of noble birth' – who organized the final details. Speaking from the dock she said:

> Not all members of the Party approved of prosecuting political strife by means of terroristic acts; but it was resolved upon nevertheless on the strength of the general conviction that the late sovereign would otherwise never alter his system of home politics . . . The accusation about the facts we do not contradict, but the accusation of immorality, of cruelty, and of contempt for public opinion I must deny. No one of those who know the surroundings and conditions of our life and work would accuse us of immorality or cruelty.

Madame Jarintzoff quotes from the memoir of one who did know the 'surroundings and conditions':

A stranger would never have believed her [Sophia Perovskaya] to be one of the chief moving spirits of a great Party. She was one of those whose gifted nature allows them to manage complicated situations as if they were the most ordinary affairs of everyday life, and to remain genuinely simple and cheerful at the same time. When other people's safety was at stake, Perovskaya would be most cautious; but when things implied danger for herself alone, she would remain strong and daring, unswerving in courage.

One of the four men on trial was Nikolai Kibaltchitch, the twenty-eight-year-old son of a priest, a graduate of the St Petersburg Institute of Civil Engineers and of the Medical Academy, who in 1875 had been charged with 'reading, storing and spreading the literature of socialistic doctrines' and imprisoned for three years. He was the Party's explosives expert and he concluded his speech from the dock by explaining:

I prepared four bombs for March 1 . . . two of which had been used . . . The amount of dynamite applied was a minimum, i.e. such that the passers-by would have been at the utmost hurt by lumps of earth and stone only . . . All the literature on the subject does not record a single instance of an explosion of 80 lbs of dynamite making a hole larger than twenty foot in diameter at its top. The aim was to explode the mine right under the Emperor's carriage. He and the escort would have perished, of course, but no one else. It would show an amazing desire for bloodshed if we acted simply for bloodshed's sake. Terror in itself has never been our aim.

At 9.0 a.m. on 3 April 1881 the four men and one of the women were publicly hanged after a long procession in an open horse-cart through the streets of St Petersburg – accompanied by five priests in closed carriages, and non-stop muffled drumbeats to attract more spectators. The pregnant Gessia Gelfman enjoyed a postponement, until the day after her baby's birth.

In February 1901 a former university student, twice expelled for 'revolutionary activities', assassinated the Minister of Education. In July 1904 the notoriously anti-Semitic and relentlessly repressive Minister of Internal Affairs, Vyacheslav Plehve, was blown away and in 1905 it was the turn of Grand Duke Sergey Alexandrovitch, described by Dominic Lieven as 'a reactionary paternalist of very authoritarian disposition'. This powerful Grand Duke – Nicholas II's uncle, married to a granddaughter of Queen Victoria – was Moscow's Governor-General, a position with viceregal status. He had blocked the reforms being proposed by a prudent Minister of Internal Affairs, Prince Peter Svyatopolk-Mirsky, who had warned the Czar, 'If you don't carry out liberal reforms and don't satisfy the completely natural wishes of every-body then change will come but in the form of revolution.' In reply, after a heavy session with Uncle Sergey, Nicholas announced, 'I will never agree to a representative form of government because I consider it harmful to the people whom God has entrusted to me.'

A team of 'revolutionists' worked on the Grand Duke's assassination. In Madàme Jarintzoff's words, 'These reckless heroes – calm in their readiness for death either on the spot or on the gallows – were daily shadowing the Duke, sometimes disguised as cabmen and pedlars, holding bombs for hours in their arms, waiting for a chance to get to close quarters with him when unaccompanied by the Grand Duchess.'

The Duke's student assassin, Ivan Kaliaiev, belonged to 'the terror-ist faction of Social Revolutionists'. Kaliaiev père could remember being sold for cash by one landowner to another; he had married a Polish woman 'of highly refined nature' whose hatred of the czarist regime equalled his own. On 4 February 1905 Ivan Kaliaiev saw his quarry driving alone along the crowded and fashionable Tverskaya Street where an assassin would have some chance of escaping in the panic and confusion. He chose however to wait until the carriage reached the almost deserted Kremlin where he could not possibly evade arrest. Then he made a short run and from three yards away threw his bomb – assembled the night before, in her one-room lodging, by a young woman who was to die in prison after the Moscow insurrection. When Kaliaiev later heard false rumours that his reprieve was being considered he wrote to the Minister of Justice: 'As a revolutionary true to the traditions of the Will of the People Party, I consider it due to my political conscience to reject mercy.'

Despite the frequency of political murders and the assassins' lack of originality, even the most obvious targets neglected their personal security. On 1 September 1911, in Kiev Opera House, Prime Minister Peter Stolypin was shot and fatally wounded by Dm. Bogrov, a Kiev academic and, according to Madame Jarintzoff, 'a gifted man, of great learning and refinement, reserved manners, deep convictions'. Nicholas II viewed Stolypin as 'the best Prime Minister I ever had'. Madame Jarintzoff viewed him as 'a cold-blooded dictator'. She assumed that Bogrov on the scaffold shared Kaliaiev's emotions, felt

> the calm enthusiasm of a fighter who has avenged hundreds of murders of innocent men and women. True idealistic terrorists always hope that they will not be killed at the moment of their attack, but will live through the exaltation which accompanies the period while they are awaiting execution, and will walk into the arms of death with a glad heart, happy to give up their lives for their cause. This conception . . . makes them blind to one part of the truth . . . 'Terrorism puts a weapon into the hands of Reaction'.

Sometimes one wonders if Madame Jarintzoff's move to England in 1904 was entirely voluntary.

In comparison with the terrorist tactics of the czarist and Stalinist regimes, the revolutionists' activities described above seem rather mild and well-controlled: an emperor here – a grand duke there – a prime minister elsewhere; certainly a moral world away from the sadistic ferocity with which Reds and Whites tortured and slaughtered each other during the 1919–22 Civil War, or from the indiscriminate terrorist attacks of our own day. However, *Russia: Country of Extremes* reminds us that the suicide bombers' mindset, which we find so bewildering and demoralizing, is neither new nor Islamic. Much nonsense is talked nowadays about suicide bombing being a peculiar symptom of Islamic fanaticism, ignorantly associated in the popular press with sexual orgies in Paradise as the 'martyrs' reward'. But the fifty men and women who volunteered to kill Alexander II were not Muslims. What they had in common with today's suicide bombers was a sense of desperation, a feeling that the extreme injustice of their situation could only be highlighted by the matching extremity of suicide. One has to discard logic to condemn suicide bombers as 'cowardly'. Several other adjectives are appropriate: callous, irrational, ruthless, fanatical. But not cowardly. A suicide bomber has to be brave – much more so than a soldier who knows he will be executed if he disobeys orders.

How would George Kennan and Madame Jarintzoff regard the notion of an international War Against Terrorism? They might point out that it takes two to war and that the numerous groups who use terrorist tactics don't have an army. They would probably argue against the use of massive military force which, given guerilla elusiveness, has to be indiscriminate and therefore counter-productive. Even the deployment of efficient intelligence services (if such exist) is a feeble anti-terrorist strategy, as short-term as chopping brambles where they appear in the garden. If you don't find and deal with the roots, those brambles will soon be back.

Over breakfast, Zoya became red with rage and torrentially voluble when I mentioned 'conscripts'. She was, Leo explained, a Mothers' Rights Fund organizer and currently engaged in helping to investigate a scandal.

In both Komsomolsk and Khabarovsk I had noticed groups of off-duty conscripts – undersized and wan, looking malnourished to the point of illness, markedly deficient in the joys of youth. Their appearance shockingly recalled photographs of labour camp inmates: the Old Russia intruding on the New. Annually, 400,000 youngsters are recruited for two years' training – a programme the army can no longer afford – and the latest scandal was the small tip of a very large iceberg.

On 3 December 2003, 194 conscripts had been flown to the Far East to act as Federal border guards, their families not knowing their destination when they left the Moscow region, dressed for European rather than Siberian temperatures. At Novosibirsk, where their plane broke down, they were ordered to sleep without bedding on a barracks floor and given no supper. That night the temperature was $-18°C$. Subsequently, during two refuelling stops, they had to stand on the tarmac, still inadequately clothed, for more than an hour in temperatures between minus 20° and minus 25°C – with a wind. On arrival at Kamchatka warm clothing was issued but by then all were ill – eighty-four suffering from acute respiratory diseases and in urgent need of hospital care. Nine days later they were flown to Magadan, one of Siberia's coldest inhabited regions, where another two weeks passed before the eighty-four were admitted to hospital. The doctors diagnosed malnutrition in addition to their multiple infections. One eighteen-year-old died after four days in intensive care. As we spoke, in mid-February, forty remained in hospital and were unlikely to be fit for 'training', said Zoya, without a prolonged convalescence on a good diet.

Had I not chanced to notice those forlorn conscripts Zoya's story might have seemed incredible. 'How could it be allowed to happen?' was my first reaction.

Another angry torrent from Zoya. Leo translated: 'My mother says it was always the same, under czars or Soviets conscripts never had value. If they collapsed or died it was cheap to get more. They're treated like serfs were by bad landowners. Now the Mothers' Rights Fund is collecting evidence, looking for punishment for officers. Putin says they will be punished but I don't believe him.'

Konstantin remembered his father's experiences as a prisoner in the Great Patriotic War. The Nazis had no problem guarding their Russian captives; even when opportunities arose, those prisoners seemed unkeen to escape. And not a few were easy to capture.

No doubt I was looking as distressed as I felt, and in an attempt to soothe me Leo explained how much easier draft-dodging is in the New Russia – given enough roubles. His attempt backfired. But I merely remarked on the context within which such brutality has survived into the twenty-first century; militarism is an inherently brutalizing ideology, whatever the political background. And, as Robert Service has pointed out, 'Stalin aimed at acceptance of a Russian national identity characterized by militarism, large-scale organization and urbanism, and by the supremacy of the interests of the state over the wants and needs of society.'

The Zhdanovs had carefully planned my forenoon. First Konstantin and Leo took me on a tour of Khabarovsk's three unexciting churches. Then Zoya showed me round a maternity hospital, clean and neat but with an ill-equipped prem unit and a permanent shortage of drugs. Our interpreter was Lydia, an English-speaking young intern. When I opined that the drugs shortage might be beneficial, and boasted of my daughter's three home-births without so much as an aspirin, Zoya and Lydia looked shocked – then sympathetic. Was Ireland like America, hospital care too expensive? Not so, I replied – a home-birth, attended by an independent midwife instead of a state-paid doctor, cost more than hospital care. At that my companions looked quite distraught – 'It's too dangerous! In problems the midwifes knows nothing, has no machines!' I began to regret my impulse to promote home-births and said in a tone of finality, 'Why expect problems? Giving birth isn't a disease.'

Then Leo arrived, wearing my rucksack, to escort me to the railway station where we were joined by Konstantin, Larisa and Irina the physics student, all bearing gifts of food. These platform farewell ceremonies are of course distance-related; one can't imagine friends interrupting their daily routine to see off a passenger on the Flying Scotsman. But from most starting points in Western Europe the 2,107 miles between Khabarovsk and Irkutsk would take you off the continent.

8

A Climate-Change Hiatus

As NO. 537 rattled across a twenty-two-span girder bridge (the Trans-Siberian's longest) I said farewell to the Amur, here a mile and a half wide though this is hard to appreciate when all the world is white and immobile.

My *platskartny*, towards the front, was full of young families en route from Vladivostok and amply supplied with books, crossword puzzles, chess sets, photograph albums – but, mercifully, no radios. And this is not cellphone territory. All their high-spirited, well-behaved children were much given to gymnastic tricks for which *platskartny* offer excellent facilities.

Soon we were traversing marshland, the crisp unsullied snow flecked with old gold tufted reeds. Then – crisis! Our hot water pipe had burst near the samovar and was leaking copiously. An agitated *provodnitsa* summoned a maintenance man laden with tools, up came the strip of coarse matting on the corridor (it would be carpet in a coupé carriage), and as floorboards were lifted cold air scythed our legs. The maintenance man switched on his miners' headlamp and small boys crowded excitedly around until shooed away by Galia, our *provodnitsa*. The leak was quickly stemmed and the boards replaced but the heating had to be turned off; something was seriously amiss, couldn't immediately be repaired. Galia ordered everyone to wrap up at once, not to wait for the temperature to drop – which it did within minutes. A rule was bent to allow us to use the next carriage's samovar and as each bunk had its pure wool double blanket hypothermia was not a hazard – though toothpaste and liquids stored near the window were frozen solid next morning.

At dawn, at a little logging town station, the maintenance man could obtain what he needed and after much banging of pipes and squealing of screws we were reheated.

That day we crossed six minor tributaries of the Amur, winding through shallow forested valleys or austerely beautiful steppe where the horizon seemed immeasurably distant. Towards sunset a long bridge took us over the Zeya, a major tributary famous for the gold to be found along its upper reaches. Hereabouts, in the mountains just visible to the north, George Kennan and his artist friend George Frost endured some of their most gruelling experiences while investigating Siberia's 'exile system'.

American journals were then competing as 'sponsors of explorers' – the *New York Herald* had started the vogue by sending Stanley to Africa – and in 1885–86 the *Century Magazine* funded Kennan's 8,000-mile, ten-month expedition. This was during the early years of Alexander III's reign, in George Frost Kennan's words 'a period of extreme reaction and uninhibited police terror'. In the 1890s, when *Siberia and the Exile System* first circulated throughout the czar's empire in German and a (banned) Russian translation, all factions of the opposition, from moderate to 'revolutionist', rejoiced to find themselves with such an eloquent, well-informed and influential spokesman. His two-volume account of a truly extraordinary journey, first serialized in the *Century Magazine*, had sold widely in the US and many popular lectures reinforced its message. As George Frost Kennan dryly observes in his Introduction, 'The book struck squarely and with great effect into that curious Victorian capacity for sympathy and indignation over evils that were far away.'

Watching a crimson and orange sky fading to purple and primrose, I remembered one of Kennan's paragraphs that might have been written in 2004 about somewhere else:

> Exile by administration process means the banishment of an obnoxious person from one part of the empire to another without the observance of any of the legal formalities that, in most civilized countries, precede the deprivation of rights and the restriction of personal liberty. The obnoxious person may not be guilty of any crime, but if, in the opinion of the local authorities, his presence in a particular place is 'prejudicial to public order' or 'incompatible with public tranquillity', he may be arrested without a warrant, may be held for from two weeks to two years in prison, and may then be removed by force to any other place within the limits of the empire and there be put under police surveillance for a period of from one year to ten years. He may or may not

be informed of the reasons for this summary proceeding, but in either case he is perfectly helpless. He cannot examine the witnesses upon whose testimony his presence is declared to be 'prejudicial to public order'. He cannot summon friends to prove his loyalty and good character, without great risk of bringing upon them the same calamity that has befallen him. He has no right to demand a trial, or even a hearing. He cannot appeal to his fellow-citizens through the press. His communication with the world is so suddenly severed that sometimes his own relatives do not know what has happened to him. He is literally and absolutely without any means whatever of self-defence.

George Kennan, so proud of being American, would feel very ashamed of Guantanamo Bay.

The next two days were hard work for No. 537 as the track zigzagged through Transbaikalia's many ranges of desolately magnificent mountains – sometimes climbing high, sometimes following wide river valleys once inhabited only by native peoples. Often we halted for thirty or forty minutes at insignificant stations to allow freight trains of prodigious length to pass – or, twice, to give way to the gleaming *Rossiya* which has several first-class carriages and an opulent-looking restaurant car flaunting curtains with frilly pelmets and flower-bedecked tables.

At the bigger stations the platform vendors of wholesome comestibles – homemade salami, grilled fish, roast chicken, pelmeni – were not allowed onto our train to compete with the junk-food trolleys of Russian Railways Inc. In 2002 such women often got on the BAM at one station – travelling free – and off at the next. This trade may be their only source of income and in winter, when many passengers are reluctant to wrap up for a brief forage, access to trains is essential. And now efforts were being made to persuade the government to repeal a 1937 law requiring all services to carry children, OAPs and the disabled free of charge or at 30 per cent rates.

I had expected the Trans-Siberian track to be smoother than BAM's but it's rougher and the notes I made en route have proved hard to read. The atmosphere, too, was more unstable; stern Railway Police and militia separately patrolled the train in pairs, peering suspiciously at everyone, though our *platskartny* (two babushki, several happy families) can't have had an aura of criminality. That said, drug merchants do sometimes recruit innocent-looking old dears walking with two sticks . . . And all trains starting from Vladivostok – not just the *Rossiya* – are assumed to be carrying heroin from North Korea.

The other babushka had come aboard at Birobidzhan and immediately taken me under her wing. Veronika was convinced that if she spoke very slowly, loudly and clearly I *must* understand Russian. By Day Two this conviction had become a little trying, especially as Veronika spurned my dictionary – using it only once, to help convey that she was going to Ulan-Ude to worship a newborn grandson. The infant's rather peculiar christening present, a coffee-table book of Vladivostok photographs with English captions, didn't make me regret bypassing that city.

Twice, as we crossed the superb Aleurskiy range, No. 537 momentarily formed a perfect 'U' on hairpin bends. Even the indigenous nomads spent little time in this chaotically fissured region – one of the main obstacles to a Trans-Siberian motor road. Between those hairpins Galia informed us that a film of Kamchatka's unique landscape was about to be shown in the restaurant car. Eagerly Veronika stood up, extending a hand to me – then looked puzzled when I remained seated. Even had I spoken Russian it is doubtful if she and Galia would have comprehended my preferring the real beauty of Transbaikalia to the filmed beauty of Kamchatka. When everyone else trooped after Galia I felt a twinge of alarm; is *Homo sapiens* approaching the stage at which cameras will be needed to render beautiful landscapes satisfying?

West of Nerchinsk the mountains receded at intervals, leaving space for agriculture – here a tragically destructive novelty. The 1960s 'Virgin Lands' campaign (rape by tractor) wrecked the habitat of many species and caused settlers to attempt the extermination of such 'pests' as marmots, spotted deer, eagles and, in the Altai mountains, snow leopards.

The afternoon of Day Three provided a shock – pollution on a truly sinister scale between Petrovsk-Zabaykal'skiy (where an iron works was built in 1790, by order of Catherine the Great) and Ulan-Ude, the Buryat capital. Tall stacks, a few miles apart, dominated this wide valley, their fumes dense and black. Broad bands of darkness obscured the horizon and a cloudless sky was dingy to the meridian. Slag heaps towered above mottled snow – recalling Vanino – and soon

I could hear our wheels saying, 'The valley of death – the valley of death – the valley of death'. I was already out of sorts, angry with myself for having badly mistimed this journey. Its final eight night-time hours would cheat me of the Trans-Siberian's *pièce de résistance* – the 200-mile stretch along Lake Baikal's southern shore and over the Primorskiy range.

Heavy industries menace Ulan-Ude, their vanguard a gigantic 1930s plant – the biggest east of the Urals – for manufacturing and maintaining rolling stock and diesel engines. While packing her bags Veronika delved deep into one and brought forth a gift for my grand-daughters, a minuscule seal made of sealskin. As we hugged I felt guilty about having been so irritated by her chattering and hoped the irritation never showed.

That was a long halt and I upset Galia – ever solicitous for her charges' welfare – by not wrapping up before standing at the open car-riage door. The Siberians take wrapping up a bit too seriously. My T-shirt-clad ten-minute exposure to a temperature of minus 19 caused a sensation; people couldn't believe that I wasn't suffering and several rushed to enfold me in their furs.

Then came a minor drama: Galia and a Railway Policewoman in confrontation. One very drunk Buryat, needing the support of two Russian friends, showed a ticket for our *platskartny* and Galia, looking disapproving but motherly, was prepared to cope with him. Then the policewoman shouted 'Nyet!' and came hurrying towards us; evi-dently inebriation invalidates a ticket. But *provodnitsi* resent their authority being challenged and Galia argued furiously that anyone in such a state would sleep all the way to Irkutsk. A reasonable argument, yet the policewoman won, loudly decreeing that in every circum-stance passengers must be protected from unpredictable drunks. Galia denounced her in ringing tones as she followed the trio back to the waiting-room. The onlookers remained silent – and inscrutable.

Beyond Ulan-Ude we chugged towards a yellowish-brown sullen sunset, following the valley of the Selenga – here a considerable river, far from its source in neighbouring Mongolia. During the descent to Baikal's shore I left my window uncurtained but soon snow came, enough to curtain it from outside. Then Galia advised me to turn in; her colleague would rouse me at 1.0 a.m.

★

A five-hour sleep left me ready to spend the rest of the night reading in Irkutsk's waiting-room, enhanced by soaring marble pillars, finely carved cedarwood doors, coruscating cut-glass chandeliers – the palatial effect only slightly marred by rows of grey plastic chairs. However, I had reckoned without the Railway Police: soon a thickset young man was curtly demanding to see my onward ticket. Dictionary in hand, I struggled to explain that I was a bona fide train-user on a round-Russia journey – I showed my sheaf of tickets, kept as souvenirs. The officer scrutinized them, then snapped 'Nyet!' None was 'onward' and his expression accused me of being a parasite, illegally availing myself of Irkutsk's warm waiting-room. (To a Russian, both my thirty-year-old rucksack and my borrowed BAM jacket would suggest 'parasite'.) Then came a pregnant pause: in the womb of possibility lay a bribe. How that was conveyed I cannot say; no words or gestures were used yet when our eyes met the message was clear. Probably this unpleasant young man had a family in dire need of the few roubles he might gain by harassing foreigners but I have an irrational loathing of bribery – irrational because petty bribe-seekers can be deserving causes. Only once have I bought a favour and that was in a truly desperate situation. As my present situation was not desperate I took a taxi to the Hotel Angara.

In 2002 I described the Angara's foyer as 'glitzy-turned-shoddy: enormous, ill-lit, almost empty'. Now it was strobe-lit with a casino decor and at 2.45 a.m. zombified citizens were playing sixteen fruit machines. I paused by Reception to consider the tariff list: cheapest room R2,400. Until moving at dawn to a friend's nearby flat it would make more economic sense to join the adolescent prostitutes around the bar and justify my presence by buying *pivos*. One teenager spoke enough English to complain that the installation of the fruit machines had hit their trade. No doubt sociologists are studying that interesting phenomenon: the gambling urge overcoming the sexual urge. I asked about AIDS, did they know how important it was to use condoms? They giggled – here was another clueless do-gooder, not plugged into the real world. No way would their clients use condoms. But they knew all about the morning-after pill and its cost was included in their fee. When I emphasized the obvious – pregnancy and AIDS being different risks – they looked uninterested. And they remained uninterested when informed that a recent United Nations Development

Programme report had named Irkutsk as one of Russia's high-risk cities where the AIDS infection rate is 300 per cent above the national average – partly because of its high heroin addiction rate, which had so alarmed me on my earlier visit.

As we talked on, Tanya the English-speaker – aged sixteen – revealed that she hoped to start university two years hence and was 'working at night' to save money to pay the bribes demanded by many professors in the New Russia. Her parents, who had lost their jobs in the 1990s, believed she was employed by Hotel Intourist as a night receptionist.

Cossacks founded Irkutsk by building a fort at the confluence of the Angara and Irkut rivers in 1651. Quite soon it became an important trading centre, then the capital of Eastern Siberia. When C. H. Hawes passed through in 1902 the population was close to 60,000 and he described the city as

> an exceptional centre of education. One met students everywhere, hurrying along with books under their arms, and quite as many maidens as youths. Many of the large and splendid schools owe their existence to private munificence, and to the presence of large numbers of educated exiles. I was told that at least 500 girls attended the gymnasium [i.e. high school] and other institutions for secondary education. They came from all parts of Siberia; many of them boarded out in families, and proceeded from here to the university of Tomsk . . . A spirit of freedom seemed to reign in the town, especially in the educational realm. There was a breadth and liberality about it that would not be permitted in Moscow, Kiev or St Petersburg.

One still meets students everywhere, though I doubt if many are maidens. Mr Hawes also reported a high murder rate, a weekly average of two in the city centre and fourteen in the scattered suburbs, where lived thousands of released or escaped convicts. He was therefore astonished when 'a lady resident' declined his offer to drive her home from a museum lecture. 'She laughingly replied, "Oh no, thank you; I am a 'new woman', you see; and besides, I *have* my revolver!"'

In Irkutsk's present population of half a million the murder rate is no higher, though mugging is said to be on the increase. For a moment one morning, in the huge new covered market, I thought I was being targeted when my purse was knocked out of my hand as I opened it. But the elderly man who had stumbled against me, then clutched my arm before collapsing, was in fact a vodka victim. On hitting the floor he had passed out and remained on his back in the middle of an aisle. I gazed down at him sympathetically: I've occasionally been there myself, though never at 10.20 a.m. or in such a public place (usually in the garden or sitting-room of excessively hospitable friends who pick me up and put me to bed and tactfully forget the incident). No one else showed a flicker of concern and on my way to the exit ten minutes later customers were stepping over the unfortunate man, treating him like some immovable, inanimate obstacle.

Russia's thousand-year-old alcohol problem is more noticeable in winter; those homeless men who in summer gather in sunny corners have to keep on the move with their tins and bottles when it's 'minus'. Outside the market another elderly man, ragged and long-bearded and wearing scarlet gloves, was pacing to and fro flourishing an empty vodka bottle and chanting verses from the Orthodox liturgy in a wavering croak. (Perhaps a defrocked priest?) A few of my babushka friends complained that 'respectable' young Siberian women are now drinking much more – and more openly, in competition with the young men.

In this third week of February Irkutsk felt almost warm: around minus 18. All over the city new snow was being shovelled off high roofs in bulk, regardless of passers-by – pouring to the ground in luminous cascades. In the central square (which is oblong) men and women laboured to clear the paths of packed snow and demolish twelve-foot-high ice constructions. Near the Great Patriotic War memorial, where burns an eternal flame, newly-weds were being photographed in noon sunshine, the bride wearing only a white crinoline gown and wispy veil; her hands, clasping a bouquet of pink roses, were purple.

Since my previous visit commerce had disfigured Irkutsk's attractively pompous pre-Revolution boulevards. There were billboards advertising motor vehicles and cigarettes, the various brands of both being associated with healthy outdoor activities in beautiful surroundings. One dual-purpose ad showed a young man negotiating a spaghetti junction in his SUV while using a mobile phone. My companion translated the text – 'You needn't lose an order because you must leave your office and get somewhere fast. With us, you're never away from your profit source'.

Recently opened supermarkets employed swaggering teenage security officers who wore ersatz military uniforms (much smarter than the conscripts') and had large holstered revolvers clipped to their belts. 'Why?' I asked. 'Are they allowed to shoot shoplifters? Or do you often have armed raids on supermarkets?'

My companion shrugged. 'It's another bit of the Americanization of Irkutsk. It goes with the SUVs.'

My four days in Irkutsk were socially action-packed; friends welcomed me back so generously that I set a personal record of four consecutive hangovers. There was however one big disappointment; Lake Baikal's southern third had not frozen normally, therefore my planned 'winter road' return to Severobaikalsk from Irkutsk was impossible. Friends advised me to try again from Barguzin, a large village on the eastern shore accessible by bus from Ulan-Ude. The Barguzin–Severobaikalsk ice was trustworthy – but traffic was meagre, Barguzin would be a gamble. I am averse to gambling with money but will always take a chance on transport. And as compensation for this hiatus, my return to Ulan-Ude would be by daylight.

9

New Year in Buryatia

ICOULD SMELL poverty as the homeless passed me, a score or so of pensioners swathed in grubby garments and clutching plastic bags, being chivvied by the Railway Police out of Irkutsk's warm station. It was six o'clock on a Sunday morning and soon a jolly crowd of young people arrived, bound for nearby ski slopes, wearing and carrying expensive gear. Several pensioners loitered outside the entrance – not overtly begging, but hoping. Most of the young ignored them, a few gave small coins.

In my uncrowded *platskartny* I sat alone by a wide window while everyone else settled down to sleep. As we climbed into the Primorskiy range snow-laden pines glimmered through the darkness and stoves were being lit in loggers' villages and a solitary engine, speeding downhill, greeted us with a cheerful 'Toot-tootle-too!' Then the first dawnlight came seeping upwards, faintly pink above the Khamar-Daban's distant rock-crests, and from the pass I glimpsed a fragment of Lake Baikal where the high mountains ahead divided – a remote colourless fragment, very far below. Then, during our descent, the lake was hidden for some two hours. This stretch of track is much admired by the cognoscenti. It was blasted out of sheer slopes and for miles it curves around mountain after mountain, overlooking deep narrow ravines. When Baikal reappears, as one emerges from the last of three short tunnels, its surface is locally stained by Slyudyanka, an appropriately ugly name for a mining town-cum-port which emits much grey-brown-black foulness.

Here we halted briefly – as did John Foster Fraser in 1901, before the completion of the Trans-Siberian. For years the best engineering brains were stumped by these mountains, the most formidable barrier between Moscow and Vladivostok. Trains and their passengers had therefore steamed to and fro on the famous ice-breakers *Angara* and

Baikal, built by Messrs Armstrong & Co. in Newcastle, assembled on the lake shore and maintained – Mr Fraser proudly noted – 'by some of the modest army of Britishers one drops across in odd corners of the world'. While aboard the *Angara*, Fraser was thrilled to see the *Baikal* come 'steaming down the lake, a huge four-funnelled vessel, white painted, by no means pretty, rather like a barn that had slipped afloat . . . [but] one of the most wonderful vessels in the world'. She was

> carrying two goods trains fully laden. If necessary she could carry three trains and 800 passengers . . . As the foregates were open I caught a glimpse of red-painted goods waggons. The ship is of over 4,000 tons, close on 300 feet long, and has nearly 60 feet beam. She has three triple expansion engines of 1,250 horse-power . . . required in the ice-breaking. She will break through 36 inches and her bow is made with a curve, so that when the ice is thicker she can be backed and then go full steam at the ice, partly climb on it with her impetus, then crush it with her weight. This means that the *Baikal* sometimes takes a week to cross the lake.

People in a hurry chose to cross by three-horse-power sledges, the traditional troika. My favourite nineteenth-century Siberian traveller, Captain John Dundas Cochrane RN, reported in *A Pedestrian Journey Through Russian and Siberian Tartary* (1823): 'We crossed in two and a half hours. Such is, however, the rapidity with which three horses abreast cross this lake, that the late governor of Irkutsk usually did it in two hours.' These troika gallops were of course hazardous, as Charles Hawes discovered in December 1902:

> It is dangerous to attempt to stop the horses, and sometimes the sledge moves faster than the steeds, overtakes them and slews round. The surface presents many . . . holes and weak places, especially at the beginning and towards the end of the sledging season. At these times the trip is undertaken at considerable risk, and prices rise in proportion to the danger, mounting to as much as 400 rubles (£42). Many lives are lost every winter.

We spent the next six hours dawdling along the shore, usually no more than ten yards from Baikal's glittering fringe of contorted mini-icebergs. This stretch of the Trans-Siberian – the last to be built – is confined to a narrow strip of sometimes marshy land at the base of the Khamar-Daban range. These mountains – all irregular chunks and long dark fissures, precipitous yet partly forested – at times seem to be leaning forward over the track. Occasionally they withdraw slightly, allowing space for small communities of fishermen, loggers and railway workers. Notoriously, those in charge of 'developing' Eastern Siberia refused to respect Lake Baikal's uniqueness, yet I was unprepared for the extent of the desecration between Slyudyanka and Selenginsk, where the line turns inland to cross the Ulan-Burgasy range. Around each of the few industrial towns Baikal was blackened and pitted and in the worst case smoke obliterated the far shore, fifty miles away. It can only be a matter of time before the entire length of the lake is fatally and irreversibly damaged.

When we stopped at Selenginsk my fellow-passengers began to yawn and stretch and look at watches: it was 1.15 p.m. Seventeenth-century Cossacks founded this large town – scarcely visible from the station, apart from factory stacks – and in 1685, when no more than a fort on the river, it was besieged by Mongols. Six years later many of the Tabunut, an indigenous Mongol tribe, migrated to Mongolia because of the Cossacks' 'offensive behaviour and impositions' (in the words of a contemporary Russian chronicler). 'Those whom the Tabunut chiefs had left behind . . . were all put to death [by the Cossacks] and thrown into the Selenga, and their wives and children and possessions were shared out and sold off' (M. N. Bogdanov, quoted by James Forsyth). Since czarist times Selenginsk has been the site of minor industries, chiefly glass-making and chemical dyes.

Until the Cossacks arrived, frontiers were not an issue hereabouts. Then, for all this region's natives, their millennia of wandering across the borderless expanses of Mongolia and Transbaikalia were brought to a close. As the czar's 'men of service' moved east, the Chinese decided that Outer Mongolia belonged exclusively to them and the empires squabbled. Their 1689 Treaty of Nerchinsk gave the steppe-lands of north-eastern Mongolia to the czar while warning him off the Amur region. But not until the 1727 Treaty of Kiakhta was the Russo-Chinese border defined and sealed, for the first time in history – and of course without reference to the indigenes' needs and wishes. One closely guarded trade route was permitted, through Kiakhta, but the normal rhythm of toing and froing between northern Mongolia and Transbaikalia's grasslands became extremely dangerous. Both imperial powers disapproved of uncountable, uncontrollable and therefore untaxable nomads. And the Cossack border patrols were always happy to shoot 'illegal immigrants' and confiscate their horses and herds.

Aside from imperial destabilizations, this whole vast area had been home-brewing conflicts throughout most of the seventeenth century, leading to frequent unusual migrations. As a result, the newly sealed border trapped many Khalka Mongols in Transbaikalia, where they eventually merged with the Buryats, whilst more than half the Buryat Khori tribe were stranded in Mongolia.

When I first noticed Todo (his nickname, which he soon invited me to use), I foolishly wondered 'Buryat or Mongol?' In fact Siberia's comparatively large Buryat population was known as Buryat-Mongol until 1958 when the Soviets banned the term, alleging that it was being used subversively by 'Buryat bourgeois nationalists' – of whom Todo was one, I quickly realized. He first noticed me and my out-spread map on his way back from the samovar. Pausing, he smiled shyly, then asked, 'Please madam, permission to sit with you?'

Professor Lopsan was short and sturdy, round-faced and white-haired with ruddy cheeks, kind eyes and a gentle voice. He had been visiting Novosibirsk where his student son lay in hospital with two broken legs. 'His skis took him over a cliff,' explained Todo. 'It's no worry, the bones have neatly broken. Tell me please about you, why you go alone?'

A quarter of an hour later Todo was saying, 'You will come to be a guest with us. Tomorrow we have Buddhist New Year, Buryatsia has Tibetan Buddhism and my wife is making a feast. My daughter Dolma talks easy English – not like me! Now she learns Chinese, that impor-tant language for this century.'

Later, Dolma told me her father's story. During Akademgorodok's heyday he had spent years doing pioneering work on the analysis of rare minerals. But Akademgorodok, the Soviet Union's intellectual powerhouse in Western Siberia, was unplugged from its funding at the dawn of the New Russia. In 1993 Todo moved to Ulan-Ude's Academy of Sciences and now, towards the end of a distinguished career, he was travelling *platskartny*.

Gazing out at the wide flat Selenga valley, I wondered what lay beneath the anonymity of all that smooth snow.

'Very much good grass,' said Todo. 'Here Buryat people fed thou-sands and thousands of horses, cattle, sheep. I talk about before I was born, before collectivization. Stalin stopped them owning animals, they must work in Ulan-Ude's new factories. Making war goods, mostly, and after 1991 many stopped making. Then people have nothing or work trading across the border. Some trade with drugs to make more profit for feeding and educating children. That's bad, dangerous for other men's children. But when I have nothing, you have nothing – which children we put first?'

Significantly this was the first time a Siberian had mentioned Stalin's name in conversation with me, as distinct from alluding to his terrorist regime. And even allusions were infrequent. As Catherine Merridale has written, 'The history of Soviet repression remains incomprehensible. Like all atrocities of its kind it is hard to face.'

At 2.38 p.m. precisely we halted amidst the dismal sprawl of a station designed to serve much heavy industry. Todo led me across four sets of tracks and up three long flights of cracked concrete steps to a tram stop on pot-holed ulitsa Revolutsii 1905. I had firmly declined taxi transport but he apologized for the discomfort of tram travel; the No. 7 – slow, jerky, chilly, noisy - belonged to Ulan-Ude's original 1930s fleet. I reassured him as we rattled uphill through canyons of high-risery; whatever its motive, such municipal frugality deserves praise and support.

No. 7's terminus is visible from the Lopsans' four-roomed ground-floor flat in a six-storey red-brick block – eye-soothing, after so much bleak concrete. This salubrious row of five blocks, on the city's edge, faces a long, low ridge dotted with *izbi* in large fenced gardens. Higher ridges, pine-clad or built over, rise in the middle distance and beyond them lies the steppeland that soon becomes Mongolia.

Mrs Lopsan (Pema) looked astonished though not displeased on being introduced to her foreign guest. Dolma registered delight at having an English-speaker on the premises but Geser viewed me as surplus to his requirements. A one-year-old long-haired white tom, with glowing amber eyes, he was the most loquacious cat I have ever met and engaged his besotted family in endless dialogues. 'During winter we must talk to him,' explained Dolma. 'For cats it's boring not to go outside.' Pema spoke no English but Dolma's fluency was remarkable and Todo boasted that she had recently come first in her Chinese language test – first of forty-seven.

The late lunch awaiting Todo was hastily divided into two despite my truthful protestations that I never eat lunch. As in the several other Buryat homes I'd visited, this was a challenging meal: overcooked pasta, coarse pickled cabbage, thin grey strips of some very tough meat so tasteless the animal was unidentifiable. Given the same ingredients the average Russian Siberian cook would have ingeniously made them palatable. One imagines similar meals being served to gulag prisoners in the privileged category.

In the good old Akademgorodok days Pema's original research into toxic waste disposal had been appreciated and rewarded with two trips to international conferences. Now she was employed to advise (code for monitor) Ulan-Ude's few remaining chemical industries. When her reports exposed excessive levels of pollution heavy fines were demanded but rarely paid. And anyway those penalties were not nearly severe enough, in Pema's view. Here was a source of marital discord. Todo argued that heavier fines would mean more factory closures, more citizens reduced to alcoholic idleness or drug-smuggling. Ulan-Ude offers limited scope for legitimate trading and the available opportunities are allegedly being monopolized by a fast-growing mafia. Dolma sided with her mother. I said nothing, not because I was being diplomatic but because this cruel dilemma defeated me.

The distinctive Buryat language (of the Mongolian group) is a happy hunting ground for etymologists who revel in ferreting out its many Turkic, Chinese, Sanskrit, Manchurian, Tibetan and other borrowings. Of all Siberia's indigenes only the Buryats were literate, using the ancient vertically written Mongolian alphabet, a legacy from the Uighur Turks. In 1926, when Buryats formed 44 per cent of Buryatia's population and colonists 53 per cent, it was agreed that Buryat and Russian would enjoy equal status. But a price had to be paid for this 'concession' and in 1933 Moscow ruled that the Roman alphabet must replace the Mongolian. Six years later the Cyrillic alphabet was abruptly imposed, to the hopeless confusion of a generation of schoolchildren (including Dolma's grandparents) who had just mastered the Roman script.

It is not known when exactly the Buryat-Mongols moved north towards the taiga and historians have heated arguments (you can almost hear their raised voices) about whether or not Buryat horsemen fought in Chingis Khan's bloody campaigns. Undoubtedly their grasslands formed part of his empire in the thirteenth century and four hundred years later the Russians found Buryatia's well-trained and ferociously accurate marksmen their only serious opponents in Siberia – though these opponents were still armed only with bows and arrows. (That soon changed as Russian explorer-entrepreneurs defied a czarist decree by trading guns for pelts.)

Until the sixteenth century shamanism was the religion of all Mongolians. However, its complexity among the Buryats (they worshipped a pantheon of ninety-nine divinities) made the practices of Siberia's tiny tribes seem quite primitive. The central Buryat ritual involved sacrificing a white horse to the sky god Tengri and hanging the skin on as high a pole as could be found. (Joining two poles was not allowed.) In Severobaikalsk's Buryat Cultural Centre, in 2002, where strenuous efforts were being made to reconnect Buryat children with their past, I had noticed equal emphases on distant shamanism and recent Buddhism.

Mongolia adopted Tibetan Buddhism in the late sixteenth century, Buryatia a century later – and even then the forest Buryats, west of Lake Baikal, clung to shamanism. This minority, long isolated from steppeland culture, had by then regressed to illiteracy while retaining their oral tradition of folk tales and folk poetry, including an immensely long epic about Tibet's legendary hero, Geser Khan.

As the Russians discovered to their chagrin, Buryatia was not a class-conscious society vulnerable to 'divide and conquer'. Neither, however, was it classless. Pre-colonization, ordinary clan members were expected to obey their powerful hereditary chiefs whose herds might number tens of thousands. But – a crucial point – no one owned land, all grazing was communal. And deprivations, aside from those caused by natural disasters, were insured against by each clan organizing an equitable system of mutual assistance. Less equitable was the Buryats' treatment of smaller tribes, notably the Samoyed, Ket and Ewenki. Where available, these were forced to pay fur tribute to Buryat chiefs and to provide armed men in times of conflict.

In 1902 Charles Hawes left the train at Ulan-Ude and sledged 116 miles through deep snow to visit 'the Buryats' Vatican' where dwelt the Khan-po Lama, regarded by both Mongols and Buryats as next in rank to His Holiness the Dalai Lama. This Gelung Nor monastery treasured a priceless collection of ancient Tibetan texts and Hawes was much impressed by

> the three-storied temple of the Lamaserai . . . Its style is Chinese, and the white walls contrast with brightly painted, vari-coloured wood work of the galleries, adorned with gilt plates. Smaller temples, of one story only, surmounted with a bowed roof and called *sume*, contain each a sacred *burkhan*. The lamas are indignant at these being called idols, and disclaim any notion of the worship of what they regard as material representation of saints. Around the *sume* clusters quite a little town, comprising the dwellings of the lamas and seminarists.

The Orthodox Church acquired few Buddhist adherents and Charles Hawes quoted Graf Keyserling, a German Buddhist scholar:

> The Russian priests are opposed by a faith that has struck deep into the roots of the Buryat nation, and the moral principles of which are held as beyond all doubt. They have to do with a Church which is more firmly organized than their own, and they find in the lamas opponents who are more variedly intellectual and – unfortunately, it must be added – more moral than they.

It seems odd to describe Buddhism as a 'Church': but perhaps that was a translator's error. Who could have foreseen, in 1902, the total destruction, by 1931, of Gelung Nor and all its treasures?

The Buryats, being by far the most numerous Siberian natives, presented Stalin with a special problem. And their belonging to one of the world's great religions was an added difficulty. Moreover, they had an inspiring literature and were well aware of being a nation – as the Ewenki, for instance, were not. To compound that hazard, they were ethnically close to the Mongolians (first cousins, you could say) and culturally linked to Japan and China who strongly encouraged them to remember – whatever the punishments or blandishments from Moscow – that Buryats are Asiatics. However, Buddhism was not immediately attacked. It seems Moscow realized that in unfamiliar Buryatia, where the mood was becoming increasingly anti-Russian, a temporary tolerance of the Buryats' religion would save trouble. Besides, as the new regime was unable to provide medical and educational services throughout Transbaikalia it suited them to leave Tibetan folk-medicine practitioners and lama schools unmolested until 1928 – by which date anti-religion fanatics were ravaging European Russia.

Then it was Buddhism's turn. The Buryatian League of Militant Godless (why 'godless'? – Buddhists worship no god) was turned loose on forty-seven monasteries and 15,000 lamas, most of whom had studied in Mongolia. Within a year their number had been halved and the buildings looted and razed. The only survivor was Aga datsan, Siberia's internationally renowned centre of Buddhist scholarship – closed, but not vandalized and burned. Even by current standards the League's sadistic ferocity, and public glorying in sacrilege, became so shocking that in 1930 its zealots were demobbed. The 'Sovietization' of Buryats then proceeded more circumspectly.

Secular institutions did not escape. In the early 1930s the Buryat-Mongol Learned Society, specializing in Buryatia's history, geography and ethnography, was abolished; six learned journals were banned; the language itself was radically reformed to weaken the Buryat-Mongol cultural bond. Not long after, an area of Buryatian territory close to the Manchurian frontier was said to be heaving with anti-Soviet saboteurs and put under the control of Chita province. Four other 'suspect' areas, west of Lake Baikal, were made subordinate to Irkutsk province. The mathematically accurate statement, 'Buryatia is one and a half times the size of Britain', tends to mislead, evoking an image of a compact homeland which Buryatia is not.

Now for the good news. According to Moscow's reliable census figures, Buryatia's population increased by some 67 per cent between 1959 and 1989.

The Lopsans were a devout family. When I presented them with a slab of chocolate, after lunch, the first square broken off had to be taken by Dolma into her parents' bedroom and laid beside a tiny aluminium butter-lamp at the feet of a miniature Buddha. In happier times, that lamp would have been silver.

Buryat was the domestic language. Both Pema and Todo grew up in villages on the Uda river, an environment less Sovietized than the capital, and like many Buryat children Dolma started kindergarten at the age of four speaking only her own language. Although as sweet-natured as her mother she was less attractive-looking, perhaps because of permed and ginger-dyed hair – which understandably irritated her parents. Nature knows what it's doing and Buryat-Mongol features need straight black hair. Having overheard her father complaining to

Moscow: in the beginning was 'The Dog', seen here at the entrance to my BAM carriage

Anna Zvegintzov helped me to heave the book-filled Dog on board

In frozen snow on Lake Baikal's northern shore children carve out play areas and adults like to be photographed in them. Severobaikalsk's municipal central heating plant fumes in the background

Fishermen drill through three feet of ice to feed their families

Severobaikalsk's railway station allegedly influenced by US 'Born Again' church architecture

The Russian headmaster of an Ewenki boarding school with three pupils

An Ewenki elder and an Irish elder. Even the poorest Siberian homes are overheated in winter

Ice sculptures overlooked by Khabarovsk's City Hall. In every town and city ice inspires local artists

An Irkutsk bridal couple risking hypothermia. Their photographer is sensibly dressed

Two small Buryats (human and equine) establish a relationship near Ulan-Ude's war memorial on the Buddhist New Year's day

Above: A much revered tractor: it opened BAM's route through the taiga

Left: A young flamingo affectionately preening his foster-mother's hair. He was blown far off course, then rescued and reared in Severobaikalsk's 'tropical garden'

With friends in Nizhneangarsk, a lakeside town (originally Buryat) where most *izby* façades now display typical Russian fretwork

Left: Rostov-on-Don's newly restored cathedral

Below: As the Neva thaws in April St Petersburgers swim between the ice floes

me, Dolma defended her coiffure: it was a precaution, not a foolish surrender to fashion. While interpreting in Moscow for an American dental clinic, to earn the fees for her Chinese language course, she had been repeatedly hassled by the police. 'Putin has made them think any young person not European could be a terrorist. I guess they saw me as Chinese and now there's a scare about Chinese coming to destabil-ize Russia and occupy our Far East – maybe parts of Siberia, too. That's why I learn the language, maybe one day they'll be my new government! I haven't told my parents about the police, they'd worry when I go back to Moscow to earn more.'

It seemed to me – but I could be wrong – that Dolma would not greatly object to swapping a Russian for a Chinese government.

When Todo invited me to accompany him to Ulan-Ude's new datsan Dolma came too, though mother and daughter had earlier per-formed their New Year's Eve rituals. A twenty-minute taxi-ride – past straggling low-rise homes, then up and around pine-clad slopes – left us on the flattened summit of Ulan-Ude's highest hill. To me this gleaming white building, surrounded by fake concrete chortens and mounds of rubble, seemed a poignant travesty of a Tibetan temple. But my companions rejoiced to have a datsan in their capital, the New Russia offering something positive.

All the day's ceremonies were over but two young monks, with the aura of security guards, patrolled the premises. Rows of electric 'butter-lamps' semi-circled the base of a gross gigantic gilded Buddha and mass-produced t'ankas flanked the altar. A score of young people and a few elders were making obeisance to the Buddha, spinning prayer-wheels, stuffing money into the large Heinz mayonnaise jars interspersed among the butter-lamps. In Severobaikalsk (part of Western Buryatia, outside the Transbaikal heartland), one of my Buryat friends had opined that resurgent nationalism rather than relig-ious fervour explains the high percentage of devout young Buddhists. (The same is sometimes said of the devout young Russians seen at Orthodox services.) Todo, however, rejected this theory, insisting that Buryatia's Buddhism had only been hidden by the heavy snowfall of Sovietization. When the thaw came it flowered again, as quickly and exuberantly as the taiga in springtime.

On the datsan verandah we paused to worship the sunset, a heart-stopping fiery expanse filling half the sky. In wonder I exclaimed,

'This is unique!' Dolma chuckled and said, 'Ask my mother! It's the beautiful result of all the pollution!'

At the arched gateway, where nylon prayer-flags fluttered, Todo dropped a donation into a collection box; the datsan planned to erect a memorial to one of Ulan-Ude's chief lamas, Agvan Dorzhi – exiled to Leningrad in the 1920s, brought back to Ulan-Ude in 1937, preposterously labelled a 'Japanese spy' and soon after found dead in his prison cell. 'Not from disease,' said Dolma, 'but from cruelty.'

Ulan-Ude's 1938 show-trial victims included M. N. Yerbanov, the Communist Party Secretary, R. Dampilon, President of the Buryat Republic, and fifty-three other Buryats, all accused of conspiring to make Buryatia a vassal of Japan and executed. The nine hundred lamas who survived this purge were among thousands of Buryats and Russian settlers despatched to the Gulag.

Over supper we talked politics in a fumbling sort of way. Todo and Pema tentatively favoured an independent Eastern Siberia because Moscow's centralization of power damages everywhere east of the Yenisey. This idea has been around for almost two hundred years, a nebulous aspiration floating above the hard reality of Moscow's interest in Siberia's natural resources.

'It should be possible,' Dolma said, 'Siberia's rich enough – but only under the ground, not in population. And we don't have enough of the kind of people who know how to get themselves organized or know about "people power". I read about that in Moscow, in English papers and magazines. There's not much about it in our media. My friends are not political, just want to get on with enjoying being young – as much as they can on a few roubles. Some are a bit afraid of Putin going backwards away from democracy. But not afraid enough, not understanding about democracy being complicated. For them it's simple – freedom to make money.'

Todo frowned slightly, poured himself some more tea, then said in his gentle voice, 'People forget now what has been known for thousands of years. It's good to have enough money, bad and dangerous to have too much. Very rich people are not free, live in their own sort of Gulag.'

As we talked on I marked Todo's calm acceptance of the political shift that had changed his and his family's life. He regretted being unable any longer to use his particular talent (Ulan-Ude's Academy of

Sciences is not a powerhouse) but his regret seemed impersonal, linked to Russia's loss of his expertise rather than to his own loss of income and status. I recognized where he was coming from: Tibetan Buddhism at its most 'developed'.

During the Second World War Stalin switched off his anti-religion machine, judging it expedient to enlist religious leaders in the defence of Mother Russia. The Aga and Ivolga datsans were then reopened and in 1946 the Party reconstituted Buryatian Buddhism, appointing docile lama figures in lieu of the 'disappeared'. It was their duty to interact with those foreign scholars who visited Ulan-Ude's newly-founded Centre for the Study of Buddhism – *study*, as distinct from practice. Buddhism was now being presented as one of several intel-lectually interesting relics of Siberia's past.

Traditionally datsans occupied isolated sites and at sunrise the four of us set off for Ivolga, some twenty miles south of the city – a New Year's Day pilgrimage I couldn't have avoided without giving offence. 'This is Ulan-Ude's only tourist attraction,' said Dolma, meaning (but failing) to whet my appetite. Ivolga was rebuilt in 1972 after a fire that may not have been – Dolma hinted – accidental.

I sat beside our minibus driver the better to view the landscape. In the middle distance, low grey-blue mountains bounded an empty plain, its whiteness unbroken (apart from an occasional chorten) until Ivolginsk appeared. At this large village everyone else disembarked and when the golden tiers of the temple roof could be seen, burnished by the early sun, my companions began to wrap up. 'It's minus nineteen,' observed Dolma. 'My mother says you should wear more clothes.'

I patted my knapsack. 'Here are more, if I need them.'

Soon I did need them, as we slowly processed around the circle of widely spaced metal prayer-cylinders and stone chortens and stupas, at each pause scattering grains of roasted barley and symbolic one-kopek coins (less valuable than the euro one-cent piece but, when collected, more than symbolic). This compound reminded me of Gelung Nor in Charles Hawes' day: the same high picket fence, *sumes* surrounding the main temple, the monks' neat *izbi* in the background, faded votive rags (shamanism enmeshed with Buddhism) hanging from dwarf birches. We were the first pilgrims and in the bright frozen silence each creak of the cylinders – some so stiff they had to be forced to revolve – sounded loud. Then two young monks in maroon robes appeared on a roof gallery far above us, under the datsan's curved eaves, carrying a trumpet seven feet long, an instrument for centuries associated in Tibet with special solemn rituals. While one youth held the trumpet at shoulder height his companion sent a mournful summons to prayer across the plain. The trumpeter needed more tuition (a lot more) yet that sound overwhelmed me with nostalgia, taking me back forty-one years to the Dalai Lama's so-called palace in Dharmsala – in fact a simple bungalow.

'You look sad,' said Dolma. 'Why are you unhappy? Do you think we are silly superstitious people?'

Startled, I could only say, 'It's complicated, we'll talk later.'

Villagers on foot and a few minibuses were arriving as we entered the datsan, well proportioned but without dignity or beauty. A backwoods amateur dramatic society might devise such a stage set for a play about Tibetan Buddhists: gilded pillars – scarlet banners – blue and yellow bunting – plastic flowers – paste jewels – hundreds of mass-produced mini-Buddhas flanking the gigantic, spotlit, vacuous-looking central Buddha. Below his dais, the Chief Lama presided over the daily two-hour reading of the scriptures, which were laid open on a long low table between two rows of monks – nine to a row, mostly young, ordained by the Dalai Lama on his frequent visits to Ivolga. The latest electronic equipment was being used to relay this ceremony to an empty compound.

'When I was young,' said Todo, 'here were many old holy things hidden in Stalin's time. After the fire . . .' He gestured despairingly.

Prayers were being sold like consumer goods – as Masses for the dead still are, to this day, in Ireland, and no doubt elsewhere. The Lopsans each took a slip of paper from a pile, filled in their names and the amount donated, handed the docket and roubles to a young woman in a kiosk selling pious kitsch. The roubles went into the till, the supermarket-style receipts were stapled to the dockets – to be presented, with elaborate obeisances, to an overweight lama sitting on a throne-like chair near the entrance. Does the amount of the donation determine the length or intensity of his prayers? There is a peculiar nastiness about trading in places of worship, be they Irish parish churches, Anglican cathedrals or Buryatian datsans.

Pilgrims came and went like people to whom the datsan was an extension of home – sat for a time near the ceaselessly intoning monks, wandered out to perform devotions in the compound or *sumes*, returned to light candles and pray privately before a life-size photograph of the Dalai Lama. One bearded young man – uncommonly tall and wild-looking, with tangled locks below his shoulders, wearing a home-made sheepskin coat – lay full length on the floor. Everyone ignored him as he began to drag himself towards the spotlit Buddha in a series of prostrations, as Tibetans used to approach the Potala.

I remained seated on a low bench, watching the slightly swaying monks, being soothed by the hypnotic rise and fall of their voices. At intervals a small boy appeared, a maroon-robed neophyte carrying a very large kettle from which he refilled, with difficulty, each monk's tea mug. Brash mugs those were, advertising branded beverages or depicting Disneyland notables: a sad contrast to the tiny wooden bowls, with antique silver lids, which every Tibetan lama kept tucked away, between temple services, in the folds of his voluminous chuba.

Suddenly something unexpected happened. Against all odds, Ivolga seemed to be generating for me an authentic link with the mysteriously calming influence of Tibetan Buddhism. Was the chanting literally hypnotic or was I being absorbed into the quietened state of mind of those around me? A state in which the datsan's visual vulgarity and sordid commercial practices were brought into proper perspective as part of the irrelevant material world. Later, as we left the datsan, Dolma exclaimed, 'You look much happier!'

More minibuses had arrived and now the lock-up kiosks within the compound were displaying their home-knitted sweaters, shawls, socks. Outside the picket fence stallholders had unpacked their crates of souvenirs, including a datsan-shaped electric wall clock made in China. An elderly lama with notebook in hand moved between them collecting 'ground rent'.

Dolma commented, 'They collect too soon, it should be in the evening when people know their profits.'

Todo said sharply, 'They shouldn't collect any time. Outsiders help them, foreigners who like Buddhism and are sorry for us. Traders get no help.'

I was tempted to ask, 'When you know the score, why do you buy prayers?' But that would have been both unkind and an exposure of my own incomprehension of what goes on, for people like the Lopsans, at Ivolga.

Ivolginsk is a miserable village of unpainted *izbi* and, it seems from a distance, several gaunt ruins – in fact half-built four-storey blocks, abandoned in 1992. From cramped stables children were leading bony black cattle, caked with their own dung, and turning them loose to forage on the plain where only scattered clumps of dead brown reeds and yellow bog-grass flecked the snow. Dolma explained: nothing was left of the previous summer's drought-stricken hay crop, though all livestock had been on short commons since October. People, too, were going hungry. Little had grown in their vegetable plots and the essential harvest of wild berries and fungi had been frighteningly meagre. River transport had also been affected in regions where there is no alternative. Upstream from Kirenga, the Lena ran too shallow to take its usual summer traffic of steamers and barges.

However, some Ivolginsk cows were still yielding a few pints daily and three small boys approached our minibus stop, pulling one-gallon churns on sledges. They had shadows under their eyes, sores around their mouths and anxious expressions. Two passengers had brought empty bottles and as these were being filled I said, 'Surely these children need the milk themselves?'

Dolma shrugged. 'Even more they need money for bread – remember we've been Russified, we must have bread!'

Ivolginsk is one of the settlements, Todo explained, into which Buryats were herded as collectivization began. Then 90 per cent were still nomadic or semi-nomadic with a cattle-based economy and Todo's mother vividly remembered the 1929 decree, appropriating hundreds of square miles of clan chiefs' land, which provoked a spontaneous uprising throughout Buryatia. Many Party officials and policemen were killed or badly maimed and this rebellion's ruthless repression left the Buryats without hope. They then slaughtered most of their own livestock rather than see them confined to the animal gulags of collective farms. Within three years cattle numbers fell by some 65 per cent and never fully recovered. After the Great Patriotic War sheep farming became important, on collective and state farms, but since 1991 it has been declining.

Todo's mother, 'Babushka', came to lunch. A keen-witted, voluble eighty-six-year-old, she had taught for forty years in her home village school and still occupied the *izby* to which collectivization had condemned her nomad parents-in-law.

Babushka's spirited evocations of times past tested all Dolma's interpreting skills. In her youth Ulan-Ude felt much more Buryat though colonists were always in the majority. (Some Russian families had been trading with China since the late seventeenth century, when Cossacks built a wooden fort where the Uda joins the Selenga.) Then industrialization brought hordes of immigrants from beyond the Urals; 5,000 arrived en masse to man the railway repair works. As a teenager Babushka noticed Buryats and colonists briefly drawing closer than either would have thought possible, being united by their shared resentment of the newcomers. Soon after, a not-quite-Communist system was introduced, with higher pay and more perks, such as bigger flats, for workers east of Lake Baikal. In 1939 further hordes swelled Ulan-Ude's population to 130,000, some 20 per cent of whom were Buryat. (It had been about 10,000 – mainly Russian – in 1901.) Most Buryats eschewed factory work and did their bit for Mother Russia in those rural settlements they so detested. A few, like Pema and Todo, took advantage of Soviet-provided educational opportunities and made their mark in academia. Now only one-twelfth of Ulan-Ude's 380,000 citizens are Buryat.

When Dolma proposed taking me to a New Year's Day performance of Buryat folk-dancing and drama Babushka demurred. The performance would be misleading; *she* could remember the genuine article, before Sovietization imposed European standards of choreography and choral techniques which made such displays fit only for tourists. As was proper, Dolma deferred to her babushka. But on the tram she said, 'Let's go to the theatre – it's fun! And I don't mind misleading you!'

In the city centre a relaxed 'bank holiday' air prevailed. Family groups strolled along wide, sunny, tree-lined streets – treacherously icy underfoot. Pony rides were on offer but most of the gaily caparisoned steeds stood idle. 'People don't have enough roubles now,' remarked Dolma. 'When I was a child we all went racing on the big streets.' Essentially the Buryats are horse-people; colonization forced them to concentrate on cattle.

In 2004 the Buddhist New Year chanced to coincide with one of the Russian Federation's eight national holidays: 23 February,

Defenders of the Fatherland Day – recently renamed 'Men's Day', to counterbalance International Women's Day on 8 March. However, two shoddy department stores were open and Ulan-Ude's free marketeers ('mostly Chinese,' said Dolma) had hijacked the Buryats' New Year, aping the West's Christmas ploys, piling their windows with tinsel-decorated displays of plastic toys, comically horrendous greetings cards, beribboned baskets of shiny confections, gift-wrapped 'French' scents and 'Italian' scarves.

The city's main square is famous for its gigantic head of Lenin, a gentleman everywhere prominent but normally *in toto*. Colin Thubron estimated, 'If I stood on its beard, my forehead might touch its nostrils.' When I asked Dolma, 'What do you know about Lenin?' she replied, 'He was bad, made us Communist, but to move his head would cost too much.'

I needed a ticket for the morrow's move to Ust-Barguzin and our walk to the bus station took us past an agreeable mix of finely fretworked *izbi* and mid-nineteenth-century merchants' mansions, some of their red-brown façades garnished with 'classical' statues – a pleasant antidote to the pretentious excesses of soul-dead architects dominating ploshchad Sovietov.

Without Dolma's guidance I might never have found this terminus; in road-challenged Siberia such places are inconspicuous and no vehicle was visible nearby. When eventually we penetrated to the unmarked booking-office, on the third floor of a rambling, grimy old building, Dolma had difficulty rousing the woman clerk from her torpor behind one of a row of sealed guichets. My bus might or might not leave at 6.30 a.m., depending on the heaviness of the expected snowfall. The ticket cost seventy roubles, which would carry you very much further by train.

The Buryat Theatre of Opera and Ballet is striking – but one doesn't enjoy being struck by it. A colossal black and white edifice, straddling a low ridge above ploshchad Sovietov, it prompted me to ask Dolma if she knew of any explanation for Soviet gigantism. Dams, factories, theatres, power plants, hospitals, government offices – all were designed as though the Planners suffered collectively from a permanently overactive pituitary gland.

'They wanted to frighten Russian people with size,' replied Dolma. 'And make other people think they were clever and strong.'

Approaching the entrance we could hear enormous drums slowly booming – the 'overture', for me another nostalgic sound, recalling the years when I lived among Tibetan refugees. Cheerful Buryats thronged the foyer, many older women wearing traditional monotone gowns: royal blue, cinnamon brown, old gold, plum red, the design similar to the Tibetan chuba. They giggled slightly self-consciously while trying to control their heavy skirts on the way upstairs. A few men looked ridiculous in full evening dress at 2.30 p.m. 'They're the new Buryat mafia,' whispered Dolma. 'They've been to Moscow.'

In the quarter-full auditorium an incompetent artist's white horses (life-size) galloped around the walls. On stage, psychedelic lighting jerked to and fro, disconcertingly, over the twenty-person orchestra of conches, cymbals, triangles and those two eerie drums. Their cacophony, amplified merely because that technology exists, made me appreciate 'Babushka's' advice. 'These are our youth orchestra,' said Dolma, a trifle defensively. 'They're still learning.'

A *tsam* followed, what we might loosely describe as a mystery play, a contest between good and evil spirits. Now the musicians, no longer aspiring to be an orchestra, were more effective. At appropriate moments individual instruments intervened to heighten the tension as weirdly masked figures charged around the stage leaping and shrieking – then suddenly standing still, assuming grotesque postures. Mightily antlered reindeer confronted red-eyed bears, a death's-head pursued long-bearded, long-horned mythical creatures. Vampire-fanged demons challenged open-jawed tigers while the audience groaned or laughed, clapped or stamped their feet – and a few small children, squealing with terror, hid their faces in maternal skirts. Finally an unmasked, gorgeously attired figure sprang from the wings, wielding a bejewelled dagger. Then the instruments united in a frenzied crescendo as he, the good guy, swiftly vanquished all the baddies – apparently by virtue of being armed. But it must have been more complicated than that; for once, Dolma's interpretative skills were overstretched. However, her understanding of the symbolism suggested roots more shamanist than Buddhist. On our home-bound tram I commented that there had been no evidence of 'European choreography'. Nor was there any resemblance to the gracefully disciplined, stylized dance-dramas put on in Dharmsala in the early 1960s by Lhasa-trained groups not long out of Tibet.

'I think you love Tibetans,' said Dolma, thus encouraging me to confide that Tibetan Buddhism has been one of the most powerful influences in my life – though not obviously so – and therefore the gradual but inexorable destruction of Tibetan civilization, by external forces, deeply distresses me.

Dolma looked puzzled and worried and exclaimed, 'But we have the Dalai Lama!'

I decided not to mention the seventeenth-century prophecy, by a high reincarnation, that the Fourteenth Dalai Lama would be the last.

Over supper I shared recollections of my Buddhist New Years elsewhere. In 1964 I celebrated in Mussoorie, India, among thousands of refugee children newly exiled from Tibet; funding was scarce but the occasion was joyous. In 1969 I celebrated in my Irish home where a distinguished Tibetan, Rinchen Dolma Taring ('Amala'), was staying while writing her memoirs. In the small hours after a memorable Tibetan banquet cooked by Amala, the Tibetan noblewoman and the wife of a senior Anglican clergyman were photographed dancing unsteadily together as their hostess refilled beer tankards in the background. Three years later I took my small daughter on her first mountain trek, into the Swiss Alps, and there we celebrated with older Tibetan children who had left their homeland as babies, then been orphaned. That was rather a melancholy occasion; the adult carers seemed to have no heart for the festival, the children sang without feeling.

'They were facing the other way,' said Todo, 'towards the future. And that was wise.'

Before retiring I wrote in my journal:

Perhaps the Buryats' New Year never much resembled the Tibetans'. Or perhaps Sovietization did more damage than Todo can admit, even to himself. It seems the Party strove only too successfully to have it both ways, forcing conformity on minorities while enabling them to retain selected and modified elements of their own cultures as 'proof' of 'no repression'.

10

Suspense and Some Solitude

A T 6.30 A.M. our battered little bus stood alone on the acres-wide station forecourt, ready to go but lacking a driver. It had been snowing for hours, he was seeking information about road conditions. In the dimly lit, cavernous waiting-room my shyly friendly fellow-passengers – all women, middle-aged or elderly – chatted quietly in Buryat, though Ust-Barguzin is mainly Russian. They had been to Ivolga on a New Year's pilgrimage – women only, I later learned, because the local Buryat male (more thoroughly Sovietized) prefers to celebrate at home amidst bottles.

By 7.15 two babushkas had lost their nerve, to the amusement of the rest. Our driver returned then and ordered us to board; he looked grumpy, had perhaps been hoping for a day off. That snow-bright, silver-grey dawn seemed to last for hours as we climbed into the Ulan-Burgasy range where one could see only a hint of the magnificence of these close-packed mountains, their heights and depths blizzard-blurred. Most passengers slept as we negotiated a series of passes – very cautiously, for this road doesn't carry enough traffic to merit snow-plough treatment. The few vehicles we met coming from Slyudyanka (timber trucks and petrol tankers) were moving snailishly and again I wondered, why no snow-chains? Nobody I asked could explain. Maybe Siberians regard them as wimpish – my attitude to cycle helmets. We descended to the Selenga valley at 10 m.p.h.: I could see the speedometer from my front seat.

At river level the road to Ust-Barguzin branches off, going north, and as we crossed a long, lowish, unlovely bridge I remembered Ekaterina Konstantinovna Breshkovskaya, known as 'the Granny of the Russian Revolution', who served part of her sentence in nearby Nesterovo. As a young noblewoman-student she had joined the 1870s 'Going to the People' movement. This entailed settling among illiterate peasants and attempting to arouse their interest in social and economic reform by introducing them to the thinking of Darwin, Spencer, Hobbes, Marx – an impractical project, but not criminal. Yet Ekaterina Konstantinovna was detained for four years without trial, then convicted and exiled, first to the infamous Kara goldmines – the czar's private property, where many political prisoners, both men and women, were driven insane and/or committed suicide. While confined to a camp near Nesterovo she wrote: 'I was like a wild falcon in a narrow cage. I grew almost frantic with loneliness and to keep my sanity I would rush out in the snow shouting passionate orations, or, playing the prima donna, sing grand opera arias to the bleak landscape – which never applauded.'

Subsequently Ekaterina escaped and, before being caught, had walked 600 miles through the mountains, with two companions – her goal the Pacific coast. That defiance earned a transfer to a camp near the Arctic Circle from which few returned alive. But Ekaterina did and then for seven years became a 'forced colonist' in a half-Buryat village – now the town of Selenginsk. On her release in 1896 she not surprisingly described herself as 'an embittered revolutionist'. Back home, she helped to organize the assassinations of Count Vyacheslav von Plehve (1904) and Grand Duke Sergey (1905).

Probably little has changed in Nesterovo since Ekaterina's time, apart from the village's fringe of collective farm buildings, long since looted and vandalized. Here we brunched in an *izby* with a window-less café annexe and everyone ate fast and vastly: soup, fish, potatoes, pasta, bread. By the light of twenty-watt bulbs I peered at the pictures around the walls, copies of eighteenth-century lithographs of nomad camps during winter and summer. This region around the Selenga basin was Buryat territory when the Cossacks arrived but soon a string of colonists' settlements – Ust-Barguzin among them – had separated the lakeside Khori and Barguzin clans from the Aga clans farther south. During the next two centuries either the Buryats or the Russians absorbed most of the Ewenki clans who had roamed between Lake Baikal and Mongolia.

We emerged into brilliant sunshine though the Ulan-Burgasy summits remained cloud-wrapped. For an hour the road ran level across a dazzling plain between pine-crowned ridges – twin ridges, perfectly matching. Then suddenly we were on Baikal's shore, the nearby surface quite furrowed. Perhaps a *sarma* was tossing the water as it froze – that dreaded squally wind which rises without warning, can reach 100 m.p.h. and has been known to fling cattle into the lake and sink large trawlers. Here we passed a minibus whose Buryat passengers had disembarked to hang votive ribbons on three wayside bushes and bow reverently towards Baikal – which means 'the rich lake' in Buryat.

In the 1690s a pioneering band of Russian fur traders settled on Baikal's shore within reach of the then sable-rich Barguzin range. A detachment of Cossacks came along too, enough to subdue the region's scattered Buryat clans, yet the Buryats have never quite let go. Some of their most sacred shamanist sites derive their significance from Lake Baikal's presence, and to this day Buryats who have deftly intertwined shamanism and Buddhism (as the Tibetans did with their ancient Bon-po beliefs) come here as pilgrims.

All along the shore new snow softened the angles of multishaped ice sculptures and twice, just offshore, translucent furrows of pale green ice – a rare phenomenon, wondrously beautiful – caught the noon sun.

Then the road swung inland and upward, through steep, darkly forested mountains – its surface treacherous where loggers' trucks had churned up previous blizzards to create 'speed bumps' of compacted snow. On the descent to Ust-Barguzin I glimpsed a minibus lying on its roof some thirty feet below the verge. It was now 2.30 p.m.: we had spent seven hours covering 105 miles.

Ust-Barguzin sprawls agreeably over a square mile or so, overlooked by a crescent of low hills. At various street intersections passengers got off, leaving me alone when we reached the 'bus station', a padlocked log cabin at the end of the road where a wide snowfield merged into Baikal. The bus quickly turned and disappeared, its driver still looking grumpy, and there was no one in sight – as is often the case in Ust-Barguzin, in mid-winter, despite its 9,000 inhabitants. An Irkutsk friend had given me a letter of introduction, the address clearly written in Cyrillic, to the only local English-speaker – Yaroslav, a blow-in (as we say in Ireland) from Novosibirsk. But how to find him?

Walking through silence towards the centre, I fell in love with this almost car-free town. Excluding loggers' trucks (not often seen), only forty-three vehicles were then registered – the majority ageing saloons, retired from service elsewhere and little used in winter. The temperature (−24°C) prompted brisk walking but conditions underfoot slowed me; children enjoy one-legged scooting over the packed snow, zooming along on boards, making the streets lethal.

Quite soon a young man appeared, pulling a milk-churn on a sledge, going to draw water from one of the communal wells. Initially he seemed reluctant to talk to a stray foreigner but my 'helpless babushka' situation softened him. Yes, he knew the way to Yaroslav's home and with typical Siberian kindness abandoned his sledge and guided me along three wide streets of quite prosperous looking *izbi*. I considered a tip − he was poorly dressed and dentally handicapped − but the risk of giving offence seemed too great.

Yaroslav was tall, dark and ruggedly handsome; his wife Irina was tall, fair and austerely beautiful in a Nordic way. When tea had been brewed and a bowl of toffees laid before me, both apologized, in unison, for not offering me a bed. Yaroslav's sister and brother-in-law and Irina's brother and sister-in-law had just come to stay for a skiing holiday. However, accommodation was available in Ust-Barguzin's Ski Lodge − 'What we have instead of an hotel, not comfortable but our visitors don't come here for comfort.'

The transport news was frustrating; only the day before, a minibus taxi with two empty seats had left for Severobaikalsk. Yaroslav couldn't predict when any vehicle would next take 'the winter road' − a short trip, a mere 220 miles, but dependent on the weather. That taxi had left a day earlier than planned because of the blizzard warning. On hearing that I had a week to spare, Yaroslav promised to publicize the presence of a dotty foreigner bound for Severobaikalsk; someone would eventually be delighted to earn $200.

The ramshackle wooden Ski Lodge was built in the 1970s by urban skiers who lacked their ancestors' skills and were using scrap materials − hence numerous loose floorboards and the repair patches on roof and walls. It was frugal rather than uncomfortable; Siberians might find the heating inadequate yet a few extra garments made my room feel cosy. It was furnished with the most important items, a table and chair conducive to diary-writing when the feeble bulb had been reinforced by two candles. Conveniently adjacent was the one loo (for fourteen rooms) − often malodorous, Ust-Barguzin's water supply being erratic. The communal *banya* provided a mere trickle of warmish water but what more can you expect for $3.30 per night? Those who exhort me 'Spoil yourself, stay in a decent hotel!' don't realize that for me staying in what they call 'a decent hotel' is the reverse of spoiling myself.

Ust-Barguzin grew slowly before the first Five Year Plan introduced more widespread and mechanized logging and two wood-processing plants. BAM-building brought hundreds of newcomers to satisfy that project's timber needs and some stayed on. Now logging continues apace but drastically reduced processing has led to mass unemployment and alcoholism. Nevertheless, within twenty-four hours of arrival I was rejoicing to have missed that taxi.

Boiling water wasn't available in the Lodge and I set off on a tea-hunt as pupils and teachers were walking to three schools – stark ugly blocks, spoiling an otherwise low-rise town. More snow had fallen during the night and some teenagers were sledging little ones to kindergarten. Everyone noticed the strange 'man', wearing a balaclava and BAM jacket, but no one showed friendly. The only traffic was almost soundless, a few sledges loaded with jerrycans of water or sacks, the horses' unshod hooves quietly clip-clopping on the soft snow. One man stopped to collect his animal's valuable donation of steaming manure.

I failed to find tea; the restaurant, attached to a large but sparsely stocked general store, functioned only from 12.0 to 2.30 p.m.

Baikal was not as readily accessible as I had supposed. When an unknown snowfield is untrodden you keep off; safe routes are trodden by fishermen, and even close to a town people can be trapped in drifts. Eventually a rough path led me directly onto the ice and I had a clear view of the far shore, the Primorskiy range, some fifty miles away but overwhelming. Out of Baikal's still, white immensity rose dusky-blue slopes and above them soared symmetrical snowy summits – aloof, severe, serene, seeming part of somewhere else, an ethereal vision powerfully demanding reverence. No wonder this has been sacred territory, for Siberia's many tribes, since time unrecorded.

I walked in a shamanist trance, worshipping this vision – until it faded at noon when clouds reassembled. No ordinary clouds, these, but a slowly shifting panorama of complex shapes and layers, as variously tinted as a sunset sky – banks of shell pink towards the meridian, a shoal of navy-blue cloudlets to the north, coppery-green tinges to the west, a black billowing above the southern horizon, presaging another blizzard.

On the way back to the Lodge I got lost; only someone with a laughably defective sense of direction could get lost in Barguzin. Those wanderings corrected my first impression of an egalitarian little town of solid, tidy *izbi*. Some dwellings were cramped shacks, a few were new two-storey homes with dormer windows or sunroof balconies, their fretwork of medieval intricacy – surely the work of craftsmen not paid by the hour. Slightly irregular cedar trunks (or parts thereof) were neatly stacked outside several gateways – lumber company rejects but not, I was relieved to hear, for burning. Self-employed joiners sell cedarwood furniture in Irkutsk and Ulan-Ude.

The Baikal forests have long been renowned for their cedar groves, especially those in the Khamar-Daban range where the most ancient specimen on record was felled at the age of 1,400. The edible nuts yield a valuable oil to anyone not deterred by labour-intensive processes. The bark oozes a clear gum which native Siberians have always chewed – 'an uncouth habit', jeered the early settlers, whose descendants now compulsively chew bubble-gum. Over the past decade or so, in the Ulan-Burgasy range, Chinese criminal gangs have been felling cedars by night and making off with them while forest rangers turn an eye blinded by a carefully calculated 2½ per cent of the trees' value. In Ulan-Ude's railway station these gangs brazenly load their loot onto hired freight wagons.

During the 1960s a natural (?) disaster devastated Siberia. Cedars are peculiarly vulnerable to *shelkopriad* ('silk weavers'), the caterpillars of the tiny Siberian moth, and for a few years these plagued the taiga, killing uncountable square miles of cedar groves. They attacked in their billions, destroying cedars no less quickly and completely than forest fires. (Many silver firs, larches and pines, though stripped equally bare, revived after a few years.) As is said of locusts, their mass-chewing was audible from a distance. Insecticides, lavishly sprayed over vast areas, left the *shelkopriad* unscathed while fatally contaminating the fungi and wild berries on which Siberians are so dependent for a balanced diet. Yaroslav, who told me this horror story, was a relative of its ultimate hero, Professor Evgenyi Talalaev, an Irkutsk biologist. The professor observed that in certain areas these caterpillars were stricken at intervals by a mysterious killer disease and after much experimentation the hitherto unknown *dendrobacillus* was identified, isolated and found to be lethal only to the *shelkopriad*. Moreover, it spread rapidly within a colony. Soon the afflicted taiga was being repeatedly smothered with a mixture of dry earth and *dendrobacilli* – alas! to no immediate effect. Vigorously the *shelkopriad* chewed on while Moscow's timber-conscious economists tore their hair out. But deliverance came a year later when all the new-hatched caterpillars died en masse, causing an unprecedented movement of forest fauna as creatures great and small fled the reek of tons of decomposing *shelkopriad*. Then began a cedar reforestation campaign which by now has repaired some of the damage; happily Siberian cedars are fast-growing as well as long-living.

This plague baffled Russia's ecologists. What had been done to so upset the balance of nature? Where were those avian predators who normally dined on the *shelkopriad*? If anyone discovered the answer, it wasn't publicized.

Back at base, I fell over a bucket and slightly sprained my left wrist. The Lodge's central 'lounge', furnished with pool table and TV, was windowless (like the Nesterovo café) and by day I had to grope through its pitch darkness; electricity came on at sunset and went off at sunrise.

I was then the only guest and Petr, the elderly manager, seemed wary of foreigners and avoided me. Every morning a taciturn young woman appeared in the little office to receive my roubles and give me a receipt, then she locked her door and wasn't seen again. Thrice weekly (weather permitting) groups of local schoolboys arrived for afternoon skiing lessons – their numbers reduced by the withdrawal of state support for such extra-curricular activities. Now children had to provide their own equipment, affordable by few. At weekends skiing parties arrived from Ulan-Ude and Selenginsk, some including the Lodge-builders' sons.

At supper that evening, following on Yaroslav's *shelkopriad* story, environmental pollution dominated our conversation. All present knew at least one youngish cancer victim in Western Siberia, which is why Yaroslav and Irina had moved to less well-paid jobs in a less polluted – though far from unpolluted – region.

★

Ust-Barguzin specializes in memorable light-effects. On my morning walk it was still snowing finely, as it had been all night, yet I could see the rising sun disguised as a harvest moon. En route to the nearby taiga I passed 'the other Ust-Barguzin', the industrial addition, invisible from the original settlement; only one of four stacks was smoking and the gigantic sawmills have long been under-used. Lines of four-storey prefab apartment blocks, housing imported workers who no longer have work, blemished Baikal's shore. What committee of crass bureaucrats decided to transport concrete panels to timber-rich Ust-Barguzin?

By lunchtime I was hungry enough to sample the restaurant – long, narrow, low-ceilinged, its twenty small round tables unlaid. The monotone decor – everything baby-pink – gave it a nursery-school feel. The place was empty and the two young women who at last responded to my tapping seemed disconcerted by a foreigner seeking food. When they chorused 'Nyet!' I persisted and twenty-five minutes later was punished by a tea-plate of lukewarm mashed potato out of a packet and a dry mini-rissole – mainly minced gristle. Cost: $1.

Thus fortified I returned to Baikal but visibility remained poor and the Primorskiy range was hidden. Being confined to Ust-Barguzin's blemished shore was tantalizing when the Barguzin Nature Reserve (Russia's first, set up by the last czar and at present snow-blocked) lay so close. I considered taking a taxi next morning to that Buryat bush-shrine and trekking back on an unblemished Baikal.

Near the Lodge a long-haired ginger and white kitten, sitting on a garden wall, mewed a greeting as I approached. When I moved towards his *izby* gateway there came from under it a cocker-sized mongrel of Rottweiler ferocity and cruise-missile velocity. His needle-sharp teeth drew blood from my right shin through three layers of clothing – a notable achievement. I had to walk away backwards, brandishing my stick. That was an unfortunate coincidence; Ust-Barguzin's numerous mongrels seemed generally amiable. The most obvious genes were husky, terrier, Alsatian, spaniel, sheepdog and poodle. I saw none of the professional guard-dogs, unloved and permanently chained, on duty where Siberians are richer. The more hirsute liked to dig deep hollows in fresh drifts, then curl up happily in the sun at −20°C. Even here both dogs and children were excited by new snow, despite its being so readily available, but the former remained ever alert lest one of their family might emerge needing company on a walk.

At the Lodge an elderly visitor awaited me, a great hulk of a fellow with long ragged moustaches, a prehistoric brow, bloodshot eyes and a knee-length bearskin coat probably inherited from his grandfather. He would be pleased to take me to Severobaikalsk in his truck-taxi on the following Sunday, weather permitting. I said 'No thank you'. My trusting nature does not go all the way. Yaroslav later commended this decision, flicking his thumb against his throat.

Yaroslav was not, in fact, Ust-Barguzin's sole English-speaker. At sunset Fyodor – his English on a par with Todo's – knocked on my door and invited me to his *izby* 'to eat something'. He, too, was a blow-in, a 'forestry engineer' (to me a new species) who had been posted to the Barguzin area in 1988 and made redundant in 1998, by which time he couldn't imagine not living beside Lake Baikal. His attempt to start a tourist agency failed. 'Here is too far from the railway and too poor for rich people.' Sometimes he considered moving across the lake to Listvyanka, a village already on the beaten track, but there he might be lonely. His twenty-seven-year-old son was settled in Ust-Barguzin, after three years' army service, and had a small government job, a teacher wife and two children. His own first wife had died of cancer at the age of thirty-five, one of a 'cluster' of cases around their then home, near Magnitogorsk, where lung cancer rates doubled during the 1980s. (This steel city admitted in 1988 that it was producing annually 865,000 tons of air pollutants, including levels of toxic benzene and sulphur compounds unprecedented even in Western Siberia.) Fyodor's second wife, a native of Magnitogorsk and mother of his twin daughters, now aged sixteen, had died of thyroid cancer in 1997.

For all his limited English, Fyodor perfectly understood my yearning to be more alone with Baikal than is possible in Ust-Barguzin. Looking conspiratorial, he revealed the existence of an isolated hunters' hut some six miles up the shore where I could commune with Lake Baikal in solitude. But he didn't want to be involved; the authorities might disapprove of a non-hunter, a foreign babushka, using this hut. It had a wood-stove and a supply of logs which hunters replenished before they left; leaving roubles instead would be OK. But could I cope with a wood-stove? Yes, nothing else heats my home. Candles would be needed – did I know about being very careful when using candles in a wooden hut? I assured Fyodor that I knew all about candles, had in the 1960s written two books by candlelight on a tiny island off the west coast of Ireland. He then sketched a map: I couldn't get lost, a little-used loggers' track led to the hut. But I mustn't go wandering off on vague inland paths through the taiga; those could be obliterated, as one walked, by a sudden snow-squall. I promised to keep close to the shore and decided to enjoy two reclusive nights; according to the weather forecast, there would be no 'winter-road' traffic before the weekend.

'If you start early,' said Fyodor, 'no one sees which way you turn.'

The hut track began not far from the Ski Lodge and I was on my way by dawn, at −21°C, under a clear sky. The first climb was steep – and suddenly the taiga seemed hung with golden lanterns as the rising sun burnished each pine's frozen burden. On the ridge-top I hesitated and without Fyodor's sketch map would certainly have gone astray – straight ahead instead of sharp right. For a mile or so the lorry-wide track ran level on this long ridge: easy enough walking despite deepish snow. The stillness was absolute: not a bird fluttering, not a pine cone falling, no sound but my own squeaky-crunchy footsteps – until someone coughed hoarsely. I paused, slightly startled: no other prints marked the track's virgin snow. Looking towards the sound, I saw amidst the trees, scarcely twenty yards away, a large dark brown bear lumbering through snow almost up to his belly. Simultaneously the bear saw me and also paused, perhaps to consider this unexpected source of protein after his winter fast. Sensible Baikal bears hibernate until at least the end of March (I had checked with Fyodor) but perhaps the previous snowy day's warm noon hours – up to −13°C – had misled this one. Siberian bears like their meat and are six to seven feet tall when upright, a posture occasionally adopted to kill reindeer or people. As this fine specimen of *Ursus arctos* stood staring at me, most probably with no ill intent, I felt seriously frightened. Vividly I recalled advice given me forty years ago about the Himalayan black bear, also occasionally homicidal and sometimes encountered in those days (but probably not now) on mountain paths high above Dharmsala. 'Lie with your face to the ground, feigning dead. Don't try to run away, you'll lose the race. Bears like to amble but can move

fast when they choose.' Snow had drifted to the side of the track
between the bear and me and when I dropped out of his sight and lay
flat I could hear my heart thumping with terror. It sounded louder
than a gradually receding rustling crunch as the 'Master of the Taiga'
went on his way. He was coughing again – could a chest infection have
roused him prematurely? Reassuringly, his way was not my way; an
hour later I saw his prints crossing the track. I assume he was a 'he'; a
'she' would surely have looked in cub.

Opinions differ about the disposition of *Ursus arctos* (varying in
colour from black to brown) and about the most prudent reaction to
chance encounters. Some fear the creatures simply by virtue of their
being very big carnivores and recommend shooting on sight – or, if
you're silly enough not to be armed, lying low as I did. Others, like
Yaroslav, believe *Ursus arctos* to be timid unless attacked, wounded or
with a cub. 'They're harmless,' he asserted. 'They always run away if
a person walks directly towards them – but not too quickly, that might
panic them.' However, he personally had never tested this (to my
mind) crazy theory. The bears he quite often saw – sometimes on the
motor road – were always at a distance. I told him then about my two
Severobaikalsk friends who have each lost a relative (bar the bones) to
a bear in the northern Barguzinskiy range.

In pre-colonial times the Master of the Taiga enjoyed a unique
status, being regarded as the embodiment of justice on earth. Some
tribes so revered him that his name had to be avoided and such nick-
names as 'the old man with claws' used instead. Other tribes – Charles
Hawes mentions the Ulchi and Nivkh – trapped cubs and reared them
to maturity for ritual sacrifice. Bear meat was occasionally eaten as a
delicacy and James Forsyth writes:

> In order to justify this, the bear spirit had to be propitiated by a special
> ceremony to ensure that it would not take vengeance on its killer and
> that there would always be more bears. This custom was shared by all
> the peoples of Siberia, but the 'bear feast' was particularly developed
> among the Mansis and Khantys, where it was performed up till the
> early twentieth century. The dead animal was welcomed by the vil-
> lagers who performed a ritual dance round it. Inside the successful
> hunter's house the bear's skin was spread out on the table with its head,
> decorated with a red cloth, lying between its paws, and food and drink
> set before it. The bear was the 'guest' during a feast at which the

village people, wearing masks of birch-bark, pantomimed the bear hunt, touched the bear while making vows, told tales and sang songs. After several days of celebration the bear's flesh was cooked and eaten. The skulls of bears treated in this way were impaled on a post in the village.

A century ago, when bears were much more numerous, travellers quite often heard of mothers with cubs using one forepaw to kill human intruders with a single skull-smashing blow. Near Uskovo, Hawes met a peasant settler who, while driving his two cows to pasture, stopped to light a fire to brew chai, as Russians will. Sometime later he caught up with his animals – both lying dead on the track, a mighty bear standing astride the half-eaten one. Angered by this interruption of his meal, 'Bruin fell upon the man, and before he could escape planted his great claws in his shoulder, making such holes that you could get several of your fingers into them'.

Not only the indigenes had a special relationship with *Ursus arctos*. Charles Hawes noted, 'The brotherly feeling of the Russian peasant towards him is expressed in the pet names they give him – Mishka and Master Petz. One not infrequently comes across the cubs kept as pets. I have seen them housed in a kennel in a yard, and even tied up to the side of a shanty by the wayside, where the bystanders might be seen trying to give a friendly pat before receiving a less amicable return.'

Until my track descended to a treeless shelf of level land, almost on the shore, I saw only taiga. Silver fir, pines, larches, a few young but already stately cedars – no sign of undergrowth, though when the thaw comes it grows fast. Between the trees, and criss-crossing the path, many tiny footprints – and a few not so tiny, perhaps deer or wild goat – belied this forest's stillness.

The hut – some fifteen feet by eight, with four plank beds – stood to one side of the treeless shelf not far above Baikal's ice barrier of high slippery chunks, beautiful in their coruscating contortions but formidable obstacles on the way to one's lake walk. Near the shore a tall isolated pine, an old twisted tree, was festooned to its topmost branches with rags, ribbons and small faded prayer-flags. And the silence was profound: a tree shedding its snow load sounded loud.

First the stove had to be lit and the big kettle stuffed with snow – when melted, on my return, it would just about fill the teapot.

No visible path descended to the barrier so I slid cautiously down the easy gradient on my bottom. The weather was being kind, the vision on the far shore if possible more wondrous than when first seen. I thought, 'Happiness is being alone with Baikal'. Yet this solitude was complicated, reminding me of the Kalahari desert, another place of great peace and beauty and silence. There, too, one feels only physically alone. In the 1960s, when industrialization was increasingly menacing the Hallowed Sea, Valentin Rasputin wrote:

> It's impossible to give a name to the regeneration that occurs in people when they're near Baikal . . . Here he stands and looks around, is filled with something and carried off somewhere, and can't understand what's happening to him . . . Something in him cries, something exults, something plunges into peacefulness, something becomes orphaned.

On my return the tea snow had melted but boiling water needed much more stove-stoking. Then the hut felt cosy and all evening I read Valentin Rasputin's *Siberia! Siberia!*, swapped in Irkutsk for Eric Hobsbawm's *Interesting Times*. This deal made me feel rather guilty, the Rasputin being far more valuable, in monetary terms, than the recently published Hobsbawm. But bibliomaniacs are notoriously unscrupulous, their guilty twinges no guarantee they won't do it again.

On Day Two squally snow-showers, brief but frequent, limited my perambulations. Now the silence was sometimes broken by a wind whining through the pines and soon snow piled up against the door; I had to force it open every few hours to avoid departure through a window – one window was obviously designed as an emergency exit. This half-expected setback gave no cause for alarm; the loggers' distinct track, between low banks, was immune to a mini-blizzard. Meanwhile I enjoyed watching the squalls drawing curtains of silver muslin across Baikal – then venturing out, never very far, when the sun did its harvest moon impersonation.

That evening I wrote in my diary:

> Is my need for solitude eccentric or does everybody need interludes alone with themselves? I suspect the urgency and frequency of my need is a bit odd. No doubt there's some convoluted psychological explanation which doesn't interest me. We are what we are.

In general Siberia's regional weather is consistent: the same day after day, week after week. But within the Baikal basin moodiness prevails and I woke to a cloudless dawn, the lake wearing a new ruffled quilt, spread by the wind. Leaving the hut, I wondered what the next occupants would deduce from the presence of 500 roubles on the stove top and a drastically diminished log stack. They wouldn't, I suspected, be pleased. My return journey took five instead of three hours, a measure of the new snow's depth.

That afternoon Yaroslav gave me the bad news. A crack had been reported by radio from Davsha, seventy-five miles north of Ust-Barguzin, a lakeside settlement of two dozen scientists, of various disciplines, dedicated to studying Baikal literally in depth. 'Crack' suggests a minor flaw but Baikal's cracks are something else, explosions audible over a considerable distance and weakening the ice for unpredictable miles around the crack's epicentre. So a 1,700-mile train journey must replace 220 miles on the winter road.

My room at the Lodge had been taken by weekend skiers but Fyodor promptly arranged for me to move up-market. His friends Vasily and Lidya Belyakov, proud owners of a new villa, were planning to offer three-star B&B accommodation ('homestay' in the current jargon) to foreign tourists. I could be their first guest: tariff 500 roubles per day including three meals. I noted in my diary:

> Actually the US 'homestay' is more appropriate in Siberia than our B&B. Immediately the guest is absorbed into the family, eats with them around the kitchen table, never feels like a commodity in tourism's marketplace. But this abrupt transition from the Lodge/hut ambience to a New Russia villa has thrown me slightly.

The Belyakovs, in their early forties, had a sixteen-year-old son, Sanych, an elderly black cat, Zola, and a young, untrained status symbol dog, Misha – apparently half Tibetan mastiff, half Newfoundland. Misha hurled himself at everyone as they came through the high gate, not fiercely but in an ecstasy of affection which, given his bulk, was seriously destabilizing.

Fyodor stayed for supper, to interpret, and after my iron rations at the lakeside the meal seemed a banquet: fried sausages, braised potatoes, the usual pickles, bread, rusks, biscuits and deliciously tart forest-berry jam with our tea.

Vasily's close-set eyes and heavy villain-of-the-piece moustache were misleading; given his generosity as a host, the family seemed unlikely to wax fat on tourism. For years he had worked as a customs officer on the Chinese border where he met his wife, then a daring independent trader regularly travelling on her own to Harbin and Japan. Now Vasily was a building contractor and self-taught architect responsible for most of Ust-Barguzin's new wooden homes, none as large as his own six-roomed breeze-block villa, plastered and cream-washed and looking sadly out of place.

Lidya, still a part-time 'biznizwoman', also practised as an 'alternative' doctor, having studied traditional Chinese medicine for three years. She had long opposed the abuse of antibiotics but now it distressed her to see patients in real need of such treatment being unable to afford it. However, 'Health Reform' was stimulating a revival of interest (and belief) in certain proven folk remedies. One particular lichen, most commonly found in the Khamar-Daban range, had been saving lives centuries before the term 'antibiotic' was invented. Now known to contain a complex set of powerful antibiotic elements, including arsenic, it is stored as a yellow-brown powder and must be administered with great care.

From the same Khamar-Daban mountains – a famously rich source of medicinal plants, for complicated climatic reasons – comes the moss *Lycopodium*, locally popular as a cure for alcoholism and easy to use. Boil the moss for ten minutes (not more), dose the patient with the hot liquid followed at once by a stiff vodka. The violence of the consequent vomiting is the cure.

Vasily was touchingly proud of the new family home, especially the spiral stairway, designed and carved by him and suggesting (as proved to be the case) a teetotal household. Even half a litre of *pivo* would disqualify one from this corkscrew-tight, varnish-slippy ascent with no handhold and a nasty drop onto mock-parquet tiles. Every conceivable manifestation of electric and electronic food-related technology furnished the biggish kitchen/dining-room where a table with barely space for four was squashed into one corner, as though the apartment-block lifestyle has by now been genetically imprinted. But why, in an area of throwaway cedarwood, have walls of blue-grey plastic 'planks', with matching 'planks' concealing the radiators? (Two to a room, the whole house felt like a *banya*.)

Eight months previously, when the Belyakovs moved in, Sanych had acquired the full range of state-of-the-art computer equipment and was keen to be photographed standing beside it wearing a Master of the Universe expression. He flushed with rage when Vasily cheerfully explained that as yet no one knew how to manage websites and suchlike. This was a five-TV family – each set switched on all day, the volume lowered but the screens' incessant movements and hectic colours creating a feverishly restless atmosphere. Only in the guest-room and the very cramped bathroom could one escape. After supper two home-made videos of family trips around Baikal's shores were kindly screened for my entertainment, accompanied by some yowling US pop group. I retired even earlier than usual.

Without my photographs of the upstairs sitting-room's pictures and ornaments, mainly souvenirs from Japan, I might here accuse memory of a betrayal. This was kitsch taken to an extreme verging on the morbidly interesting – for example, a huge crimson 'flower' embossed on cotton and closely resembling an ox-heart ready for cooking. That conceit hung on a wall of fawn-coloured plastic bricks above a foam-rubber sofa upholstered in nylon 'bear fur'.

The guest-room had a many-mirrored dressing table, a wardrobe containing reindeer antler-shaped hangers and a reclining easy-chair that almost flung me to the ground when I touched an unnoticed arm button. To compensate for the lack of a writer-friendly table and chair, literature was provided – real literature, Colin Thubron's *In Siberia*, almost certainly Ust-Barguzin's only English-language volume. I photographed it, propped on the bedhead under a sentimental landscape in a pea-green plastic frame from which depended a panel of the same material inscribed DREAM LAND in English – and from that hung a dozen long shiny nylon tassels, also pea-green.

All Ust-Barguzin homes are electrified, if someone can pay the bill, but for water many depend on deep wells, slowly and laboriously winding the bucket up on a steel rope. According to Yaroslav, wood-processing chemicals have long since dangerously contaminated all the town's water, both tap and well. This insidious form of pollution, a long-term threat to children's health, particularly enraged Lidya.

Every Sunday morning the Belyakov parents (leaving Sanych to enjoy a lie-in) collected their week's supply of drinking and cooking water from a pure mountainside spring that rarely froze. Before we left the house Lidya tucked a little bag of bread bits into my pocket, as

Pema had done with roasted barley before our pilgrimage to Ivolga. Both Vasily and Lidya were pure-bred Russians of early settler stock – apparently early enough for shamanism to have rubbed off. We drove a little way towards Ulan-Ude, then turned onto a narrow track at the base of an almost sheer mountain. Near the spring – gushing through a hollowed-out tree trunk, protruding from a snowdrift – votive rags had been draped around the doorless entrance to a log-cabin shrine which, mysteriously, I was discouraged from visiting. Before filling the jerrycans we laid our bread offerings on a rough-hewn trestle altar – a picnic table, in summer. I marked the incongruity (obscurely reassuring) as Vasily emerged from his beloved Japanese saloon car – long and sleek, silver and turquoise – and bowed towards the shrine-hut before hanging a shred of yellow ribbon on a bush. Two other cars arrived as we were loading up and those families, too, made bread offerings to the spring's tutelary spirits. The local fauna must look forward to weekends.

Vasily dropped me off in the centre, to book a seat on the morrow's bus. Ust-Barguzin's centre is not in fact central but close to the shore where taiga forms the background to the municipal offices and the Second World War memorial – a simple white obelisk, topped by the red star, listing hundreds of names. New wreaths had been piled around it on Defenders of the Fatherland Day: so many victims from a small remote town – reminding me of the opinion of an Irkutsk friend, an academic born in 1940 who never knew her naval officer father. 'The Soviet *Union*', she said, 'was created by our Great Patriotic War. That's what united us. Until then all was psychological chaos – state terrorism, ideological conflict, resentment of new hardships, blurring of Orthodox identity. When twenty million died their blood bonded the survivors. We had acted bravely together, we were proud of our victory as the Soviet *Union*.' An interesting retrospect, with which other of my Siberian friends would vehemently disagree.

Having failed to rouse anybody at the bus terminus, I was dandering towards Baikal when something unusual caught my eye, a small crowd gathering around a stationary lorry. (Down the length of a Barguzin street one rarely sees more than two or three people.) Curious, I changed direction and came close as the ancient lorry moved off, very slowly. This was the local hearse, its sides and tail-board lowered, leaving visible an open coffin with two women (widow and daughter?) kneeling beside it, their faces impassive, sur-rounded by bicycle wheel-sized plastic wreaths. Gradually the cortège was joined by another score of mourners on foot, by a snow-caked military jeep (the first I'd seen of Ust-Barguzin's hibernating gar-rison), by four beat-up private cars and by another loggers' lorry carrying grey metal railings to fence the grave.

Everyone processed silently for half an hour; here was none of the subdued chatting usual in Ireland where hundreds attend small-town funerals and may be meeting friends not seen for weeks or months. Beyond the tarred road a rutted track led to the cemetery, Ust-Barguzin's most colourful corner by far. Masses of artificial flowers 'bloomed' on those snowy acres, protected from the day's piercing wind by dense taiga.

The coffin was not closed until the very last moment. Then the hammering of six nails into cheap wood took on a huge significance because there was no other ceremony, no ritual sacred or profane. Only that sound of hammering acknowledged the final separation. As the coffin was lowered the gravediggers, who overnight had thawed the ground by coal-fire, stood at a little distance puffing on cigarettes. Then they came to shovel in the yellow-brown lumps of frozen earth that banged like stones on the frail lid. Two of the male mourners helped them and now, for the first time, the widow and daughter were dabbing at tears. No one approached them; there were none of the hand-shakings and murmurings of sympathy and mumblings about the great qualities of the deceased that mark this moment in Ireland. Perhaps such comfortings happen at another time in rural Siberia. And there was a further contrast with Ireland, where people have recently succumbed to various reality-dodging strategies. Now a bright blanket of ersatz grass coyly covers the inevitable mound of gloomy-looking earth and graves are filled in only when the mourners have dispersed. All these mourners lingered mutely, watching every last lump of earth being shovelled in. Then a few helped to erect the railing (another half-hour's work) and on it hang the wreaths.

Meanwhile I was touring the cemetery and wryly observing myself being slightly disconcerted by the lack of a ritualistic farewell. Religious burial or cremation services are intrinsically nonsensical to unbelievers yet they do have a certain soothing poetical quality. The stark depositing of a body in the ground, without any ceremony, seems somehow ungracious, too curt. But maybe, in this case, that is how the deceased wanted it. And it is a serious violation of a person's integrity, an insult to their memory, to impose on them ceremonies out of harmony with their beliefs – something too often done, now-adays, by next-of-kin without the courage of the corpse's convictions.

Personally I go along with M. S. Ol'minskii, a Central Committee member who wrote in July 1924:

> Comrades, I am a long-time supporter of the funeral ritual which the Party advocates. I think that all survivals of religious practice . . . are nonsense. It is more pleasant for me to think that my body will be used more rationally. It should be sent to a factory without any ritual, and in the factory the fat should be used for technical purposes and the rest for fertilizer. I beg the Central Committee most seriously on this matter.

Comrade Ol'minskii begged in vain. By the time of his death nine years later the Central Committee had devised its own rituals, as Catherine Merridale describes in *Night of Stone*.

> Members of the elite did not have any choice about the manner of the funerals. They could not rot in peace, and funerals for them were state occasions. Ol'minskii's body was laid out in the appropriate Bolshevik fashion, surrounded by expensive flowers and palm fronds, in the Central Executive Commission's building . . . on Red Square. It was then cremated in Moscow's new crematorium, and the ashes were buried in the Kremlin wall.

For the proles, however, things were very different. In 1931 S. Mackiewicz, a Polish political journalist, wrote a remarkable little book about Russia as Stalinism tightened its grip. In *Russian Minds in Fetters* (1932) he noted:

> Passing through the streets the funeral procession has had no religious character whatever, but, if the family is pious, it will ask a priest to cele-brate the proper rites over the body, and he, and even the other priests who may be waiting in the cemetery, will receive an alms . . . the only source of livelihood of the innumerable Orthodox priests whose churches have been suppressed . . . The communal shops in Moscow hire out coffins only for the funeral procession: the corpse is carried to the cemetery . . . where it is dumped into the grave and the coffin is returned.

Clearly Mr Mackiewicz deplored this ecologically admirable 'dumping', now possible in Britain if one plans a woodland burial.

As I meandered around the cemetery deep snow cut me off from the older graves but other pathways had been kept open by the traffic of loving relatives and their dogs. Even in winter, brief graveyard gatherings happen on special occasions. And in summer family members (usually women) often visit their plot to keep the dead company while chatting and knitting and picnicking – hence the little tables and benches within many enclosures. A graveyard's silent history lessons have fascinated me since childhood. On different headstones within the same enclosure were Communist red stars and hammers and sickles, and Christian icons and dwarf angels – the conflicting symbols sometimes, though not always, explained by dates. One railing sported a new length of red star bunting, no doubt because the most conspicuous occupant of this five-grave plot had died on 25 February 1984, aged fifty-two. His head and shoulders photograph, set in a tall marble slab, showed a thin-lipped army officer. Several new wreaths, incorporating military insignia, also marked the twentieth anniversary. Most family plots reflected national statistics; in general, husbands predeceased wives by a decade or two. Simple white-painted crosses marked children's graves – too many recently dated.

My generation has witnessed the arrival in Ireland of the 'deathcare industry'. Forty years ago, when my parents died, home-deaths were as common as home-births, funeral parlours (a suitably odious phrase) were unknown and embalming only happened in exceptional circumstances. Now the bereaved are often made to feel it is disrespectful, or rather indelicate, or just plain stingy to dispose of an intact corpse that looks dead. But why try to slow down the natural consequence of dying, which is immediate decomposition? This makes no more sense than trying to hide the natural consequence of living, which is inexorable ageing. How have we been bamboozled into such a mindset, wanting to see dead people looking like live people? Are we attempting to postpone the impact of separation? In funeral parlours one hears mourners exclaiming admiringly over an open coffin – 'Isn't he (or she) lovely, just like him (or her) self! Wouldn't you think s/he was asleep, not a bit of a change there!' But by that stage, left to his or her own devices, s/he would already be imperceptibly rotting. And surely it must be less stressful, emotionally, to bury or burn what looks like a corpse than what looks like a 'Loved One' dressed up for an evening out. ('Loved One' – another odious phrase.) Isn't it healthy and necessary to accept the difference between live and dead bodies, as part of the grieving process? This shouldn't be something we pay to evade.

On my way back to the town I thought about President George W. Bush, as I quite often do in a variety of agitating contexts. What brought him to mind on this occasion was his lucrative association with a major section of the death-care industry. Not many of my readers will nod knowingly when I mention Service Corporation International (SCI), yet some are likely to have had dealings with one or more of its 35,000 employees. SCI owns take-under companies (variously named) on five continents and these annually manage more than half a million death-care events. Its CEO, Robert Waltrip – based in Houston, Texas – has a close and meaningful relationship with the Bush dynasty. SCI contributed unspecified amounts to the Bush Junior presidential campaigns and Robert Waltrip personally donated $100,000 to the George Bush Presidential Library, a monument to Bush Senior. A few years later SCI and its CEO were the defendants in a lawsuit involving allegations that Bush Junior had rallied round his friend Robert to block an investigation, by Texas's regulatory agency, into SCI's modus operandi. However, SCI is not narrowly partisan. During the 2000 presidential campaign, Al Gore's campaign manager, Tony Coelho, was an SCI director who owned shares in the company worth $450,000.

The death-care industry's polluting power is rarely publicized. In the US, more than 800,000 gallons of embalming fluid are buried annually. Formaldehyde causes neurological illnesses, chronic rashes and asthma; it is also carcinogenic. Embalmers and funeral parlour workers are 30 per cent more likely than the average citizen to develop cancer of the pharynx, nose or throat. As current embalming methods are non-Egyptian, rotting anyway begins quite soon, and two or three years later a witches' brew of toxic substances is leaking into the surrounding soil and watercourses.

In Britain now 73 per cent of bodies are burnt (sixty years ago the figure was 4 per cent) but cremation solves no problems. Crematoria produce, according to the EU, 12 per cent of Britain's atmospheric dioxins. And according to the WHO:

Short-term exposure of humans to high levels of dioxins may result in skin lesions and altered liver function. Long-term exposure is linked to impairment of the immune system, the developing nervous system, the endocrine system and reproductive functions. Chronic exposure of animals to dioxins has resulted in several types of cancer.

Then there's mercury: at present burnt dental fillings contribute 11 per cent to the mercury vapour in Britain's atmosphere – a figure expected to rise to 30 per cent by 2020 unless people do a fast rethink on body disposal. Several countries' crematoria are responsible for 10 per cent of the North Sea's extremely toxic methyl mercury which becomes lethally concentrated as it moves up the food chain from plankton to fish. My interest in such matters was first aroused in the 1950s when mercury-contaminated seafood killed 1,400 Japanese in Minamata. Soon I was protesting against the transformation of organic Irish farming into chemicals-sodden Irish agribusiness and being mocked as a Luddite. Two generations later it is cool to go organic.

Why do I bother reeling off all these depressing death-related facts and figures? Who wants to know? It is now generally accepted that everything must be a source of corporate profit, from new-born babies whose parents are persuaded they need X number of in-essentials to dead oldies whose children are persuaded they need embalming and incinerating. Since human beings seem always to have preferred not to face the fact that a corpse of their own species is simply another dead animal, the death-care industry at present rakes in $20 billion each year in the US and £1 billion in the UK. That's how our world works. A bit scary if you stop to think about it, but little or nothing can be changed so isn't it best *not* to stop and think . . . ? Yet in fact we each can change quite a few things; a coffinless body buried in a cotton or woollen shroud (the woodland burial option) avoids being a pollutant. And surely, when we are no longer thinking beings, our proper role is quietly to rot away, at nature's speed, fertilizing the earth as we go; trees and shrubs thrive above decomposing bodies. As Kant put it, 'Whoever wills the end' – in this case less pollution – 'wills also (as far as reason decides his conduct) the means in his power which are indispensably necessary thereto.'

★

Every Sunday evening Fyodor's son Fedya and his daughter-in-law Tasha had their widowed parents to supper; Tasha's mother, Galia, worked in the municipal offices and had once spoken a little English when a railway clerk in Ulan-Ude. (Fedya's half-sisters, the teenage twins, preferred to spend their Sunday evenings at the home of a computerized friend.) As Fyodor had included a written address in my invitation I went direct from the cemetery, in rather a chilled condition; I had spent too long moving too slowly between the graves at minus 31 with a wind. But thawing was rapid in that solid *izby*, the walls of massive pine trunks, the external fretwork pale blue and white, all four rooms overheated by a five-foot-high tiled stove.

Fedya's military uniform, worn out but carefully laundered, took me aback; hadn't he long since left the army? His father, looking a little awkward, explained, 'At home he likes always wearing it, to make him feel important and strong.'

The grandsons, aged two and four, were romping with Fyodor when I arrived and at once accepted me as another romper; small Siberians are uncommonly outgoing. Already both Galia and Tasha were fretting about the boys' career prospects, 'Education Reform' having so depleted local resources.

We ate in the kitchen, tight-packed around a cedarwood table, the meal traditional Siberian: pelmeni, sun-dried omul, creamed potatoes and pork liver, pickled cabbage, grated beetroot, bliny with forest jam, tea and toffees. Then back to the white-washed, Chinese-carpeted sitting-room where the TV news was showing brutality in Haiti – yelling 'security' forces kicking and beating women lying on a street. Hastily Galia switched channels. 'She's kind,' said Fyodor. 'She would get bad dreams from that.'

Galia and I were sitting together on the sofa when the two-year-old Igor toddled over to show us an armful of lovely bright video jackets cleverly extracted from the shelf under the TV. That was a memorable moment. His babushka and I leant forward, showing an appropriately keen interest in what he had to offer, and found ourselves gazing at lesbians doing innovative things with their tongues to each other's erogenous zones. Fyodor, sitting on my other side, stood up and went to pour everyone another glass of Georgian brandy. (A precious bottle had been broached in my honour.) The blonde Tasha blushed scarlet as far as the eye could see and whispered something to her mother. Fedya, busy surfing channels, noticed none of the vibes. Poor little Igor, sensing something amiss, began to whimper. Galia said it was the boys' bedtime and swept them off the scene.

Handing me my refilled glass, Fyodor reseated himself and told me about Ust-Barguzin's new Orthodox church (really a converted furniture warehouse). It had been consecrated in 1998 but the priest often went hungry, he had such a small congregation – even smaller than the Baptist church, reopened in 1906. Fyodor was devoutly but not rigidly Orthodox and deplored inter-church rivalry. If some people got what they needed from Baptists, why make trouble? Was God bothered about labels?

Shortly afterwards I made my excuses and left before the mortified Galia reappeared. Escorting me home by starlight, Fyodor stated abruptly, in a flat voice, 'We had nothing like that before, it was not possible with Soviet law to find such things.'

Soothingly I replied that to me lesbians in action seemed harmless – in fact rather comical, though perhaps a bit disconcerting for babushka types from sheltered backgrounds.

What did revolt and anger me were the numerous porn-plus-violence magazines displayed in railway station kiosks (and elsewhere), often at child's-eye level and interspersed with juvenile comics. Typically the covers show naked contorted women wearing psychopathic expressions. Certainly no such publications or their video equivalents were readily available in Soviet times, whatever may have been furtively marketed. And doesn't our own increasingly violent and sex-demented society provide enough evidence to justify the re-censorship of such 'entertainments'?

Soviet Puritanism was of course rooted in the class struggle and S. Mackiewicz studied its early growth in 1931:

Soviet writers must not write about love, or, at any rate, as little as possible; for in spite of what is said, written and thought about Bolshevik Russia, a real Puritanism prevails there. It is forbidden not only to sing but even to play gypsy songs, for it has been recognized that they are sexually exciting, and therefore 'bourgeois' in their action . . . Now there is no prostitution in Russia. It may perhaps still lurk in some dark corners, but there is certainly no open visible prostitution such as exists not only in Paris, Berlin and Warsaw, but also in London . . . As for the facility with which, it is alleged, sexual relations are established, I cannot see why it should be greater in Bolshevia than in Europe. On the contrary, the general poverty and misery, the perpetual standing about in sometimes mile-long queues to obtain anything, the insufficient nourishment, all militate against any exuberance of eroticism.

Sometime later I told my story of Igor to a young woman friend who remarked that many Russian wives buy such videos because their husbands are more easily excited, pre-coitus, by lesbian frolics than by the heterosexual variety. When she asked, 'Is it the same with Irish men?' I had to admit that I'd done no original research in this field. But privately I worried a little about those Russian husbands – has pollution got to their libido? We've heard a lot recently about declining sperm-counts . . .

While dating my diary entry (29 February) I remembered that this was the sixtieth anniversary of Beria's grimly triumphant telegram to Stalin reporting the deportation, within one week, of all Chechens to the Kazakhstan steppes. Almost 400,000 had been packed into some 12,000 troop train carriages and despatched from Grozny because, according to Stalin, they had been collaborating with the Germans – who never reached Chechnya. Within four years, more than 150,000 had died of cold and hunger. In 1957 Khrushchev ended the survivors' exile but the crop of hatred sown sixty years ago is now being harvested.

Vasily rose at 6.0 a.m. to prepare my breakfast: three fried eggs, cheese, bread and jam. Then he insisted on driving me to the bus terminus, a mere twenty-minute walk. Inside the log cabin waiting-room a vodka-pickled ancient – voice quavering, hands trembling – was poking an unresponsive stove. Inch-thick ice, beautifully patterned, decorated the inner window-panes. Before the bus arrived seven other elderly women and three unhealthy-looking young men had assembled. On board we paid our fares to a jovial woman wearing an outsize *shapka* – her face doll-like, framed by its massive furriness. The ticket-issuing was labour intensive. First, each passenger's name (and Russian names are long) was inscribed on an A4 sheet of flimsy pale brown paper. Then, with nail scissors, each name was neatly cut out and presented to its owner. My name had to be copied from the Cyrillic version on my visa and its shortness caused a momentary unease – could it be *genuine*?

On this local service only one other passenger was going to Ulan-Ude and we often stopped to put down or pick up taciturn unshaven men wrapped in pungent layers of bedraggled fur and felt, usually carrying ice-fishing tackle or rudimentary snares, and canvas bags from which bits of small animals protruded.

The few villages were surrounded by ruined kolkhoz (collective farm) buildings and the stripped skeletons of gigantic machines that had never made sense in this region of limited cultivable acres. In most yards one or two emaciated cows and maybe a yearling calf listlessly nosed at stacks of grey hay. A miasma of demoralization and incompetence hangs over Siberia's rural settlements. When Soviet control ended without warning thousands of kolkhoz were looted, often by their Directors, and many were also burned down by angry, suddenly destitute workers. In Irkutsk I had met a young man, now employed by a foreign NGO to 'regenerate agricultural communities', who described how it was. 'My father was Director of a big kolkhoz. We don't see each other any more. I said then, "Let the workers have time to reorganize themselves." But he and his friends took everything. They were in charge and no one was in charge of them. Everyone grabbed what they could. I was sixteen and I was against my father anyway for other reasons – looking back, maybe that's why I stood with the workers. Many believed then they could have learned to keep the co-ops going in a new way but they never had a chance, all was looted so fast.'

It was my karma to be thwarted on crossings of the Ulan-Burgasy range. At Nesterovo a score of heavily laden passengers came aboard and their bulky sacks and boxes restricted my view of all those towering mountains, rounded summits and long ridges. The forests seemed as yet unmolested – though some fierce conflagration had swept a few slopes, leaving thousands of tall black boles standing out against the snow with a melancholy sort of grandeur.

Down in the Selenga valley much snow had fallen and bright new hillocks lined Ulan-Ude's streets. The driver kindly dropped me off near the railway pedestrian bridge, high above a complicated sprawl of sixteen tracks and innumerable offices and warehouses. As I crossed, free entertainment was provided by two invisible railway staff, male and female, one at either end of the station. Furiously they argued by loudspeaker, exchanging what sounded like accusations and denials, jeers and insults, the decibels rising until the system couldn't cope any more and the voices lost their human quality, became crackling snarls. I paused in the middle of the empty bridge to savour this surreal moment – the harshly utilitarian city spread out below, the setting sun dim amidst more snow clouds, the bleak platforms deserted, the silence broken only by a very public private row.

In the ticket hall-cum-waiting room a group of Tajiks, uninterested in scores of vacant chairs, were huddled on the floor in one corner surrounded by what immediately struck me as a defensive barrier of battered cardboard cartons and bulky striped nylon holdalls. The three bearded men wore loose Afghan-style turbans; their wives – two pregnant – wore flimsy headkerchiefs knotted at the back, concealing neither their hair nor their handsome features. Between them, they had five small children and two suckling babies. Everyone's clothing was adequate for survival but patched and soiled. The adults looked stressed, exhausted and underfed; the children looked scared. I wondered why they were so far east; most Tajiks head for Moscow. They come from the poorest and least developed of the former Soviet Republics, which has become even poorer since independence was followed by a vicious little civil war. In Soviet times Tajiks were rarely seen (or heard of); now half a million out of a population of six million are desperate and unwelcome 'economic refugees'.

Among Soviet citizens the Tajiks were unique, as Monica Whitlock points out in her important book, *Beyond the Oxus* (2002) – particularly important since recent oil rivalries have flared high, bringing Central Asia out of the romantic shadows into a dangerous limelight.

> The Tajiks are Persians . . . heirs to a shared and famous literature, since Persian has been a written language for at least three thousand years . . . Modern Tajiks have retained many features of classical Persian in their everyday speech . . . Their language alone made them unusual citizens of the USSR: Tajikistan was the only one of the fifteen republics to share a language with a whole country outside the Union.

I was lucky to get a *platskartny* place: only one remained. My train would depart at 7.0 a.m., arriving in Severobaikalsk forty-seven and a half hours later.

Ulan-Ude's three-storey, 1950s Buryat-owned Hotel Baikal, from which Lenin's head may be enjoyed in profile, had threadbare carpets, dicey plumbing, Buddhist motifs throughout (kitschy but oddly endearing), a friendly staff and a caravanserai atmosphere very unlike the average dour formerly Soviet hotel. Going to my room, at the end of a thirty-room corridor, I passed many open doors through which Buryats were holding cheerful shouted inter-cameral conversations. The savoury smells of suppers cooking on camp-stoves sharpened my appetite.

In the 100-table ground-floor restaurant, lit by twinkling cut-glass chandeliers but lacking condiments and napkins, my only fellow-diners were five elderly men evidently nearing the end of a prolonged feast that had been two parts liquid to one part solids. An atlas-sized menu listed dozens of dishes – almost all of them 'not on today', which became a joke between me and an attractive chubby waitress. She advised me to go for 'beef broth and fish salad' – simple-sounding, yet the time lag was one hour and forty minutes.

This might have irked me but for Semyon's arrival. He stood beaming down at me and said, 'I know you! I saw your photo in Raisa's home in Irkutsk, you are her friend from Ireland and I am her cousin so now I am your friend!' (In 2002 Raisa was my hostess in Irkutsk.)

Semyon was short and slim and obviously Korean with an infectious effervescence and fluent English; he had spent two years in the mid-nineties sampling Harvard life, then decided he preferred the academic scene in Irkutsk – which got us off to a good start.

Semyon considered himself as 'Siberian' as any Slav and more so than many. Two great-grandparental couples had been among the thousands who fled to the Russian Far East in 1910 when Japan occupied Korea. Those farmer-refugees, skilled and industrious, were just what the czar needed to populate Ussuriland and they were readily accepted as subjects – unlike the would-be settlers from China, always suspected of being up to no political good. Most Koreans soon went over to Orthodoxy and during the First World War more than 4,000 fought for the Russian Empire. During the Civil War they tried to remain neutral, as a community, while making plain their opposition to Sovietization. However, almost all (about 170,000) took Soviet citizenship in 1925; they then made up 25 per cent of settlers in the still sparsely populated Vladivostok district and 80 per cent of the city's Komsomol membership. When post-Civil War reconstruction started, they were reputed to be the hardest and most enthusiastic workers. At around this time, in the mid-1920s, Semyon's grandfather migrated north to work in the newly discovered Aldan goldfield in Yakutia (now the Republic of Sakha) where Chinese and Koreans made up one-third of the workforce. There grandpa, outraged by the miners' living conditions, helped to form a soviet – in effect, a trade union – which wrested some few concessions from the Party mine bosses.

In 1930–31, Ussuriland's Korean farmers – mild by temperament – resigned themselves to collectivization. But then newcomers from Russia and the Ukraine, their endemic racial prejudice in top gear, physically attacked Korean communities, alleging unfair distribution of land, animals, machinery, seeds. In one such attack, Semyon's aged great-grandfather was killed. Party leaders in Khabarovsk had to intervene, condemning 'Great-Russian chauvinism' and sending militia to restrain the rabid Slavs – most of whom, we must remember, had recently endured extreme hardship and multiple tragedies back home and didn't want to be in the Far East in the first place.

During the 1937 'Japanese spy' mania – in certain ways similar to McCarthyism – 63,000 Chinese disappeared without trace. They died in the worst of Northern Siberia's prison camps, according to Solzhenitsyn. He adds, 'Spy mania was one of the fundamental aspects of Stalin's insanity. It seemed to him that the country was swarming with spies. He would rather that 999 innocent men should rot than miss one genuine spy.' Instead of being 'disappeared', the privileged Koreans were now deported en masse from comparatively lush Ussuriland and the Amur valley to arid Kazakhstan, a 4,000-mile journey almost as hellish as that of the Chechens seven years later. Semyon's father, aged twelve at the time, grew up on the steppes among the survivors; the numerous casualties of that deportation were never counted. By the time Semyon was born in 1960 the Koreans were regarded as Kazakhstan's intellectual elite (the competition was not keen) and in due course he became a palaeopedologist – a useful discipline, given the current race to exploit natural resources found very far down.

Semyon had already supped in his room and he watched sympathetically as I took the edge off my hunger with a soupçon of broth, served in an imitation Tibetan tea-bowl, and an interesting but not addictive mush of fish flakes, mayonnaise, walnuts and lemon, the portion small enough to fit on one dainty lettuce leaf.

In the New Russia, Semyon told me, Eastern Siberia's cities have a linking network of Korean entrepreneurs – 'not exactly mafia, not often killing each other, but like a secret society, a brotherhood only for Koreans'. Through this network it is possible to buy imported goods wholesale at half-price if customers can prove they are bona fide Koreans, not only able to speak the language but having some acquaintance with esoteric traditional medicines and ancient folk beliefs. 'Seems strange', said Semyon, 'that a century after being Christianized, then Sovietized, there's this valuing of our own past – now so distant. I saw the same in the States, people tuned in to where their folks came from a hundred years before. I don't understand it myself, I feel all Siberian.'

I didn't voice my suspicion that this 'secret society of entrepreneurs' might have more in common with a mafia than Semyon liked to recognize. As we stood up he glanced at my bill ($2.30) and muttered, 'Too much!'

We would meet again in the morning; Semyon was taking the same train as far as Irkutsk.

11

Reunion with a Bicycle

A T 6.0 A.M. Lenin was looking quite Islamic, his new skullcap shining silver in the street lights. Efficient municipal workers were out in force, snow ploughs grinding, men and women shovelling vigorously, adding to the high kerb-side ridges. Come the thaw, Siberian cities can't be nice to live in but I would very much like to see the ice breaking up on rivers and lakes – especially the Lena and Lake Baikal.

In the waiting-room, now half-full, the Tajiks were getting themselves organized, repacking primus stoves and bowls in cartons, thrusting querulous children into warm garments – the adults by now looking haggard, snapping at one another, making me feel inanely guilty about my comfortable seven hours' sleep. A whiff of dirty nappies came from their corner and was ostentatiously commented on by three women sitting opposite me. When we moved out to be checked into our carriages the Tajiks joined my queue. Hauling their bulky luggage on board, while coping with all those fractious toddlers and wailing babies, was the stuff of parental nightmares and our *provodnitsa* compounded their difficulties by scrutinizing each ticket and travel document (they had no passports) extra-closely. The adults were now shouting at each other and I tried to help one of the pregnant mothers as she struggled to pull an awkward load up the high ice-slippy steps, whereupon the *provodnitsa* scowled at me and yelled angrily at the young woman. As did her husband, already on board, who should have been dealing with that load. Here were all the stereotypes in action: bullied wife of authoritarian Muslim husband, anti-Muslim Slav, feebly intervening Western European . . . At last everyone was in place, the Tajiks occupying six rear bunks. Thereafter they caused no more hassle, were so quiet between Ulan-Ude and Taishet that I suspected some sedation of the children. Who knows what tranquillizing herbs grow on the banks of the Amu?

At 6.55 I saw Semyon hurrying along the platform towards his coupé carriage. He had volunteered to visit me, to come down-market since I wouldn't be permitted to move up.

My bunk was mid-*platskartny*, by a window, and four young soldiers, en route from Khabarovsk, occupied the opposite bunks. They looked scarcely less wretched than the conscripts I had seen along the way and it seemed they had been celebrating all night. As Moscow's Standing Interdepartmental Forensic Psychological and Psychiatric Board would put it, 'they were in a transitory, situationally induced, cumulative psycho-emotional state'. Neither their over-indulgence nor their insistence on keeping a transistor going at full blast would have been tolerated by any BAM *provodnitsa* I encountered – which rather supports the BAM loyalists' claim that the Trans-Siberian is, in comparison, an ill-disciplined, insecure and generally inferior service. Beyond Ulan-Ude the quartet collapsed onto their bunks one by one, muttering woozily, and I took it upon myself to switch off the sound.

Conveniently, the teenager in the bunk above mine awoke only as we approached Irkutsk, leaving a seat available for Semyon. At first we talked of Kazakhstan and he explained why he never wanted to return to his nuclear-polluted birthplace. Then we were down to the Selenga delta and I looked forward to the next 200 lakeside miles, some compensation for missing that 'winter road' drive.

Since my return to the Baikal basin I had been exercising mind-control, repressing surges of anger and grief, rejoicing to receive the riches Baikal still bestows, refusing to dwell on the lake's desecration as there was nothing I (or, apparently, anyone else) could do about it. But now, in Semyon's company, that sensible stance could not be maintained.

Selenginsk's deadly plumes, fouling a cloudless morning sky, were reminders of the even deadlier discharges flowing into Baikal. Semyon gestured towards the smoke stacks and said, with a tremor in his voice, 'It's more than forty years since this started, to make cardboard out of cellulose. Have you heard of Grigory Galazy? Very brave, Director once of the Limnological Institute near Listvyanka – over there on the far shore. A hero, you should write about him, he tried to block these developments, then was punished as "an abettor of imperialism" and "an enemy of the Buryat people". The Party boasted about a pulp and cardboard complex bringing prosperity for Buryats. Now it's being neglected and doing even more damage – look!' He pointed to a line of pines and birches beyond the station buildings – all dead. 'And so many birds gone over the past half-century – no more grey geese, swan geese, bean geese. No more cormorants, black storks or bustards – instead we have cellulose and cardboard.'

Slowly we chugged along the shore, Selenginsk's ugliness behind us, Baikalsk's ahead but not visible, the Hallowed Sea a tranquil expanse of unflawed whiteness – its tranquillity an illusion. Under the ice industrial effluents were relentlessly destroying a unique ecosystem twenty million years in the making. For the rest of creation *Homo sapiens*, suddenly technologically powerful but morally irresponsible, is a horrible plague.

During his student days in Irkutsk Semyon had been a passionate eco-warrior; now he was a mere observer of Baikal's destruction, cynical and despairing. Bitterly he reviewed various battles, some fought before he was born – all lost. Around the time of Stalin's death (which should have been a good omen) people noticed, for the first time, dwindling omul catches – perhaps a result of over-fishing? During the near-famine of 1941–49, thousands of tons of omul had been delivered to state depots – and 'private enterprise' was always possible along Baikal's remote and sparsely inhabited shores. But few believed in the possibility of over-fishing, given Baikal's legendary abundance of many species, not just omul (and including sturgeon, now almost extinct here as elsewhere). Soon Baikal's defendants exposed the truth. Indiscriminate logging, started around the Baikal basin immediately after the Second World War, had destroyed the spawning rivers – blocked them by floating timber to the lake, poisoned them with chemicals. Yet this form of river transport was not banned until 1969.

By then a new town, Baikalsk, had been built in a hurry to serve the infamous Paper and Pulp Combine. Its establishment had aroused white-hot opposition throughout the Soviet Union and far beyond. As we passed its gigantic plants Semyon recalled an odd happening in 1985: the presentation of a special UN award to the Soviet Academy of Sciences 'for its activities in preserving the pearl of the natural world – Lake Baikal'. Yet at that date, nineteen years after Baikalsk's opening, the lake's pollutants were manifold. In addition to the Combine's toxic discharges chemical fertilizers were being washed down from distant farms, the Angara valley's proliferating heavy industries were producing lethal airborne emissions, the Selenga river was carrying uncalculated tons of poisons from Ulan-Ude and elsewhere, clear-cutting in the taiga was causing erosion havoc and forest fires – and BAM, the latest violator, had attacked from the northern shore. Moreover, the final decision to build the Combine had been taken by Academician Nikolay Zhavoronkov, head of the special 'commission of experts' set up by the State Planning Committee in 1966. So here we have yet another example of UN perspicacity.

Clouds had been gathering around the Khamar-Daban range and as we left Baikal the first flakes floated down, then a wind rose and a white-out gave our crossing of the pass a pleasurable eeriness. Yet in the Angara valley no new snow had fallen – but soon it would, the sky seemed almost touchable. On my way to the loo I noticed that the Tajik women had changed into richly embroidered versions of the shalvar-kameez – clean though well-worn – while the men had groomed their beards and tidily rewound their turbans.

When we halted in Irkutsk the four conscripts came to, pulled on their boots and hastened out in shirt sleeves to the nearest liquor kiosk. (The temperature had soared to minus 9.) Having said goodbye to Semyon, and sent fond greetings to his cousin, I watched the Tajik wives who had gone to fetch drinking water from a platform tap. Returning, they coincided with the conscripts at our carriage door and were elbowed aside while the young men boarded. Perhaps fortunately, their husbands didn't witness this.

Beyond Irkutsk the afternoon sky looked almost as white as the flat snowfields – then suddenly flocks of crows appeared, a dramatic black multitude wheeling in formation between the two motionless whitenesses. Minus 9 – was spring on the way?

That transistor was on again, at full volume, some pop star moaning 'I wanna be where the sun is shinin', I wan you there beside me, I wan you hot with me . . .' As I considered an approach to our *provodnitsa* another sufferer took action, a middle-aged man with a down-turned mouth, a bad limp, a rasping voice and enough clout to cow the young conscripts. One of them then turned to me, a Muscovite who spoke a little English and was soon bragging about his marksmanship. In

Chechnya he had killed twenty-three Mussulmans – one for each year of his life, plus two . . . (Twenty-three *Mussulmans* – not 'terrorists' or 'rebels' or even Chechens.) In what precise circumstances, I wondered, had those twenty-three been killed? Throughout Chechnya war crimes are a daily event and officers habitually cover up for their men while the 'international community' looks the other way. Tricky negotiations about pipelines must not be made trickier by criticizing military terrorism.

In Kosovo NATO launched its first ever war (or 'humanitarian intervention', in Blair-speak), ostensibly to rescue Kosovo's Muslim Albanians from Serbia's uniformed criminals. So why not rescue the Chechens? The brutality of Milosevic's anti-Kosovar campaign seems almost trivial compared with the Russians' conduct in Chechnya. If Milosevic had had a few nuclear weapons stashed away, would NATO have felt equally solicitous about the Kosovars? Such weapons have their uses. Doesn't every country need one nowadays, with the US on the march, explicitly describing its programme for the twenty-first century as 'full spectrum dominance' – that is, military, political and economic control of the whole world. (See the Pentagon's 'National Security Strategy' document of September 2002.)

Incidentally, as an interesting side-effect (?) of that NATO attack the Pentagon now has its biggest permanent European base in Kosovo – in 2006 still part of the sovereign state of Serbia. As Richard Heinberg has reported in *The Party's Over* (2003):

> The Balkans is not a resource-rich region but one essential to the transfer of energy resources from Central Asia to Europe. It is also the site of Camp Bondsteel, the largest 'from-scratch' foreign US military base constructed since the Vietnam War. Located on farmland seized by US forces in 1999, it lies close to the US-sponsored Trans-Balkan oil pipeline now under construction. A Houston-based contractor that is part of the Halliburton Corporation, the world's largest supplier of products and services to the oil industry, provides all Camp Bondsteel's support services including water, electricity, spare parts, meals, laundry, and firefighting services.

At intervals the Tajik women passed us on their way to and from the samovar (only then did their presence register) and always the soldiers stared at them insolently, whispered to one another and sniggered. Within the confines of a railway carriage they dared not be more overtly hostile. But what showed in their eyes was disturbing. I jotted in my diary: 'Conditions in Tajikistan must be v. grim to have driven so many into a country where they are so resented and despised.'

Anna Politkovskaya (surely Russia's most courageous journalist) commented in May 2004:

Russia now faces the question, as the US did at the end of the Vietnam War, of how to view its soldiers and officers who every day are murdering, looting, torturing and raping in Chechnya . . . Five years into the Second Chechen War, more than a million soldiers and officers have passed through the experience. Poisoned by a war on their own territory, they have become a serious factor affecting civilian life. They can no longer simply be left out of the social equation.

The next white-out came as we entered an immense forest which in the autumn of 2002 had enchanted me (though some find it boring). Hereabouts the heating system went wrong – so wrong that I couldn't sleep. As my sweat streamed, the limping man with clout angrily challenged our *provodnitsa*. But the situation was out of her control, the defect could only be remedied in Taishet – where we arrived at 2.20 a.m.

I felt then as one expects to feel five hours past one's normal bedtime. The vaulted glossy waiting-room was three-quarters full, this being such an important junction – of the BAM/Trans-Siberian lines. Although its black welded-together metal chairs were not sleep-inducing most males were asleep, empty bottles clustered around their ankles. When I stretched out on the floor, where I could have slept soundly, a Railway Policeman – a beardless youth, relishing his power – insisted that I must *sit*. The Tajiks, too, were bullied into chairs. Their train came soon: why were they going to godforsaken Ust-Ilimsk, far to the north? Perhaps they had connections there. When trains were announced women roused their menfolk, some wives having to drag all the luggage because their man could barely get himself onto the platform.

Thinking positive, I contrasted this clean warm waiting-room with the railway junction scenes, immediately after the Civil War, described in H. H. Fisher's *The Famine in Soviet Russia*. 'The peasants who had left their homes in panic became marooned. They waited for trains which never came . . .' Professor Fisher quotes then from the report of a Russian observer, a man working for the American Relief administration:

> Imagine a compact mass of sordid rags, among which are visible here and there faces already stamped with the seal of death. Above all one is conscious of a poisonous odor. It is impossible to pass. The waiting-room, the corridors, every foot thickly covered with people, filthy rags swarming with vermin. The typhus stricken grovel and shiver in their fever, their babies with them. Nursing babies have lost their voices and are no longer able to cry. Every day more than twenty dead are carried away, but it is not possible to remove all of them. Sometimes corpses remain among the living for more than five days . . . Only once it was decided to clean the railway station . . . [and] fifteen wagons of every conceivable filth were hauled out. These inhabitants of railway stations are refugees, homeless, starving. It has proved impossible to clear them out, although *thirty-six decrees* ordering it have been issued. No registration is attempted. Whence they come and whither they are going, no one knows . . . One attempt was made to establish a rest house but at the end of the week it became rather a death house and was finally closed as a spreader of contagion. It is impossible to close the railway station. There is no way to stop this great wave of starving peasants who come to the city to die.

The train for Severobaikalsk was not due to depart until 10.18 a.m. and those eight hours passed very, very slowly.

Again I had a window bunk, opposite three talkative men and a young woman who sat primly upright, never raising her eyes from a blockbuster romance and replying only in monosyllables if addressed. The men were drinking tins of whiskey mixed with Coca-Cola, or so the English labels claimed – another form of pollutant.

A foot of new snow had fallen and over the first eighty miles a snow-plough engine preceded us through dense taiga, shallow valleys, marshy expanses – all with that dancing, diamondesque glitter peculiar to fresh snow in strong sunlight. Near the lumber depot of Sosnovye Rodniki a long bridge spans the Chuna and far below I could see an articulated truck, loaded high, crossing the frozen river – evidently very frozen, to bear that weight. This region has no motor roads, only loggers' tracks; in summer timber for Rodniki is floated 750 miles down the Chuna from southern forests.

Around noon, cloud banks along the eastern horizon suddenly swelled – then moved fast to capture the sun. By then only the novel-reader was awake. Vera, our brisk, cheery, double-chinned *pro-vodnitsa*, had long since put a stop to whiskey-and-Coke drinking and advised the trio to lie down.

In mid-afternoon we halted at Vikhorevka, a big town where food-hawkers worked the platform and business was brisk around the open carriage doors. From the nearby row of kiosks – their occupants invisible – a hand often emerged, scattering crumbs. Wherever humans generate warmth, half-tame pigeons and sparrows thrive throughout the winter. Just outside my window Vera dumped a bag of beer bottles and a big bucket of hot coal ash into a five-foot-high metal bin. A pensioner was hovering nearby, a babushka who couldn't see into the bin but probed doggedly, clouds of ash rising around her head, until she had retrieved all eight bottles – each worth a few kopeks. Her boots were falling apart but the quality of her fur coat indicated that in times past she could never have foreseen herself foraging in bins.

I prefer to forget the next few hours; this region around Bratsk was the Soviet Union's biggest industrial site. We crossed the dam as the sun sank into a mass of brown-fringed cloud that soon became slate purple while the clear sky above remained weirdly apricot-tinted. Then an almost full moon took over, hanging pale gold and high in a dusky blueness – but still, to the west, long ribbons were faintly pink. Ribbons of cloud or of factory smoke? I couldn't tell.

Stretched out on my bunk, I reread the apposite passage from *Siberia! Siberia!* Thick tomes have been written to explain the Soviet Union's economic failure – unnecessary tomes. Valentin Rasputin, writing in 1984, says it all in a few paragraphs:

> The Bratsk dam alone flooded more than half a million hectares of the most valuable agricultural land along the Angara. [A few of those hectares belonged to the Rasputin family who had been settled on the river bank for almost three centuries.] The aluminium and cellulose smelted and turned into pulp, at the expense of Siberia's rivers, are sold for hard currency which is used to buy grain – the same kind that was grown recently in these very river valleys . . . Just before the Trans-Siberian was built, Western Siberia alone had more than eleven million head of cattle. Siberia could produce enough grain for all of Russia. In 1898 it exported 2,682 tons of butter, in 1906 54,000 tons. The region had an abundance of poultry, game, fish, honey and pine-nut oil . . . and it could increase production, as with butter, several times

over within a few years when there was a demand . . . Today Siberia gets grain from Canada and Argentina, meat from France, poultry from Hungary and Australia, butter from Finland and Denmark, potatoes (a shame to admit, but a sin to hide!) from China, red currants from Poland . . . A few decades changed Siberia from a land of rich agriculture restricted only by the market into a land of risky, bankrupt agriculture, a parasite, a spendthrift that squandered its own share of Nature's legacy and now steals what belongs to its grandchildren and great-grandchildren.

Being back in Severobaikalsk after my five-week absence felt like a return home – the same hurrying to catch up on friends' news.

Anna and Ivan had astonished themselves by buying a two-storey wooden house: a bargain suddenly came on the market, too good to miss . . .

Two other young friends were absent, having had to fly to Irkutsk with their two-year-old son who needed emergency treatment for a rare kidney condition.

The Yasins had been shocked by a neighbour's misfortune. When their old friend Lazar opened his hall door one afternoon, two masked men threw him to the ground and kicked him until he revealed the whereabouts of the family cash. He owned two small fishing-boats, was reputed to be rich, and was known to be about to visit St Petersburg on business. He remained in hospital; one broken rib had penetrated a lung. Locals were pretty sure of the robbers' identity but the police seemed reluctant to get involved. A deplorable story yet unremarkable; in Ireland old people are sometimes murdered for small sums hoarded in isolated rural homes. Rashit, however, had been quite shaken; in Severobaikalsk this was a new and frightening crime. Then, smiling wryly, he added that such intruders used to be the secret police, who only beat you up in prison.

Another friend was upset because her nineteen-year-old daughter had announced without warning that in June she would marry a divorced forty-two-year-old Irkutsk man suspected by the distraught mother of . . . a thumb flicked her throat.

The friends with whom I was staying, Roza and Nikita Volkonsky, were now able to offer me a bed because their two sons had recently migrated to Moscow's gold-paved streets.

★

The Volkonskys lived scarcely ten minutes' walk from the shore in what I have described elsewhere as 'Severobaikalsk's Hampstead', a small privileged suburb on high ground overlooking Baikal. Theirs was another owner-designed villa, spacious and quirky, built in 1994 as though in celebration of the family's escape from half a century of confinement to identical flats. From one side of the wide, wood-panelled hallway a spiral metal staircase led to the conservatory where, throughout the winter, Roza grew an astonishing variety of flowers and pot plants for the local market. At the other end of the house a short, steep wooden staircase led directly into my L-shaped bedroom, separated from the conservatory only by a Venetian blind 'wall'. The semi-basement boasted a deep sauna, permanently full of warm water, but the shower was dysfunctional. In the baronial kitchen/living-room (much wood carving everywhere) I again noticed that 'tiny dining-table' syndrome.

A short walk, towards the railway, took me to Anna and Ivan's new home, eight-roomed with an underground heated garage and a very cold cellar. Built seven years previously in simple traditional style, it had half an acre for food-growing, a large glasshouse with raised beds, a large frame for a plastic tunnel – set up each spring – a *banya* hut in one corner, a firewood shelter, a hen-house and a rabbit-house both already occupied and a goat-house soon to be occupied. Asking price: one million roubles, reduced to 800,000 (approximately $27,000) because of slight earthquake damage to a gable wall. (In August 2003 an earthquake, 5.5 on the Richter scale, was severe enough to have thrown the baby Ilya, then a few weeks old, from bed to floor. But such seismic events are so frequent hereabouts they cause little comment, one of many reasons why oil or gas pipelines around Baikal's shores are such a bad idea.)

The house-warming party, on the Sunday after my return, was an eating marathon such as I have never seen elsewhere – not even at an Indian wedding. All the guests (thirty-two relatives and friends) brought festive dishes and each would have taken umbrage had their offering been overlooked – or under-eaten.

Venison came in many guises to honour the occasion though normally, nowadays, it is kept for children. Anna explained, 'We believe deer won't eat or drink anything contaminated or polluted so it's our only safe meat – except what we breed ourselves.' (But, I asked myself, does the contemporary deer have any choice?) Throughout the Baikal basin hunting is supposed to be strictly controlled. Men buy a ten-day licence and if out of luck lose their roubles. If in luck, as is usual, they have secured a few months' meat supply on the cheap. Often deer are lamp-dazzled by night – a nasty trick, but this is hunting as a survival mechanism, not a sport. The licensing law is enforced erratically, Ivan admitted, and often to the detriment of the poor, who infringe it simply to feed their families. Commercial hunters, the real threat to wildlife stocks, can afford to bribe or will have the necessary 'contacts'.

The variety of edible fungi fascinated me. (Incidentally, a minority of Siberians, perhaps over-reacting to Chernobyl several thousand miles away, believe all fungi to be by now nuclear-contaminated.) Each fungus seems to require a particular treatment. Some, resembling our field mushrooms, may be eaten immediately, raw or cooked. Others must be soaked in cold water for three days before being stored in salt for at least six weeks. Still others need to be thoroughly dried, suspended over the stove, before pickling. And no fungus, however treated, should be fed to a child under five. I thought of Valentin Rasputin when Anna's mother mentioned a study done by Swedish nutritionists who concluded that Siberia's native products (animal, vegetable and mineral) provide a perfectly balanced diet: no imports needed.

Next morning I was puzzled to see every pedestrian laden with expensive bouquets of flowers, outsize boxes of chocolates or trays of multicoloured confections. Then the kopek dropped: this was International Women's Day, another long weekend for the Federation when government offices and banks close though schools and shops open to hold impromptu parties. In the two-storeyed covered market, an embryonic shopping-mall, the atmosphere was reassuringly relaxed; Severobaikalskians were not yet so profit-enslaved they couldn't put trading in second place for a day. Tea parties with lots of squidgy cakes and sticky buns were usual near underworked tills as staff and their regular customers celebrated together. Visiting the more basic outdoor market of independent stallholders, I was invited to join Buryat women enjoying vodka and dried fish parties. Muslim men – Azeri footwear merchants, Uzbek pirate video vendors – looked on censoriously.

Even on 8 March, with the presidential election less than a week away, Severobaikalsk remained unpostered; nor did any of my friends (all 'average citizens') show the slightest flicker of interest in the outcome. Of course Putin would win; there was no genuine contest and no widespread wish for one. This baffled me, given the extent of dissatisfaction with Eastern Siberia's present situation.

According to one young man, the Kremlin/Moscow scene, viewed from beyond the Yenisey, seemed ludicrous, couldn't be taken seriously – so many gangs on the make, calling themselves political parties, none interested in the Federation's well-being. Another friend more kindly likened the parties to 'babies, not even toddlers – they can't find their way around what's supposed to be a democracy'.

Referring to Severobaikalsk's unemployment rate (above 50 per cent), one young parent wondered, 'How will it be for our sons in 2020 if there's no revolution against how it is now? Most political leaders have never heard of Severobaikalsk or Buryatia, there's no link between us and the Moscow people with power. So why should they go on having all that power? They only want our resources, as people we don't matter.'

A friend of my own generation to some extent associated unemployment with the Russians' preference for imported goods, their conviction that everything Russian-made, from cars to electric kettles, was inferior. Yet I also heard it claimed – and was shown the proof – that a simple thirty-five-year-old Russian refrigerator was more efficient and durable than a gadget-enhanced five-year-old South Korean model.

Many Siberians were bothered by the 'brain drain', especially from east of the Yenisey though it affects the whole Federation. One thwarted scientist met in Irkutsk (aged twenty-eight, seeking a US visa) complained, 'Pay is too low and opportunities too limited. Our clever people who could be good scientists, factory managers, skilled workers all leave – or else join some mafia to make quick money.'

The refrain 'They only want our resources' is almost as old as the colony itself and autonomy, in one form or another, has been glimpsed at intervals – but only as a mirage.

In the 1760s Catherine the Great, daunted by the sheer extent of her property, toyed with the notion of Siberia as a self-supporting dominion, minting its own currency – an idea abandoned within twenty years.

From the early nineteenth century the possibility of following the example of Britain's former American colonies was widely discussed, especially after the Decembrist exiles arrived in 1826. But no action was taken until the 1860s when Siberian students at St Petersburg University advocated independent economic development and more humane treatment for the indigenes. Several were arrested in 1865, following the discovery in Irkutsk and Omsk of 'seditious documents promoting an "autonomous republic of Siberia"'. The sentencing of two leaders to years of hard labour ended open discussion, yet Siberia's intelligentsia continued furtively to debate a change in the colony's status, many favouring the Canadian model.

Six weeks before the October Revolution, in August 1917, an anti-Bolshevik alliance of Mensheviks and Socialist Revolutionaries met in Tomsk, called themselves the First Siberian Congress, hoisted a white and green flag symbolizing tundra and taiga and voted for autonomy. When the Congress met again two months later, to lay the foundations for a parliamentary government, Bolshevik agents broke it up. Then the Civil War started and the Congress was replaced by the fascist-style Provisional Government of Siberia, equally opposed to Socialist Revolutionaries and Bolsheviks.

Seventy years later echoes of autonomy talk were audible – but muffled echoes. A few hopefuls quoted from Mr Gorbachev's *Perestroika*, 'The type of relationship inherited from the past, with a metropolis being on one side and colonies on the other must give way to a new type of relationship.' Yet by now Siberia's twenty-first-century fate is evident: to remain a valued part of the Federation until resources give out, those resources not to be fairly shared with the Siberians.

As the temperature went up, to minus 7 or 8, the snow came down in quantities new to me and unpredictable. The 9th of March I won't soon forget. At the beginning of my lake walk the morning air was still and the sun visible though veiled. I was quite far from the shore when a sudden wind enveloped me in a fast blinding mass of snow. I turned to retrace my footsteps, already obliterated – but surely, by walking in a straight line, I'd eventually reach the shore. The deepening snow slowed my pace, then it seemed I wasn't walking in a straight line. No ice barrier blocked my way, long after it should have. Panic loomed: would I spend the rest of the day wandering around in circles before dying of hypothermia during the night on the bosom of Lake Baikal? (I can think of worse ways to go – but that's a retrospective thought.) Sometime later – half an hour or so – the wind abruptly dropped, the whiteness became less . . . and less . . . and less, until the cliffs' reappearance showed that I had been walking not in circles but parallel to the shore, towards the naval base. So even had the blizzard persisted I would have reached safety – an undeserved safety, some might say.

That afternoon I collected my bicycle, Pushkin, from his long-term lodgings in the Yasins' garden shed. I had been looking forward to our reunion, not having ridden him since my second Siberian accident in August 2002, but road conditions (black ice or deep new snow) prompted me to wheel him to the railway station by way of avoiding a third accident. In the freight-shed office my BAM-driver friend was awaiting me; he had volunteered to expedite the paperwork involved in despatching a solo bicycle direct to Rostov-on-Don. Boringly, I had to go via Moscow. My plan to buy a Moscow–Venice Aeroflot ticket, by courtesy of Rashit's internet, had been over-optimistic. Instead, I must present myself and my passport at an Aeroflot office in Moscow.

On the eve of my departure I sat alone by the lake, the afternoon sun warm on my face, not needing gloves, sadly drinking a 'Farewell to Baikal' tin of *pivo*. There was no one in sight, no sound but the occasional croaking of ravens and the single hoot of a train on its way to the Pacific – a ridiculous little noise in relation to BAM's achievements, like the brief husky whimper of a child with a sore throat. I found it hard to believe that never again would I look upon the Hallowed Sea. Well, probably never again . . . Having known Lake Baikal in summer and winter, it would round off our relationship to witness the dramatic spring thaw. Maybe a holiday in Severobaikalsk with my granddaughters, when they are a little older? Such comforting fantasies are harmless.

12

On the Way to the Thaw

For this five-day journey I was travelling coupé; the dim *plats-kartny* lighting limits reading and unlike most BAM passengers I can't sleep eighteen hours out of twenty-four. As my friends were dispersing, after a series of emotional farewells, an elderly woman arrived late in great distress. Only two hours previously she had heard of her daughter's death in Moscow – her only child, aged forty, killed by a hit-and-run driver. (Next day it was being rumoured in our carriage that the unfortunate woman had in fact been robbed and murdered, during the small hours, on the stairway of her apartment block.)

Xenia was tall and bony, ginger-haired and asthmatic and in an extreme state of shock. Sobbing convulsively, trembling violently, her teeth chattering despite an overheated carriage, she couldn't steady herself enough to make up her bed. Our *provodnitsa* – near retiring age, her appearance not enhanced by a bulbous nose and a mean little mouth – glanced at her impatiently, then moved on. While I made up the bed and unlaced Xenia's dogskin knee-boots she seemed unaware of me as an individual. Then she curled up, pulled the blanket over her head and sobbed until she slept – a long time later.

I stood in the corridor as we crossed the Baikalskiy range, by now so familiar and loved – the many sheer escarpments below pointed peaks, the twisted outcrops on sloping shoulders, the serrated ridges overlooking short, deep canyons – always different, seen by moonlight and dawnlight, by noonlight and starlight, in summer, autumn, winter.

Kuzma, a young man from Nizhneangarsk, joined me and spoke enough English to discuss the possibility of his becoming a tour operator. His father's fishing boat could take eight tourists across the lake and he planned to advertise Baikal's annual seal hunt (21 April–5 May) on the internet. I tried to explain that while nerpa-hunting may be acceptable as an integral part of the locals' way of life, seal-kills would not draw the average Western tourist seeking a fun holiday. Kuzma might soon find himself dealing with an unsavoury gathering of psychopaths and perverts, plus animal rights fanatics who would never concede the Baikal peoples' right to maintain their traditions.

Kuzma stared at me, looking in turn bemused, disbelieving and mildly annoyed. Yet again I marked how out of touch are the Siberians – for all their satellite TVs and cyber cafés – with contemporary 'Western' attitudes. Attitudes *and* information: I was horrified by the amount of accessible asbestos visible in newish Severobaikalsk homes. No one I met was aware of this material's unwholesome properties – not even the BAM museum's curator who proudly listed expanding asbestos mines among Eastern Siberia's natural riches.

This was an old train with worn corridor carpets, defective insulation around the windows and a cramped restaurant car serving only dried omul snacks and *pivo*. As if in compensation, baskets of plastic flowers hung between the windows and irritating blue and yellow half-curtains curtailed one's view even when pulled back. Just outside our coupé a trapdoor under the carpet revealed the carriage 'cellar', a long coffin-like box full of perishables being refrigerated by Siberia – mostly sacks of precious omul, for trading at the biggest stations by BAM staff. From time to time someone raised the trapdoor and with a hooked stick hoisted out a bag for immediate use; delicious smells often came from the *provodniki*'s base, furnished with camping-gaz. During some halts staff crawled under the carriage to add to the box.

By the following morning, to my relieved astonishment, Xenia had outwardly recovered her composure. No one joining us would have noticed anything amiss, though they might have thought her 'a bit depressed'. I asked myself, is this the fabled Russian stoicism or an unusual individual's resilience? The former, I guessed: a stoicism to be respected and wondered at but also pitied as a measure of how tough life has been for so many Russians over so many centuries. In Xenia's position I suspect I would become more disintegrated by the hour – instead of finding the strength, overnight, to seem reintegrated.

Kuzma proved to be a kind young man. Realizing that, for obvious reasons, Xenia lacked the customary food basket, he brought her breakfast. Then I reassured him; with the farewell gifts from my support group I could feed the whole carriage all the way to Moscow.

A blizzard blurred the industrial ghastliness around Bratsk where the snow was being discoloured even as it fell, a gruesome phenomenon. Kuzma, on his way to Irkutsk, now appointed himself my interpreter. Thus I learned that Xenia, a widow living alone, was aged sixty-seven and had never known what it feels like to be in full health. She belonged to a generation (born c. 1930–50) most of whom were permanently debilitated by childhood malnutrition and other hardships. Before the age of thirty she had lost all her teeth; she suffered from asthma and chronic digestive problems; her sight had always been imperfect. I knew from personal encounters, and my friends' references to parents' and grandparents' ill-health, that she was not exceptional. It is easy to forget the long-term consequences of disasters, natural or man-made, as the media shift our attention from famine to earthquake to war to drought to flood. Yet many disaster victims have been given a life-sentence. (Most harrowingly, all those babies and small children brain-damaged by prolonged malnutrition, then physically resuscitated by Western medical know-how – enabled to continue living but not enabled to fend for themselves as adults.) And now, in the New Russia, most of Stalin's victims are deprived of free diagnosis, treatment and medication.

However, those Oldies are on their way to the exit, their plight pitiable but less tragic than that of Russia's younger generation of TB sufferers. The Soviet Union ran an ever-vigilant Sanitation and Epidemiology Service (SanEp) untrammelled by human rights' considerations. Vaccinations were compulsory, blood tests for syphilis and chest X-rays happened annually, infected individuals were separated from their families, by force if necessary, and kept isolated from the healthy community until cured. Unlike all those economic Five Year Plans, SanEp's system worked. Sufficient drugs were produced and efficiently distributed; the remotest Eastern Siberian sanatorium got what it needed and TB rates dropped steadily throughout the last century – until 1990. According to the World Health Organization, between 1990 and 1996 the rates doubled; according to Russian estimates they almost trebled. In 1996 alone, 111,075 new cases were recorded, of whom one in five was carrying multidrug-resistant tuberculosis (MDRTB). Since then the incidence has been steadily increasing, with possible long-term consequences for continents far from Russia.

This epidemic is not entirely owing to SanEp's collapse and the IMF's 'Health Care Reform'. When job security was no more, tens of thousands of young men took to petty crime – in general non-violent 'against property': thieving, forging cheques, running small neigh-bourhood scams, distilling gut-rot in abandoned factories – minor crimes compared with the oligarchic *piratizatsiya* (piratization) that had left the New Russia unable to sustain SanEp and drug manufacturing. Since 1991 the prison population has more than doubled while the Ministry of Justice's budget has been shrinking. By 1998 a million Russians out of a population of some 150 million were in prison, a ratio only matched by the US. Everything favoured a resurgence of TB: gross overcrowding, insufficient food, poor ventilation, a scarcity of drugs, X-ray film, masks, syringes. Prison doctors went unpaid for months and were too overworked to emulate their 'outside' colleagues by running private practices. The International Committee of the Red Cross reckons that TB causes 80 per cent of prison deaths.

Indefinite detention without trial is now illegal but all those petty crime cases have jammed the courts and many young men are infected before ever they come to trial. If acquitted without treatment they bring the infection home, as do thousands of uncured patients released at the end of their sentences. GUIN (the Department of Prisons) has been overwhelmed by the epidemic. It set up 'TB Colonies', special hospital jails for convicted prisoners – and then took to isolating MDRTB victims behind barbed wire, a desperate strategy to limit the spread of the deadly bacillus to 'standard' patients. Meanwhile Yuri Kalinin, then head of GUIN, admitted in 1995 that conditions in the pre-trial detention centres could be 'classified as torture under inter-national standards; that is, deprivation of sleep, air and space'. The Siberian TB rate tripled between 1992 and 2002, some families having been infected by young men found innocent of any crime after pro-longed detention.

Irregular treatment (in Russia's case because of drug shortages) assists the tubercle bacillus rapidly to become drug resistant; thus 'stan-dard' TB mutates fast into MDRTB and since not all the standard cases are receiving appropriate treatment the percentage of MDRTB cases rises inexorably.

MDRTB treatment is longer than the 'standard' (about two years rather than six to nine months) and the essential second-line drugs are up to 100 times more expensive. Therefore that chilling phrase 'cost-effective' was heard in 1996 when GUIN realized they couldn't cope and opened Russia's prisons to foreign medical NGOs and 'international experts'. The latter argued that in 'resource-poor countries' (like oligarch-ravaged Russia) 'the treatment of MDRTB patients with second-line drugs could not be considered "cost-effective"'. WHO described those drugs as 'prohibitively costly' in the Russian context. According to a World Bank calculation, in China an effective first-line course costs less than $100 and a second-line course tens of thousands of dollars. World Bank consultants emphasized that they always opposed the use of second-line drugs in countries receiving 'Aid' – the post-1991 fate of the Russian Federation. In one city I met an over-wrought prison doctor who was shedding tears of rage as she condemned her government for heeding such 'experts'. Despite all its failings, she remarked bitterly, the Soviet Union had never, during her lifetime, sunk so low as to think of certain medicines as being 'not cost-effective' because the patients were poor. 'What about the *reason* behind these off-patent drugs' high prices?' she added. In response I quoted Paul Farmer, Professor of Medical Anthropology at Harvard Medical School, 'Much of the MDRTB epidemic can be traced to the pricing mechanisms and social policies current in the "free world".'

As the tubercle bacilli were rampaging through Russia in the early 1990s, more than $1 billion was being spent to eradicate New York's comparatively minor MDRTB epidemic, its main source prisons and shelters for the homeless. Writing in the *New England Journal of Medicine*, T. R. Frieden and his colleagues noted: 'Despite the cost, which may reach several times $1 billion, efforts to control tuberculosis in the United States are likely to be highly cost-effective.' The US not being 'resource-poor', its citizens are obviously entitled to protection from dire diseases. MDRTB carriers wandering around New York might infect people of consequence. MDRTB carriers wandering around Russia don't pose the same threat – at least, not yet.

For more than a quarter of a century IMF reforms (Structural Adjustment Programmes: SAPs) have been causing debilitation, despair and death on three continents – my own eyes have too often seen this. However, Russia now is something else. MDRTB moves around. Rich World citizens can (and mostly do) ignore SAPs-related suffering in faraway places but distance won't protect us if Russia's epidemic rampages on. As Paul Farmer has observed in *Pathologies of Power*: 'Russian prisoners with an airborne disease have become yet another reminder of the "unsustainability" of any approach [to public health] based on differential valuation of human life.'

By 1998 half of the infected prisoners were not responding to treatment and Alex Goldfarb of the US Public Health Research Institute (a Russian-born microbiologist) persuaded the financier George Soros to contribute to a TB-control programme. Mr Soros then invited Professor Farmer, the world's leading authority on the effective treatment of MDRTB in poor communities, to help with his project. Since 1999 the Farmer-founded 'Partners in Health' NGO has been working with the Public Health Research Institute, MERLIN, and several Russian government agencies to treat prisoners. Paul Farmer has reported, 'In 2000, the Tomsk DOTS-Plus Programme began treating fifty-two patients. The importance of this programme goes far beyond saving the lives of these young men. It will serve as a stepping-stone to an equitable, comprehensive approach to TB treatment in Russia as a whole, and beyond it, in other countries where MDRTB continues to spread.'

Next morning Novosibirsk's platform thermometer registered −25°C; beyond the Baikal basin one notices the temperature dropping. This was 14 March, Presidential Election Day, and I wrote in my diary:

> From the Gulf of Finland to the Pacific Ocean citizens of the Russian Federation are now (give or take eight hours) doing their democratic thing. Or are they? Can they? Not really. Putin has it all stitched up and that seems to be OK by most citizens. Democracy doesn't happen simply because the new label appears on an outwardly new regime and some percentage of an uncomprehending population then jumps through electoral hoops.

In April 1990 Boris Kagarlitsky, a prescient young political journalist, was elected to the Moscow Soviet as a Popular Front representative. In *Farewell Perestroika*, he observed:

> The opportunity to form hundreds of new parties did not generate much enthusiasm among a population weary of standing in queues. For a majority of people, democratic rights remained abstract and

useless if they did not allow them to defend their immediate interests
. . . If democratization is still a game for professional politicians and
intellectuals, then nothing good can be expected from the changes.

How right he was! Fourteen years later, only the self-deluded could
believe that the Russian Federation was having a democratic election.
I flicked back through my diary, seeking the relevant comments of
BAM acquaintances.

In the restaurant car between Irkutsk and Taishet I had sat with a
thirty-ish woman, a translator for a foreign oil company (not named)
who flatly declared that she wouldn't be voting. 'Putin will win, it's
not a real election. He likes the Communist way of dictating. I would
like a woman president the way you have in Ireland. Russia needs that
for its women. We are not free of men like you. They try to keep us
down, want us to earn money in outside jobs and still be in the kitchen
in their minds. My husband will vote but the rest of our two families
won't. We say, "Why vote? It can make no difference." We hear half
the US voters say the same. Most Russians are not interested in
democracy so it's easy not to give it to them. My husband votes
because he likes strong men. He says it's good Putin doesn't go running
around the country begging for votes like politicians do in the West –
he's so strong he doesn't have to. I like to annoy my husband saying
Putin's not really strong, only doing things the old way.'

Between Bratsk and Ust'-Kut I had met Andrei, a Tomsk-born
electrical engineer based in Ust'-Kut for the past eight years. Since
1992 this big town – where I stayed in 2002 – has been declining even
faster than most such industrial bases. Yet Andrei greatly admired
Putin's leadership skills. True, the economy was doing badly, especially
in Siberia, and people wanted more jobs, higher pay, better schools and
hospitals, more security about their future, no more *piratizatsiya* leading
to rising bills for lighting, heating, telephones. But Putin is a strong
man (that word again!) who knows how to control those Mussulman
terrorists in Chechnya. (This of course was six months before the
Beslan school siege which to some extent tarnished Putin's image as a
terrorist-controller.) Andrei expatiated on the need for Putin and Bush
to stand shoulder to shoulder in the 'War on Terrorism'. Yet again I had
to listen to the Iraq/Chechnya comparison ('We need our army in
Chechnya the way Bush needs his in Iraq') – a comparison revealing

total though unsurprising ignorance of the nature of both conflicts. The Putin and Bush regimes are equally aware of the importance of keeping their citizens uninformed – or, better still, misinformed.

Now, on election day, our carriage was enlivened by three English-speaking Novosibirsk students bound for a Moscow seminar on IT, their university subject. Olga was a friendly, vivacious blonde, the two youths were at first more inhibited about conversing with a native English-speaker but a *pivo* session helped them to unwind. They, too, were indifferent to the election; of their fellow-students who voted, most would go for Putin so why bother voting against him? Yet they detested and distrusted their President. 'His *face* is old KGB,' said Olga. 'You can see it in his *face*!' One of the young men added, 'He's dangerous. He has most Russians blindfolded, not seeing where he's leading them.'

I remarked that democracy is partly about voting against detested candidates – though while speaking I could already hear the response. Olga said, 'Vote for who else? We see no better person with a chance of winning. We know Putin has the power to keep the power. It's not like in your countries where people don't know the winner before the votes are counted.'

A young man said, 'We don't have enough people interested in professional politics to give a choice of good candidates, though students everywhere have many political groups. Some like the free market – some are fascists, all nationalism and Orthodox religion – some want back to Communism. All together they're only a minority. The rest are same as us, no energy for politics, thinking about studies and careers and personal and family problems.'

Tentatively I suggested that their personal problems and Russia's political problems might often be linked, but any such connection was dismissed with shrugs – a disquieting end to that phase of our conversation.

As Putin's KGB methods become more obvious, perhaps Russia's masses will tear off their blindfolds. In December 1988 Boris Kagarlitsky wrote:

> Soviet people, weary after decades of generalities and fine slogans, are primarily interested in a concrete programme which is not just polit-ical but social and economic as well . . . Socialist ideas, despite the changes in the political environment, are so firmly rooted in the public consciousness that any organization not advancing socialist slogans is

perceived by the broad masses as suspicious, if not downright dangerous. The gulf between the pro-capitalist sentiments of part of the privileged Moscow intelligentsia (from where dissidents used to recruit
their supporters) and the spontaneous socialism of the masses was one
of the major reasons for the isolation and unpopularity of dissidents
during the Brezhnev era.

This sheds some light on the New Russians' confusion. The 'defeat of
Communism' gloated over by the West was not a defeat of the socialist ideology – though so many free marketeers work hard, with considerable success, to conflate those two terms in the public mind.

The last word on democracy must go to a youngish mining engineer, met between Khabarovsk and Ulan-Ude. He said, 'Western
peoples wants us to be democratic, do things same as they do. They
don't know here we need strong leaders. Without strong men China
will come to our Far East and Eastern Siberia while we have fights
about voting. Russia is too big for democracy. In US, also a bit big,
they don't have it. Dollars make who's next president. Democracy's
only OK for little countries like Germany and Britain.'

At Ekaterinburg – a long halt – the students requested me to wrap
up; they craved a two-way 'photo opportunity' on that historic platform where Nicholas II and his family ended their last railway journey.
(Not that my young friends knew about this association: a reference to
it brought blank looks.) All three were downcast because I had no film
left – so they wouldn't feature in the Siberian album to be shown to my
family, friends and acquaintances. By way of consolation I explained
that in our world one doesn't bore people with photographs; mine are
personal souvenirs, to be shared only with small granddaughters whose
interest in my doings is flattering and whose boredom threshold is high.
The students looked flummoxed. How could anyone be bored by
photographs, especially of distant regions and their inhabitants?

Siberians (maybe all Russians) are compulsive camera-users as
though everything needs the added value of being pictured, isn't
otherwise quite real. One friend had been looking forward to making
a super-snowman, with all the trimmings, when the spring snow
became sufficiently adhesive. 'I want a photo of Max [aged two]
beside him,' said the fond mama – one of many examples of this com-
pulsion. I had to waste much film because friends would have been
offended if I didn't want the picture they thought I should want, of

some trivial event or banal scene. Nor are 'natural' shots appreciated; everyone must comb hair, adjust or change garments, rearrange furniture, toys, tools and facial expressions. It seemed people felt my possession of those photographs could somehow consolidate or prolong inevitably transient relationships – which might be so if I looked at them, back home, as often as Siberians pore over their albums.

For a few hours next morning large soft flakes floated down from a low silvery sky. 'European snow!' said Olga. Then the sun shone on flat land overcrowded with the town-sized dacha settlements of urban dwellers, factory stacks, railway depots, villages, traffic-busy tarred roads. This overcrowded impression was of course a post-Siberia hallucination; to a Dutch traveller, European Russia would appear virtually uninhabited.

By mid-afternoon, in a thawing zone, messy black slush surrounded each station, wellies had replaced *valenkis* (knee-high felt boots) and most people were discarding gloves, scarves and *shapkas*. After my two glittering ice-bound months all those pools of murky water looked sordid. From Kirov station we could see a colossal bulldozer on a wide street smashing long high ridges of packed snow and flinging it into trucks for dumping in the Cheptsa river. 'This is Kirov's first thaw day,' observed Olga. 'It comes suddenly and no one likes this wet time.'

Miles of taiga extend beyond Kirov and towards sunset the silver birch boles on either side shimmered rose-pink – a fairytale effect, magical things could happen in that radiant forest. Olga was standing beside me at a corridor window. She said, 'Now mostly we live in cities. But we need *this* Russia, where there is beauty for every season. Our souls belong to the forests and the steppes and the rivers' flow. Being a city person makes me less Russian.'

It was my turn to be flummoxed, those were not the sentiments expected of a twenty-year-old IT student.

Laying a hand on my arm, Olga asked, 'Are you sad about leaving Siberia?' I nodded, then was beckoned into the students' compartment. 'In Ekaterinburg we bought many beers, now we'll make you less sad.' And so they did. But Russian-brewed *pivo* is benign and at dawn I stepped clear-headedly onto a Kazan station platform.

13

Debacle at Rostov-on-Don

A N IRISH PUB in Moscow on St Patrick's Day . . . My companion and I were genetically programmed to order pints of Guinness and our tankards came with green shamrock images neatly imprinted on their fawn heads. Imbibing, I wondered what lethal chemical goes into the making of that dye. The pub was festooned with shamrocks, leprechauns, harps, hurleys and Tourist Board posters of Irish beauty spots – their beauty now fled, banished by 'amenities'. I recalled another St Patrick's Day, in California in 1979, where a roadside bar served green beer (entirely green, not just decorated froth), and the town's street surfaces had been sprayed green, and giant leprechauns hung from trees and eaves and for the first time in my life I wanted to deny my Irishness.

My companion was a thoughtful and charming young compatriot who for the previous five years had been monitoring religious freedom in the New Russia. Having travelled widely throughout the Federation, she reckoned the numbers of foreign evangelical groups actively proselytizing in Russia was exaggerated, often by the groups themselves. The Orthodox Church resented and scorned them but reserved its deepest hostility for the Vatican.

The Orthodox equivalent of the Vatican is a General Synod, also keen on control, conformity and centralization. Since the rapprochement legislation of September 1990, abolishing most restrictions on religious activities, the Orthodox rebuilding campaign has been conspicuous, its involvement in social needs less so. Individual young priests who show concern for their flocks' earthly problems get little support from bishops and are often reprimanded for taking their eye off the heavenly ball. In recent years the standard of clerical education has gone up slightly (starting from near zero) with stricter seminary entrance exams; but it is unlikely the Church will ever again be allowed to exercise any influence in state schools. Legally it is free to establish private fee-paying academies, though official antipathy to such institutions raises almost insuperable bureaucratic barriers.

In search of maps showing minor, bicycle-friendly roads, I toured Moscow's main bookshops and met with consistent unhelpfulness, sometimes verging on rudeness. My friends (both Russian and foreign) were not surprised, having themselves observed that as Muscovites participate more frenetically in Western consumerism they become increasingly xenophobic. 'Which is only superficially a paradox,' said one English friend. 'Even young Russians are sensitive about their empire's dissolution – of course associated with *us*. So the more they ape our way of life, while their own Federation looks like a "failed state", the less they like us.'

A Muscovite friend sensed a link between the xenophobic trend and Putin's 'strong leadership'. Gloomily he pronounced, 'We're not going back towards Brezhnev but towards Stalin.'

As I read the *Moscow Times* that evening the 'failed state' label seemed, sadly, not too inaccurate. A front-page photograph showed the debris of a nine-storey apartment block in Arkhangelsk. The gas explosion which demolished it (thirty-two dead, many missing) had been caused by two homeless men stealing bronze lids off valves. Dmitry Lovetsky reported:

> Authorities found the lids missing in two neighbouring buildings, but crews were able to fix the gas leaks in time . . . Homeless men have been systematically stealing the lids in the past . . . Thieves pilfer power lines, municipal facilities and industrial equipment throughout the Federation in search of copper, bronze, and other metals to sell for scrap . . . Residents of the building had reported smelling gas to the local emergency gas service before the explosion, but its workers did not come until the blast occurred . . . The Prosecutor General's Office said neglect of safety precautions has led to frequent gas explosions in apartment buildings and public facilities.

Mid-March is when not to visit Moscow: the sky a dirty smoggy grey, the air raw and damp, the pavements and streets muddy, the parks repulsive as slushy thawing snowdrifts reveal a three-months' accumulation of dog-shit and litter. On the 18th, when my friends escorted me to Kazan station at 5.30 p.m., I could fancy myself home in Ireland on the worst sort of January day. It had been raining coldly for hours and in a gusty wind people struggled with umbrellas advertising Western brands of alcohol or cigarettes.

A non-alarmist Russian friend had warned me not to travel *platskartny* in European Russia and to beware of muggers and pickpockets in Rostov-on-Don, a city with a somewhat shady reputation. I had therefore left my journal (by this stage my most valuable possession) in a Moscow 'safe house' and taken just enough cash for a month of rural living.

By chance, all my coupé companions for this twenty-hour trip spoke English with varying degrees of fluency, a ratio never encountered in Siberia. Vladimir had recently retired from the army after twenty-five years' service and was fervently pro-Putin. 'Soon our President have restored Russian war-making capacity.' Opposite us sat Vera and Ivan, agronomists who had worked in Tashkent for ten years. When they left in 1993 their jobs were still secure – newly independent Uzbekistan needed their expertise – but they couldn't cope with the anti-Russian attitudes of many ordinary Uzbeks, now eager to express what had been muffled since 27 June 1865. On that date the keystone of Russia's Central Asian empire was laid by Major-General Mikhail Cherniaev when he seized Tashkent for Czar Alexander II.

Everyone expressed much sympathy for the Soviet Union's Cold War enemy, now also threatened by Mussulman terrorists. Vladimir quoted the numbers of Muslim settlers in Western Europe and had his figures right. Of course the Jews, too, were, as always, a threat to Russia – had collaborated to bring about the collapse of the Soviet Empire, having seen how they could benefit from an abrupt transition to the 'free market'. The US was wrong to support Israel but right to keep a tight grip on Afghanistan and Iraq. Even the powerful US military presence in Uzbekistan was acceptable, that country being Muslim. I sought their opinion of Craig Murray, then Britain's man in Tashkent. His refreshingly honest criticisms of President Islam Karimov's neo-Stalinist regime, supported and funded by the US, had enraged both London and Washington in the autumn of 2003 – and then set them sparring. (Honesty in diplomatic circles never refreshes governments.) Vera and Ivan thought ambassadors in general should be seen and not heard. Vladimir agreed with them; anyway, getting tough with Uzbek domestic dissidents was essential to defeat all those terrorists based in Afghanistan. This comment illuminated the moral and geopolitical chaos in post-Soviet Central Asia where 'hunting terrorists' is code for controlling oil and gas resources and routes. Vladimir grinned appreciatively while quoting one of Karimov's more notorious statements. Rejecting a complaint in the Uzbek parliament about suspected terrorists being systematically tortured to death, the President declared, 'Such people must be shot in the head. If necessary, I will shoot them myself.' Was this a human rights concession – a quick bullet in the head being more humane than slow torture procedures?

Our Anglophone conversation brought Nestor from next door – a tall, blond young man with violet eyes and a goatee beard. He spoke fluent English, was newly graduated as an economic historian and had an unusual ambition: to use the teaching of history to help schoolchildren to overcome their generation's particular heritage of post-Soviet uncertainty and unease. 'That will mean going back to their great-great-grandparents' Revolution-related traumas and self-deceits. Difficult! But as I see it, our future collective mental health needs an understanding of our *whole* past. How can we become a stable nation if we don't face past realities? Our children must get to know *why* we are *where* we are at this time.'

The temptation was too much. I had to ask, 'So where *are* you at this time?'

Nestor laughed. 'I think you know very well the answer! Totally fucked up in a Third World way! Moscow boasting of prestige projects, pensioners and villagers going hungry, the masses all disorientated – told lies for fifty years about being an imperial superpower, which we never were. That's why the way seems clear for a dictator promising military muscle-building.'

I glanced at Vladimir, the militarist. But he and Ivan had been sharing a large bottle of vodka and were no longer making sense in any language. Soon after, Nestor retired – he drank only fruit juice – and Vera and I exchanged meaningful looks. We had been allocated the lower bunks but clearly the men were in no state to climb up nimbly and arrange their bedding sensibly. As we settled them on our bunks, tucking them in securely, Vera observed, '*Pivo* people OK, vodka people needs always more.'

Drifting into sleep, I wondered why one so rarely has even this sort of rudimentary conversation about international affairs on the BAM, though Eastern Siberians now receive their share of satellite TV news and internet information. Perhaps the topographically insignificant Urals do constitute a significant mental barrier. Or is it the Yenisey? I don't, after all, know Western (or Northern) Siberia. Given the territory's extent, that blanket term 'Siberia' is inane.

We all awoke at sunrise, when the men silently drank many mugs each of fruit juice and tea — and by 9.15 were needing hairs of the dog. Several hairs, in tiny but frequent gulps, until at noon they slept again.

I stood by a corridor window watching grey rain sweeping across mile after mile of soon-to-be-ploughed steppe, just released from winter's prison, its brownness relieved only by lingering snowdrifts and occasional naked bushes, black squiggles against the sullen sky. A dreary landscape — had I not been able, thanks to Herodotus, to people it with Amazons. Writing in the fifth century BC, Herodotus described this landscape as 'forest with trees of all sorts. In the most densely wooded part there is a big lake surrounded by reedy marshland; otters and beavers are caught in the lake, and another sort of creature with a square face, whose skin they use for making edgings for their jackets; its testicles are good for affections of the womb.'

Once upon a time (dates are not Herodotus's forte) the Greeks beat the Amazons in a battle near the river Thermodon, then in three ships sailed off across the Black Sea with the surviving women as prisoners. However, being disgracefully sexist the Greeks saw no need to keep their female captives under strict control and very soon no man remained alive. The Amazons then had a problem; as inland horse people, they couldn't handle ships. But Fate sent helpful winds and tides which eventually deposited them on Scythian territory near the Don delta. There they hijacked a herd of grazing horses and cantered off in search of sustenance. A minor battle ensued: Amazons *v.* Scythian horse-owners. It was a draw, most of the Amazons galloping away unscathed. Collecting the few corpses, the Scythians discovered to their astonishment that the marauders, foreign in dress and speech, were women — impressive women, *very* impressive . . . Immediately the Scythian leaders thought in Darwinian terms and Herodotus gives a hilarious account of the wooing of the Amazons. (His sense of humour resonates with ours over the 2,500-year gap.) The young warriors' wooing was partly successful. Yes, the Amazons would happily bear Scythian children but, predictably, on their own terms. Herodotus records their ultimatum:

We and the women of your nation could never live together; our ways are too much at variance. We are riders; our business is with the bow and the spear, and we know nothing of women's work; but in your country no woman has anything to do with such things – your women stay at home in their wagons occupied with feminine tasks, and never go out to hunt or for any other purpose. We could not possibly agree. If, however, you wish to keep us for your wives and to behave as honourable men, go and get from your parents the share of property which is due to you, and then let us go off and live by ourselves . . . somewhere on the other side of the Tanais.

Tanais was the Greek and Latin name for the river Don. Much later (*c.* 250 BC) the Greek city of Tanais arose not far from Rostov-on-Don and its remains are at present being excavated by Russian archaeologists.

As the Don came into view – huge ice chunks moving sluggishly towards the Sea of Azov – I marvelled at the extremes offered by the Russian Federation. Around Tynda or Komsomolsk or Vanino one is conscious of being in regions of the planet only known, until a few centuries ago, by small primitive tribes – and to this day remote in spirit from 'our world'. So abrupt was its brutal colonization that its cities feel like (and are) 'foreign bodies', unrelated to the needs and skills of the indigenes. But here, close to the Black Sea coast, the roots of our European culture are discernible. Here existed sophisticated trading cities when the inhabitants of Ireland and England were on a par with (if not less developed than) Siberia's tribes.

Some three centuries before Herodotus's birth in Halicarnassus, on the south-west coast of Asia Minor, many colonies of Ionian Greeks had settled along the Black Sea. Their business was curing and packing fish for export to the increasingly populous Greek city-states and, in due course, their trading posts became stone-fortified towns, then port cities. Merchants from China, India and Persia converged on Tanais, the Don delta's first defended city, bringing gold and bronze luxury goods, porcelain, silk, spices – and ideas. The Greek colonists exported decorated pottery, household ornaments, jewellery and wine. For five centuries or so all was well, give or take a few local difficulties with the Scythians. Then came the Goths, who swiftly reduced Tanais to charred ruins. Thereafter, travelling across the steppes became so precarious that for almost a thousand years, until the Tatar-Mongol empire restored security, the Silk Roads linking China and Europe were closed.

Where the railway almost touches the Ukrainian border we passed several impoverished old villages of brick houses. In Rostov, too, most old one-storey dwellings are of brick, though the bricklayers imitated the traditional fretwork effect around windows.

At 2.30 p.m. a gale was lashing Rostov with icy rain. I had already resigned myself to a change of plan; instead of immediately fetching Pushkin from the freight shed and pedalling towards the Tanais exca- vations, I would have to spend the night in a hotel. Nestor recom- mended Hotel Turist and we shared a taxi through a city centre that needs sunshine to cheer it up.

This was the first hotel I had stayed in in European Russia (apart from Aeroflot's skyscraper in Soviet times) and compared to BAM Zone hotels the workmanship was markedly less shoddy. The staff spoke no English but were cheerful, friendly and used to foreigners – probably low-budget businessmen, Rostov not being a tourist must-see. My bedroom was enervatingly overheated yet its bathroom lacked hot water. I borrowed a kettle to make tea, then observed a sinister oiliness on the surface of my mugful. Later I discovered that Rostov has long been notorious for dangerous drinking water; in the nineteenth century it had one of the world's highest death rates from cholera.

For the rest of the day it rained without ceasing but Nestor assured me that the long-term forecast was good. Happily I had compensa- tory reading matter, found in one of those disagreeable Moscow bookshops – Neal Ascherson's *Black Sea*, which kept me awake hours past my normal bedtime.

Russia's new Railway Authority had recently favoured Rostov (a major junction) with a colossal, glossy, bright blue and yellow station building of the currently popular Lego school of architecture. It was mindlessly spacious and not yet fully operative; the ticket hall was open, the tennis-court-sized café and adjoining loos were not.

In Severobaikalsk Ivan had thoughtfully written a chit saying 'Please show Dervla Murphy the freight office where she can collect her bicycle despatched from here on 10 March'. Clutching this and my passport and Pushkin's ticket (three times the size of and six times more complicated than a human ticket) I sought guidance from the traffic policemen who swarm around the station – a force not respected by Russians. The first pointed me in one wrong direction;

within the next twenty minutes three of his colleagues had pointed me in three other wrong directions and I had walked a mile or so. Two uniformed railway officials were no more accurate. Was Rostov's station in such a critical transition phase that no one knew how to locate something as unprecedented as a bicycle sent from Severobaikalsk? Wandering hither and thither, desperately knocking on the doors of empty offices, I came upon an amiable-looking young man, one of a team of four (the others middle-aged women) who were painting old olive green carriages in the new yellow and blue Russian Railway colours. He read my chit, took pity on the distraught babushka, led me down a long platform and around two corners to the Left Luggage office in the gigantic ticket hall. There an obese elderly woman wearing a weary expression and a piled-up wig of jet black hair (it couldn't have been homegrown) scrutinized my documents, thumbed through a thick file of embossed railway invoices and said no bicycle had come from Severobaikalsk. Perhaps tomorrow? Twitching with frustration, I wondered if goods sent thousands of miles in a freight wagon came into the category of Left Luggage? Returning to the young man, I put that point. Smiling kindly, he assured me that Left Luggage would certainly record Pushkin's arrival though I would have to go elsewhere – he didn't know where – to collect my property.

Leaving the station, I resolved to think positive; at least the weather had improved, early morning drizzle replaced by intermittent sunshine. But Fate had it in for me that day. When I took a scruffy minibus to Tanais the windows were so mud-bespattered I couldn't see the landscape and in Nedvigovka, a dejected one-street village near the excavations, I was told 'Nyet!' The site was closed to visitors until mid-April.

From the bus station (beside the railway station) I walked back to Hotel Turist – an hour's walk, slightly uphill from the river, along wide streets where solid late nineteenth-century mansions recall Rostov's most tranquil era but are too often dwarfed by the banal ugliness of 'the Khrushchev School'. This is a socially engineered city of one million inhabitants and unhappy memories, a place fractured by Stalin – and somehow one senses that the injury hasn't healed.

In 1749 Rostov was founded as a garrison town. 'New Russia' then described the colony soon to be established by Catherine II on the

Black Sea's northern shore, previously under Ottoman control. Inland, this had been Don Cossack territory since the late Middle Ages, a borderless region until Russia's expanding trade needed the freedom of the Black Sea. In the 1790s these fertile steppes were sparsely populated by communities of self-governing Cossacks, mainly cattle farmers, but during the next few decades hordes of hungry peasants migrated from the much less fertile central provinces. By 1863 European Russia was producing more grain per capita than any other European country, though the yield per hectare was the lowest in Europe. And of course the dispossessed Cossacks were in sullen mood.

Come the Revolution, Rostov and its surrounding province were enjoying relative prosperity, the population an interesting mix of Cossacks, Germans, Tatars, Jews, Poles, Armenians and Greeks. Yes, the Greeks were still around, 2,600 years after those pioneering fishermen settled along the coast. It took Stalin to dislodge them. In the 1930s he closed Greek (and Tatar) schools, newspapers and publishing houses. After the Great Patriotic War he banished all Greeks, Tatars and Germans to Central Asia, forcing them to leave their possessions behind for the benefit of the Ukrainians and Russians now planted on their land. Of Rostov's original multiracial population, only the Cossacks remained. Notoriously macho and dour, their lawless antecedents were mongrel mercenaries, used by Catherine II and her successors to 'maintain order' and colonize Siberia. They specialized in massacring Jews throughout the empire. Pogrom is a Russian word meaning 'destruction'.

Because local self-government had continued until 1917 – though freedom to roam the steppes was no more – many Cossacks still feel entitled to dominate their old Don Cossack heartland. The logic of this argument escapes the Russians who point out that few Cossacks contributed much to the region's agricultural and industrial development. Year by year in Rostov, tension tightens behind the scenes.

That evening I unfolded my three excellent maps and calculated that from Rostov to Moscow is 780 miles on second- or third-class roads. Or 640 miles on the main road which would be both intolerably unpleasant and potentially suicidal, given Russian drivers' unfamiliarity with two-wheeled traffic. (One hardly ever sees a cyclist or a motor-bike. In Moscow I had been told that cycling is considered uncool.) Given four weeks, that came out at less than 200 miles a week, leaving me ample time to observe village life. But would I be given four weeks? Where was Pushkin?

At 8.05 next morning – a Sunday – the station environs were quiet but the traffic police no less numerous. Mrs Raven-Wig had just opened her guichet shutter and before I could speak she snapped 'Nyet!' Plainly she found my preposterous request irritating; when I pathetically suggested 'Zaftra?' (tomorrow) she waved me away and beckoned the next in the short queue. Her eyes were puffy and her lips, as yet unpainted, had a bluish tinge. But she couldn't afford not to work, despite obviously poor health. Wandering away, I reminded myself that, statistically, she was quite likely to have an alcoholic husband, a messily divorced child and mounting debts. She was never going to concern herself with my problem or even point me towards someone who might take an interest in Pushkin's whereabouts.

It was 21 March, the spring equinox, and as if on cue the sun shone warmly from a clear sky – felt almost hot, out of the wind. Perhaps a riverside stroll would cheer me up . . . But no: the quietly flowing Don has been so polluted for so long that as one walks along the copiously littered bank, a yard from the grey-green, ice-chunky water, its exhalations are uncheering. Rostov's masses still eat what fish have survived, Rostov's intelligentsia don't.

I sought musical solace in the Nativity of the Virgin Cathedral, its restoration recently completed, its five cupolas visible from afar (gold-plated at a cost not divulged to the general public). Entering, I felt the warmth generated by hundreds of votive candles, their distinctive aroma blending agreeably with the incense billowing from thuribles swung by two youthful deacons. The congregation represented a cross-section of Rostovians; as is usual at Orthodox services, they came and went as the spirit moved them.

After the service I watched a little girl, aged seven at most, going about her devotions, moving from icon to icon, repeatedly bowing and crossing herself before each, then standing on tiptoe to kiss those few within her reach, finally touching them with her forehead. She seemed to be alone but in the background, standing near the entrance observing her progress, was a typical babushka – a squat little figure clad in calf-length skirt, belted sheepskin jacket and tight headscarf. When her granddaughter joined her she pointed to a couple of overlooked icons in corners and the child trotted off, with apparently undiminished fervour, to give them their due. Older children and teenagers were also in action, as numerous as their seniors, praying and lighting candles before favourite icons. I remembered the comment of a Muscovite friend that from the Church's point of view the exorbitant restoration costs were a sound investment. All the gilded glory and vivid icons (laboriously executed replicas of those destroyed by Stalin's gangs), and the brightly burnished brass railings and sparkling chandeliers, have helped to restore the Church's status and – at least in the popular imagination, if not in political reality – its ancient aura of power and mystery. More frugal restorations, though seemingly more appropriate, could never have the same mesmeric effect.

Strangely, on this crowded Sunday afternoon, eight women were sweeping and mopping the floor, moving between the worshippers – a few of whom slipped on the soapy tiles, provoking the cleaners to angry mutterings and gesticulations. When I revisited the cathedral next day a similar team was busy, as well as a polishing team sweating over the yards of intricately wrought brass railings. And at noon on a Monday the worshippers were almost equally numerous and various.

In Gorky Park strolling crowds were celebrating the first day of spring. Towards the end of the nineteenth century an unusual Cossack, a wealthy industrialist, endowed the city centre with this very fine park, rich in tall trees, dense shrubberies and little streams now thaw-flooded. The designer cleverly used the lie of the land to create a long sunken garden, then added a tiny observatory – reminding me of some Georgian folly in Ireland. Sadly, the twenty-first-century municipality has allowed many garish advertising banners – echoing the streets' billboards – to overhang the main paths, stretched between trees. And equally garish junk-food kiosks abound. (There can't ever before have been a society as *visually ugly* as ours.) At one end, overlooked by the ponderously handsome Town Hall, 'amusements' happened, to the accompaniment of blaring rock bands. The omnipresent ferris-wheel rotated slowly and teenagers shrieked in delighted terror while whirling up and down on an irresponsible simulation of dangerous driving at high speeds. Old-fashioned bumper cars and a sedate wooden mini-train catered for small children – as did two ponies, their riders being photographed by doting grandparents, or maybe great-grandparents. The older couples, people who would have used horse-power in times past, seemed to derive another sort of pleasure from stroking and talking to the ponies.

I was leaving a portaloo when someone yelled, 'Irish babushka! Hey, Irish babushka!' Understandably, Nestor had forgotten my name and was puzzled to meet me in Gorky Park. 'Why are you here? Now the weather is good – where is your bicycle?'

My sad tale didn't surprise him. 'You need an interpreter,' he said, and volunteered for the job. Then his companion was introduced to me, his aunt Tina who might have been his sister; only twelve years separated them. She, too, was tall and blonde and violet-eyed. Later, when I felt free to make personal remarks, I admired this unusual eye colour and was told it had long been a family trait, could be seen even in eighteenth-century portraits.

Tina invited me to supper; her flat was not far from Hotel Turist, in a four-storey block dated 1888 with shops on the ground floor. A fourteen-year-old son and twelve-year-old daughter greeted me awkwardly, then withdrew to their computer-equipped bedroom.

After supper Nestor opened a second bottle of wine and Tina talked about her circumstances. She had been divorced ten years previously, at the age of twenty-seven, when she was a poorly paid teacher of English in a gymnasium, the approximate equivalent of an English grammar school. Then a foreign bank offered much higher pay and she felt bound to accept 'though I was happy teaching and this job bores me'.

I recognized the pattern; some of my Siberian friends had criticized foreign corporations who poach the best-qualified teachers of Western European languages, especially English. 'We must put our families first,' continued Tina. 'If our government wants good teachers it must pay them. Would you put your country's need before your children's? We have no faith in our politicians. They don't put Russia first and if I don't care for my children, who will?'

As Nestor escorted me home I noticed that the municipal flowerbeds, bare at dawn, were now flecked with the green of daffodils and tulips pushing through. My companion was speaking of his aunt with affectionate concern. Her husband – a prospering dentist – had treated her cruelly; not wanting a second child, he had accused her of deception *re* conception – then vanished in '95, having disowned his daughter and refused to pay any maintenance for either child. 'Tina lives a long lonely struggle,' said Nestor. 'For the children it's not too sad, they don't remember him. I want Tina married again and she has a man friend but never in her flat. She believes Tasha and Andrei need to feel they're *most* important in her life. She seems like a cosmopolitan lady but as a mother she's primitive – cubs first!'

Outside Hotel Turist we arranged to meet at the No. 21 trolley-bus stop, opposite the university, at 8.0 a.m.

Another sunny morning and my spirits soared when Nestor eventually found the real freight office, located not in any of the numerous empty rooms of the several new station buildings but in two unmarked discarded goods wagons parked in a remote siding and entered via a makeshift wooden stepladder. At 8.50 three women, wearing navy-blue railway parkas, frayed headscarves and heavy boots, were breakfasting off hardboiled eggs, pickled cucumbers, slanina (bacon fat) and hunks of the cheapest bread. Freight stood around: piles of sacks, enormous crates, oddly shaped objects wrapped in sheets of plastic – none of which was a bicycle. When Nestor displayed Pushkin's ticket the first reaction was incredulity. Then the woman nearest the antique telephone wiped her mouth with the back of a hand and slowly dialled a number. A long conversation ensued – the ticket number repeatedly quoted – and was punctuated by long pauses. Nestor's expression warned me that the news was bad. Pushkin's wagon, as we spoke, was having two wheels repaired in Krasnoyarsk, very far away. 'But your bicycle is safe,' Nestor assured me. That was no consolation; I'd not been worrying about his safety, only about his rate of progress. Then I had to marvel at a system which, given the ticket number, could within fifteen minutes locate one minor piece of freight in the middle of its 4,000-mile journey from Eastern Siberia to the Don delta. That's the up-side of Russian bureaucracy. But why, when a freight wagon breaks down, can't its contents be transferred to another wagon? Is this the down-side? Nestor explained: an item that starts its journey in wagon No. 8531 must end its journey in wagon No. 8531, which could not be expected in Rostov for another four days, even if all went well with the repairs. After an exasperated moment, I could see the point of this rigidity. It guaranteed Pushkin's security; in Krasnoyarsk's repair shed that disabled wagon would remain locked, inviolable.

Nestor took the No. 21 back to the university – his workplace – and I walked to the central open-air market near the cathedral, reflecting that my relationship with Pushkin was undoubtedly jinxed.

This market's seafood emporium, a hangar-like hall with scores of traders behind marble counters, should be avoided by the tender-hearted. On the street outside, aged ex-army trucks, converted to water tankers, back up to metal gates giving access to traders' stalls. An astounding variety of live fish cascade into baths of shallow water where they flounder and gasp, their gills piteously palpitating, sometimes leaping high, splashing passers-by, in their frenzied longing to return to the Black Sea. Some are more than four feet long and bulky; many are three feet. Satisfied customers depart with the contents of their plastic sacks still heaving and squirming. Mammals drown much more quickly than fish die in our element.

When I aimed my camera at the counters of the caviar-sellers – jars arranged in pyramids – angry shouts and scowls came from every side; as a foreigner I was being closely watched and not much liked. But wouldn't a photograph of Rostov's thriving red caviar trade project a positive image? My nostalgia for welcoming Siberia was renewed. Then I reproved myself – 'Mustn't generalize, mustn't make such comparisons based on a city with problems.'

At winter's end the half-acre fruit and vegetable market was limited: carrots, parsnips, beets, potatoes, all reassuringly dirty with black earth, variable in size and shape and often blemished as is natural. The fifty-yards-long potato section fascinated me, displaying a variety I had previously seen only in Peru, the home of that tuber. Bananas and oranges were scarce and expensive but an abundance of passion fruit was going cheap; somewhere had overproduced.

Near the cathedral gate six women sat on beer crates hawking litters of multicoloured kittens in cardboard cartons: fifteen roubles each or two for twenty-five. A few mongrel pups – very young but potentially enormous – were wrapped in scarves on their owners' laps (prices negotiable) and two men held aloft tiny cages containing pairs of budgerigars. Further on, several covered stalls sold up-market rubber bones and squeaky toys for dogs, and scratching boards, litter trays and belled collars for cats. Pet owners fall easy prey to consumerism. The guard-dog gear included very long, strong chains and metal-reinforced rope collars; if a guard-dog breaks loose, serious injury to a human is certain and death quite possible. The muzzles, too, were formidable – worn by the minority lucky enough to be given exercise.

Between cathedral and market is the tram terminus, designed to serve both God and Mammon. These tracks were laid in czarist times and the trams themselves have been in use since the 1920s, according to Tina. Their unmelodious yet cheery bells took me back to Dublin c. 1945. Close to the tracks – so close that customers have to move as trams pass – is one long arcade with shiny blue and white striped metal canopies arching incongruously over each stall: a brash free-market flourish in old Rostov's decaying centre. Those stalls, selling everything from deep freezers to so-called 'Swiss' watches suggest comparative affluence. Then a mere forty yards away one comes upon the commerce of desperation. Goods that even I, Ireland's leading hoarder, would bin without hesitation were laid on sheets of newsprint along broken pavements overlooked by terraced dwellings in a dangerous state of disrepair but still inhabited. Most of the hawkers – sitting on doorsteps, erratically dressed in whatever they had been able to scavenge – were elderly; each offered only a few items. Here were a broken alarm clock, chipped and cracked tableware, the guts of a transistor radio, two clumsily repaired ornate picture frames, a misshapen sieve, rusty tools, nails and screws, well-worn garments and footwear, a black-spotted hand mirror, a few damaged plastic toys and much-fondled soft toys, shop-soiled postcards of Moscow, single pieces of cutlery, an electric iron without a flex, a shoulder bag with broken zips, dented pots and pans . . . This was the sort of scene one does not photograph. Purchases were being made, the buyers as desperate as the sellers. A certain *esprit de corps* was evident; these comrades in distress joked and laughed and teased each other. Most of the men looked like vodka victims, or victims of whatever perilous vodka substitute they could afford.

On the corner of the next street, beside the ruins of a one-storey house, sat a separate group of six down-and-outs. Their stock of old clothes, spread on a plastic sheet, was augmented by three auburn wigs and made no more attractive by an accumulation of dust and wind-blown debris such as toffee-papers. The small, wiry saleswoman wore too-tight jeans and a ravelling sweater and seemed slightly drunk. Her companions were a man of her own height and build whom she addressed as 'Papa', a peroxide blonde of uncertain age with boils on her neck, two unshaven men who were squabbling over the dregs in a samogon bottle and a ragged, grey-bearded wreck wearing four Great Patriotic War medals. A fallen roof beam was their seat and behind them, on the remains of a gable wall, hung three lounge suits and three women's skirts. As I approached, the young woman (let's call her 'Kate') was loudly berating two young men who had just paid fifteen roubles for two pairs of socks. She stood angrily waving the ten-rouble note and five-rouble coin, insisting that she had asked fifteen roubles for *each* pair. But the men only laughed while pocketing the socks. As they walked away Kate yelled shrill abuse – arms akimbo, face flushed. Then, seizing a sword-length bit of window frame from the ruins, she strode after them, brandishing her weapon and still shouting, like a medieval soldier marching into battle. I couldn't understand why they didn't, at this stage, run away: they had a twenty-yard start. Instead, they allowed Kate to attack them, in turn, hitting each over the head. I had followed the trio and now Papa came running to the rescue and wrested Kate's weapon from her – with difficulty, she was a sinewy young woman. This was the young men's chance to flee but they stood their ground, still vehemently arguing. Escaping from Papa, Kate now went for them with feet and fists, repeatedly hitting them over the head and face and attempting kicks to the groin. Beyond raising their arms ineffectually to protect their heads, they offered no resistance. One had thick curly hair and yelped in pain when it was used to wrench his head backwards. The other had a crew-cut and the first blow of the sharp-edged window frame had drawn a trickle of blood from his scalp. As the three ranted hoarsely at each other Papa, white-faced, said nothing and seemed to be hesitating. Then he again tried to drag Kate away, grabbing her around the waist, half-lifting her, but again she fought him off and on resuming the attack bit one of Crew-cut's over-exposed ears. At that, Papa became suddenly vocal and shouted something so potent that Curly and Crew-cut instantly reached into their pockets and handed over another fifteen roubles. Exulting in her victory, Kate swaggered back to base flaunting the money as ample justification for a vigorous course of action. ('I see a woman may be made a fool, / If she had not a spirit to resist' – as that other Kate said.) Her friends, I noticed, had kept their eyes averted from the conflict. Had it ended badly, had that weapon put out an eye or had there been a traffic accident (there almost was), they would have witnessed nothing. But now the bemedalled veteran was loud in his congratulations and from within his rags drew another bottle of samogon to toast the Heroine of the Hour.

Why had Papa not said earlier whatever he finally said? I longed to know the background (surely not just the fifteen roubles?) and the code by which the victims were operating. Two young men allowing themselves to be beaten up by one young woman in the middle of the day in the middle of the street (the traffic had to slow down) does not accord with one's image of the Russian male. Were they afraid to defend themselves lest Kate's friends might set upon them? That however didn't explain their not running away. Later, when I described the fracas to Nestor over dinner in his flat, he said, 'It sounds like some arcane Cossack clan feud.' After a moment he added, 'Maybe – it's possible – Papa's magic words after the bite were an AIDS-related threat.'

The Hotel Turist tariff included breakfast: mini-cartons of 'mixed fruit' juice and brightly coloured yoghurt, one tiny cube of butter and triangle of sticky cheese, fresh white bread and a tea-plate of luke-warm pasta with a boiled sausage tasting only of pepper. Waitresses toured the ballroom-sized restaurant bearing mega-kettles of pallid tea and instant coffee, filling cups on request. From three of the square central pillars hung TV sets, high above the tables, relaying pro-grammes of such incomparable idiocy that I couldn't even guess what they were supposed to be.

On my third morning the restaurant was unusually busy; a delega-tion of science teachers had arrived from the Urals to attend their annual conference. Two spoke English – Rina fluently, Millya brokenly – and soon they had befriended me. We arranged to meet in the city centre that evening on my return from a day trip to Novocherkassk.

Nestor had disloyally advised me to skip Rostov's museums and take a bus to Novocherkassk's History of the Don Cossacks Museum which also has a superb collection of Scythian gold. This little city (twenty-five miles to the north-east, population about 110,000, indus-tries waning) is now the notional 'capital' of Russia's seven million or so Cossacks, a large percentage of whom have been settled in Siberia for centuries. Apart from the museum, it is unexciting – as is the factory-befouled landscape on either side of the highway.

*

Central Rostov wears a shell of affluence: stores displaying spotlit luxuries in wide windows, expensive restaurants and boutiques, the recently spruced up, exuberantly decorated mansions of late nineteenth-century tycoons – some now taken over by banks whose armed guards are conspicuous. When I met Rina and Millya they were accompanied by two English-speakers from Volgograd: Olga and Tatyana, physics teachers, also in their late thirties/early forties. All four looked stressed, after yet another failure to persuade a government minister to fund better equipment for school laboratories.

Our destination was a rather grand café, popular with the well-heeled young – a former mansion's three long ground-floor rooms, opening into one another. The off-white and duck egg blue decor, with discreet touches of gilt, respected the fanciful scrolled plaster-work: the raucous piped muzak did not. Our table was beside one of those toy-lifting cranes in glass booths – five roubles a session, proving how easily some New Russian parents are parted from their money.

Olga asked, 'Have you noticed, people like us only use places like this for treats, away from home?'

Rina looked around and said, 'These lucky young people don't know how fast their city has changed! Twenty years ago Rostov had nowhere like this.'

I nodded neutrally, thinking that twenty years ago neither did Rostov have unlucky old people sitting on pavements trying to sell cracked cups and split shoes.

My companions questioned me closely about Siberia, as though it were some exotic country on another continent, and envied my acquaintance with the legendary Lake Baikal. That 'freedom to travel' emphasized in the West as a major benefit of 'the defeat of Communism' is not much use to the average Russian. In six months I met no one who could afford to travel outside the Federation as a private individual and most can't afford to travel far within it. Tatyana, especially, had longed since childhood to salute Lake Baikal and visit Irkutsk where her maternal grandparents grew up. But any such journey would be an irresponsible extravagance; she and her husband were saving up to pay university fees. 'Now the children are eight and ten so for ten years and more we must save every kopek. We have to believe education can give them a future! They are intelligent; if Russia in 2020 can give them nothing, good education can give them jobs outside.'

Was Tatyana being over-optimistic? Several of my friends – Tina most recently – had deplored the lowering of academic standards, the blurring of the traditional distinction between 'university' and institute, reminiscent of the upgrading of Britain's polytechnics.

Two lively hours later (a few glasses of wine had de-stressed the quartet) my struggle to foot the bill was unavailing; where foreign guests are concerned, Russians forget about saving every kopek.

As I snuggled into my comfortable bed that night, I was haunted by a vignette of caricature quality. Waiting for the Novocherkassk bus, I saw several OAPs shuffling to and fro, peering hopefully into litter-bins. One old woman wore two left boots, both too big for her. From the bin beside me she retrieved a half-eaten sugary bun and an apple core. Moments earlier, a passing young man had spat into that bin, though Russian males usually spit towards the ground, quite often victimizing somebody's footwear.

Among a dozen familiar book jackets on Tina's shelves I had noticed H. N. H. Williamson's *Farewell to the Don*, suitable Rostov reading – or re-reading, for in 1970 I had reviewed the first edition. Trustingly Tina lent me her signed copy, despite its being inscribed to her grandfather, son of a former Imperial Army officer who had fought with Brigadier (then Major) Williamson in the Don Cossack regiment. This great-grandfather had also been at General Kaledin's side immediately after the Revolution and Tina showed me two damp-damaged photographs dated November 1917. In that month the Moscow Bolsheviks' declaration of war against General Kaledin and the Don Cossacks inspired a widespread workmen's uprising in Rostov. Although the revolutionaries briefly took over the city it was soon captured by Kaledin, with the assistance of Great-grandfather and Cossacks just back from the Eastern Front where (said Tina) their lack of battlefield discipline and their penchant for kidnapping women refugees had impressed nobody. However, the General could neither hold Rostov against the Reds nor bear the humiliation of losing the Cossack capital; in January 1919 he shot himself. Ten months later Great-grandfather was disembowelled by a platoon of Cossacks who had gone over to the Bolsheviks.

In the spring of 1919 Major Williamson volunteered to fight with the Don Cossacks as part of the ill-conceived and ultimately disastrous

British Military Mission. His personal journal, written in plain, restrained English, conveys the dreadful day-to-day realities of the Russian Civil War more cogently than anything else I have ever read. He simply told it like it was. The imperial government had been overthrown, the czar and his family had been murdered, all over the empire foreign meddlers were pouring petrol on the flames of revolution and anarchy prevailed. Troops who were White on Monday might be Red on Tuesday and vice versa. When an ancient empire collapses, and while a radical, incomprehensible alternative regime is struggling to take over, most people think only in terms of personal survival.

In general the peasants were not sufficiently informed to be either pro- or anti-Bolshevik. Writing of the White Army based in and around Rostov, Major Williamson observed:

> Recruits were largely awkward country youths with a tendency to tie wild flowers to their rifle barrels on the march and gape at the unfamiliar brick buildings. Some of them had even been known to shake with fear at the sight of a train. They fought well but, when their villages were freed, they had a habit of leaving the ranks to cultivate the land once more . . . Their officers were lazy, arrogant, ignorant, and often cowardly, chiefly because they knew their men had no heart for fighting their fellow-countrymen and because they had already once seen them desert and mutiny, and were firmly – and rightly – under the impression it could easily happen again.

Major Williamson supported the Whites because – he explains – as an Old Etonian what threatened them seemed to threaten him. Yet he was a fair-minded observer, equally critical of the ex-imperial generals' complete indifference to the welfare of their troops and of the British officers' reluctance to expose themselves to danger or even to the embarrassment of arguing with White officers about how best to use British Mission supplies. (Most were wasted or misappropriated.) As a professional soldier this young major thoroughly enjoyed fighting for a cause he believed to be right and it frustrated him that there were so few conventional battles and so many mass slaughterings of civilians – by both sides. (Nowadays military men are less sensitive on this issue.) But of course he was not even slightly tainted by wimpishness. Captured Bolshevik officers, condemned to die on the dubious evidence of terrified peasants, were shot within hours, having dug their own graves, and the Major commends their 'considerable sang-froid'.

The suffering caused to the general population by hunger, cold and disease occasionally moved Major Williamson to eloquence. There were of course no functioning hospitals, 'field' or otherwise, and 'starving, infected patients staggered about in quest of food'. During the Whites' mid-winter retreat, in overcrowded trains, to the Black Sea port of Novorossiisk, where thousands were evacuated by Allied navies, it was impossible to wash either oneself or one's clothes and the death rate from louse-borne spotted typhus – always high – went off the scale.

> An ambulance train with forty or more carriages of dead bodies had been seen with not one living soul aboard. One carriage was devoted to Sisters of Charity and doctors – all dead . . . The bodies of soldiers and civilians, men and women who had died of wounds or typhus, were being thrown out of the trains at the end of station platforms, where they were at once stripped of any clothes worth taking which only passed on the disease to the healthy who removed them . . . These awful heaps, grey-white and stiff and stacked like piles of timber for the engines, increased in size as each train passed and disgorged its dead . . . Everywhere bodies lay in all sorts of corners, those stricken with typhus remained just where they happened to fall. One Russian colonel lay dead for a fortnight in the cupboard where he crept when he was taken ill.

While helping to organize the evacuation from Novorossiisk Major Williamson himself went down with the fever and came to a week later in a Constantinople hospital – to find that while delirious he had been awarded an instant DSO.

A nasty example of two-tiered realpolitik concludes *Farewell to the Don*. When the invading Germans captured Novocherkassk in 1941 one of Major Williamson's friends, Pavlov, raised Cossack regiments to support the Nazis. In 1944 these were ordered to Italy where a year later, at war's end, they surrendered to the British. After much debate Whitehall delivered them to Stalin who promptly hanged several of their generals and exiled the rest to Siberia's grimmest labour camps. This Whitehall decision paralleled Field Marshal Alexander's treatment of Yugoslavia's Chetniks and other anti-Tito refugees. Immediately after 8 May 1945 the Chetnik 'irregulars' surrendered but on 20 May were among 26,000 men, women and children sent back to Yugoslavia by the British army, all to be slaughtered on arrival by

Tito's Partisans – not as enemy troops but as political opponents. In Nigel Nicolson's words, 'This was one of the most disgraceful actions that British troops have ever been asked to carry out.'

My stopping people in the street brought out the worst in the Rostovians. The reactions to an obviously lost foreigner, carrying a large city map (Cyrillic only), were uniformly hostile. Some glanced sideways with impatience or disdain, others walked straight on, ignoring me. In most countries non-English-speakers pause for a moment and smile while indicating their inability to help – and many try to help, despite the language barrier. Do Rostovians have some mysterious grudge against non-Russian-speakers? To my baffled indignation, two shops refused to serve me. By then even I knew the words for 'milk' and 'salami' but because I couldn't name the 'brands' – only point at them – the women behind both counters scornfully said, 'Nyet! Nyet!' while seeming to enjoy my chagrin.

At any time of day shop staff may decide to mop their floors, then they snap irritably or glare aggressively at would-be customers who chance to interrupt. In one general store I stood behind a young woman with babe in arms, toddler at foot and a too-small shopping-bag. When she dropped a glass bottle on the tiled floor two assistants screamed abuse at her while a teenage girl, looking mortified by her colleagues' reaction, rushed out to clear it up, muttering reassurances to the flustered mother.

In Gorky Park those private enterprise portaloos so common in Moscow had not yet sprouted and their free municipal equivalents were supervised by boiler-suited young women, one of whom demanded ten roubles from the foreigner. At that, a passing babushka seized my arm and said, 'Roubles nyet!' Her law-abiding stance provoked a vituperative outburst, verbal violence that sent the babushka scurrying on her way, looking scared. A remarkable number of Rostovians seem to live on a very short fuse.

On the Wednesday morning Tina left a note at Reception; a young friend of hers – Ilyana, eager for English conversation – would be in the foyer at 1.0 p.m. By the time this note reached me Wednesday had become Thursday and poor Ilyana had waited an hour in vain. Why, when she made enquiries, had no one given her my room number? And why had the security officer, a close observer of my comings and goings, denied all knowledge of the hotel's only foreign guest? When we did meet I ventured to suggest, 'Maybe a touch of xenophobia?' but Ilyana protested, 'No, no! It's a different problem, people with boring jobs can enjoy not being helpful for anyone, it's their way to feel important.'

Down on the ground (though not up in the stratosphere) Soviet planners deplored capitalism's discarding of machinery still in good working order just because something faster, bigger, smaller or more efficient had been invented. This mindset, seen by Western econo- mists as a major cause of the Soviet Union's 'uncompetitiveness', greatly appeals to me and whenever possible I used Rostov's trams. Very slowly they go on their way, serving the most deprived districts, the average tram passenger visibly poorer than the average bus passen- ger. Most tram-drivers are women, paid less than bus-drivers – usually men – and the fare is four roubles (buses five roubles, private enter- prise minibuses ten roubles).

During one long ride the tramline was blocked by a decrepit punctured taxi and never have I seen a tyre being changed so fast. Yet throughout this brief delay all the passengers fumed and one man shouted at the unfortunate taxi-wallah, then demanded to be set down at the next traffic lights. When the driver refused to risk being fined by an officer of Rostov's notoriously corrupt traffic police, he banged persistently on her cab and kept up a stream of insults (their nature seeming to shock our fellow-passengers) until the next official stop.

Rostov's best walks are in tram territory; the double tracks on narrow streets leave no room for motor vehicles. Here early nine- teenth-century dwellings line the streets, set in small neglected gardens. Pre-Stalin, prosperous Armenians occupied one of these dis- tricts where rows of three-storeyed, balconied wooden homes, intri- cately carved, overlook large courtyards. Now these houses are semi-derelict, held together by ingenious innovations, their occupants bottom-of-the-pile Cossacks whose malnourished children stand still to stare – half-nervously, half-defiantly – as the foreigner passes by.

At 8.0 a.m. on Thursday 25 March Nestor gallantly accompanied me to the freight office. I had suggested his telephoning but appar- ently visible documents were needed to avoid misunderstanding, ambivalence, indifference, general confusion. Pushkin's non-arrival dismayed but did not surprise me. The good news was that wagon No. 8531 had recovered, was on its way, would arrive at 5.40 on Sunday 28 March.

Later that day I had a Siberian-type experience, as I nostalgically thought of it. The wrong minibus took me into a hilly suburb of extraordinary ugliness on the left bank of the Don, ten miles or more from where I wanted to be. When the driver (an Azeri, a Mussulman) became aware of my error he tried to return the ten rouble fare. Then a fellow-passenger, a stout babushka, took it upon herself to find an English-speaker to help me, and the driver, being at the end of his run, signed me to wait in the taxi and bought me a polystyrene mug of coffee from a kiosk. Ten minutes later the babushka returned, beaming triumphantly, with an embarrassed teenage granddaughter in tow – her English minimal. But she led me into a small shop selling office equipment where one of the salesgirls was her friend and allowed her to telephone a fluent English-speaker who not only gave me exact directions but invited me to his nearby flat for chai and cake. Such an example of serial kindness seemed astonishing in Rostov.

During this week, all over the city, teams of municipal workers – mostly middle-aged women – were raking into piles many tons of newly exposed black leaves. (Rostov has inherited from czarist times a wealth of fine trees.) Beside the women, detachments of sullen undersized conscripts raked lethargically, being frequently chivvied. Recent advertisements glorifying the military life had omitted leaf-raking. The piles – much of it litter – were dumped by rusty earth-movers into equally rusty lorries and deposited where dacha-owners could help themselves to the leafmould.

Rostov's city cemetery, behind high walls almost opposite Hotel Turist, covers a square mile or more, but would go unnoticed by transient travellers. However, this trapped traveller spent a few hours amidst the dead one sunny afternoon, alone in the neglected wilderness. Trees abounded: elder, birch, ash, some fallen and obscuring headstones, others half-choked by brambles and vines. The drab dereliction was relieved only by occasional clumps of celandines and violets – and by a bunch of fresh daffodils on the tiny, well-kept grave of an eleven-month-old boy who died in 1959. Probably his mother would now be in her sixties.

Where names remained legible on vandalized headstones they were usually Jewish and I was reminded of Major Williamson's admiration for

> the keeness and efficiency displayed by the Jewish doctors, of which there were always one or two in each medical unit. This was the only capacity in which the Jews were allowed to serve [in the White army] and comparing their methods with that of the Orthodox Russians, it was easy to see the reason for the prominent position they had reached in every area and community where they had established themselves . . . It was their competence and energy, in fact, backed by their resentment against generations of ill-treatment and intolerance, which brought them so conspicuously to the front of the Bolshevik movement.

Only a minority buried here had been granted their biblically allotted span of three score years and ten. Three nonagenarians were exceptional; most Rostovians seemed to have died in their fifties and early sixties – many in their forties. The septuagenarians were almost invariably born in the 1870s and 1880s, thus reaching maturity before the Revolution.

One of the long, wide intersecting paths – muddy after the thaw – led to an unexpected open space, a neat area of military officers' graves and massive marble cenotaphs listing Great Patriotic War heroes. There was a certain incongruity about this reverently tended corner, given the present demoralization and degeneracy of the Federation's armed forces.

In another corner a ruined mortuary chapel, its roof supporting an uprooted ash tree, was inhabited by one of Rostov's many packs of homeless dogs (something I never saw in Siberia). Homeless but not hungry; obviously within their territories the locals feed them. At night, however, these large mongrels became rowdy; a seven-strong pack, based near Hotel Turist and favourably placed for food, sometimes howled for two hours at a stretch – no doubt warning off intruders less fortunate.

Finally I came to the in-use section at the cemetery's south end where a mortuary chapel had recently been redecorated and some graves were rather OTT. One eight-foot-high black marble monument was surmounted by an engraved life-size portrait of the deceased (1930–2002) – a veritable clone of Queen Victoria, at first glance I felt quite disorientated.

Back at Hotel Turist I found a note from Tina, this one pushed under my door. Would I care to join the family next day for a trip – starting at dawn, returning after dusk – to their dacha at Starocherkassk?

Of the Don Cossacks' several 'capitals', Starocherkassk is the oldest – founded in 1593, then for two centuries defended by sturdy fortifications and some 20,000 inhabitants, now dwindled to a village of market gardeners where a few Rostov families have dachas.

At 6.45 a.m. Tina, the children, Nestor, Razin and I set off by taxi; public transport to the village is erratic. Razin, clad in a quilted scarlet jacket, was Tina's despotic and asthmatic Peke. During the twenty-mile drive he wheezed and snuffled continuously and Tina explained, 'He's allergic to petrol but he can't be left alone for so long.' The original Sten'ka Razin, Nestor informed me, was a seventeenth-century Cossack hero, revered to this day, who led an unusually well-organized and prolonged peasant revolt against the imposition of serfdom in the Don region.

Rostov has extended its industrial tentacles in every direction and we reached open steppe only a few miles from Starocherkassk. Outside the dacha (no more than a two-roomed hut set in a half-acre of fertile black earth) I begged Nestor to let me explore on my own; he had serious work to do, this was no jolly family jaunt but the beginning of a season of hard labour to grow food for the following winter. Tina suggested a compromise; I would return for a picnic lunch, then Nestor would escort me around the museum.

Starocherkassk still feels like a town because of its many solid Cossack fort-houses, built to last in the eighteenth century, and its three churches – one a cathedral, dating from 1719 and more sensitively restored than most I had seen. The main street, too, had been spruced up for the benefit of summer tourists who are attracted in modest numbers by monthly 'Cossack fairs'. The atmosphere – Nestor had hinted at this – was no more welcoming than Rostov's, though several children were keen to relate to me, as beggars – the usual tourism spin-off. Beyond the main street narrow tracks and pathways, eroded by thaw floods, rambled between ramshackle *izbi* surrounded by untidy yards where faded, threadbare garments flapped on clotheslines and scrawny hens pecked for worms and small mongrels with tightly curled tails barked at me shrilly and their owners looked away when I smiled at them.

By lunchtime Nestor had a backache after three hours of potato planting. The children were looking mutinous after three hours of laying compost beds in the glasshouse. Tina's hands were blistered after three hours of setting up stakes for beans and peas. And Razin was complaining because Andrei had dropped his lunch (minced chicken) on the muddy floor and he was too fastidious to eat anything dirty. (Tina said, 'Too fastidious', but I thought, 'Too spoiled'. My three mongrel terriers, in the unlikely event of their being fed minced chicken, would eat it off a midden.)

Afterwards, as we walked to the museum, Nestor reflected, 'It will take some more generations for people like us to have the right sort of bodies for this sort of work. We're too tall and thin. Have you noticed Slav peasants are mostly small and wide with big muscles?' I had noticed.

Without Nestor, this museum would have seemed dull; with him, all its exhibits, linked to Cossack traditions and rebellions, inspired a flow of information about the region's economic history. A happy afternoon was had by both.

Back in Rostov, I invited the family to dine with me in a restaurant of their choice. But they were past eating, only wanted to go to bed.

14

When Fortune Scowls

SUNDAY 28 MARCH – Reunion Day! After breakfast I set off on foot, street map in hand, to determine my exit strategy for the following morning. Finding a minor road out of a big city is never easy but that was a good map; less than three hours later, after only a few wrong turnings, I was surveying my pot-holed road where it branched off from a busy dual-carriageway.

Tina had invited me for a farewell lunch, then it was time to collect Pushkin. After so much hoo-ha, our reunion felt a trifle anti-climactic; it should surely have involved some ceremony, instead of being accomplished within two minutes by exchanging a bicycle ticket for a bicycle. It seemed not quite right that there wasn't even one short form to be filled in and rubber-stamped.

Anxiously I tested the gears, a modern bicycle's Achilles' heel, but all was well. Exultantly pedalling along too-familiar streets, I recalled Eric Hobsbawm's paean in his autobiography *Interesting Times*:

> If physical mobility is an essential condition of freedom, the bicycle has probably been the greatest single device for achieving what Marx called the full realization of the possibility of being human invented since Gutenberg, and the only one without obvious drawbacks. Since cyclists travel at the speed of human reactions and are not insulated behind plate glass from nature's light, air, sounds and smells there was no better way in the 1930s – before the explosion of motor traffic – to explore a middle-sized country . . .

The hotel security man strongly objected to a bicycle being wheeled into the lift but I was on too much of a high to be intimidated. 'Get lost!' I said cheerfully, pushing the button.

After a farewell *pivo* with Nestor, I oiled and loaded Pushkin, then transferred most of my cash from money-belt to shoes and prepared one

$50 bill to be inserted next morning in the ultimate hiding place – reflecting as I did so that in this context the female anatomy is more convenient than the male, the vagina being in less frequent use than the anus.

By 6.30 we were bowling through a cool grey dawn. 'Light showers' had been forecast and the sunrise was a wan affair, ghostly rays stretching tentatively upwards from heavy horizontal clouds. In temperature and capriciousness the Don delta's spring weather closely resembles Ireland's but the lushness of an Irish March was missing. On the monochrome steppe ploughing had just started, a few obsolete machines working this legendary black earth, a landscape continuously under cultivation since at least the second millennium BC. Hereabouts the Scythian horsemen got the better of Darius's infantry and cavalry and in a characteristic aside Herodotus tells us:

> One very surprising thing helped the Persians and hampered the Scythians in these skirmishes: I mean the unfamiliar braying of the donkeys and appearance of the mules . . . Neither donkeys nor mules are bred in Scythia . . . because of the cold. This being so, the donkeys' braying caused great confusion among the Scythian cavalry; often, in the course of an attack, the sound of it so much upset the horses, which had never heard such a noise before or seen such a creature as that from which it proceeded, that they would turn short round, ears pricked, in consternation. This gave the Persians some small advantage in the campaign.

Traffic was limited to an occasional private car, farm lorry or commercial van, all exhaling the fumes associated with antiquated vehicles and adulterated petrol. As the first village appeared in the distance a small dented Lada overtook me, then stopped to offer a lift. This seemed odd: the young men's car was not bicycle-friendly. They were obviously brothers, blue-eyed and shaven-headed with snub noses and square chins, wearing soiled dungarees and wellies. Surprisingly, one spoke a little English. 'What your country? Where you go? Where you friends? Why you use this velocipede?'

Although feeling slightly uneasy I played friendly, explaining that I enjoy using a velocipede and thanking them for stopping. One said, 'Moscow is too far!' – then away they sped, leaving me wishing I had cycled on, ignoring them. But it is instinctive to respond positively to smiling faces.

The village was straggling and unpainted, its abandoned collective farm buildings the biggest structures, its dogs noisy, its few cows with sunken flanks, its inhabitants invisible. A Coca-Cola advertisement above one *izby* door, and crates of empties by the gate, marked a shop where milk might be available (my staple nourishment when cycling). But the door was decisively padlocked and no one emerged to investigate their guard-dog's hysteria.

A mile or so farther on the brothers again overtook me and stopped some thirty yards ahead. They were no longer smiling. The passenger stood in the middle of the road, arms outstretched. I beamed and waved and pedalled faster. The driver leant out, still in his seat, and silently pointed a revolver at me – the long sort, carried by Russian policemen. As I braked, almost falling off, the passenger demanded, 'Give dollars!' I took out my purse, holding a hundred or so roubles, and emptied it into his hand. He scowled, tossed the notes to his brother and said, 'Give *more* money!'

I shook my head. 'No more, until the bank in Voronezh.' Both brothers sniggered their disbelief and the passenger stepped close to feel under my jacket and sweater, his fingers cold on my skin, his touch professional; this was not the first time he had sought a money-belt. Deftly he unzipped the pouch and cleared it of $200 worth of small denomination rouble notes, suited to rural commerce. But this didn't satisfy him. Angrily he pointed to my shoes and repeated, 'Give dollars!' When I feigned incomprehension he bent down and undid my shoelaces; these were indeed experienced tourist-robbers, a common enough breed around Black Sea coastal resorts. The driver was still leaning through the window, his gun more a stage prop than a threat. I had no fear of being shot dead if I refused to co-operate; the Don delta isn't the Caucasus and small-time robbers (off-duty policemen?) would be unlikely to risk killing a foreigner twenty miles from Rostov. But as one man could easily overpower me I meekly handed over my shoe-stashed dollars. The gratified brothers smiled again, then went on their way – not interested, curiously, in my other possessions: Swiss knife, camera, a velocipede worth many hundreds of dollars.

Turning back towards Rostov, I felt quite shaken; being robbed is unpleasant, however mild the procedure – though in this case my having been mentally prepared lessened the shock. That apart, disappointment and frustration devastated me – but not anger, an emotion rarely stimulated when the comparatively poor rob the comparatively rich. Anger is more appropriately directed towards the greedy, those who cloak their immorality in respectability.

My options were clear: (a) borrow enough from Tina to fund the ride towards Moscow, (b) telephone Anna and ask her to transfer dollars to a Rostov bank, (c) return to Moscow by train that night. I at once discarded (a); Tina had allowed me to pay for the Starocherkassk taxi, an un-Russian concession suggesting no spare roubles. As for (b), I had by then collected an anthology of horror stories about Russian banking delays. The most bizarre concerned twenty-seven kopeks, an amount too minuscule to be translated into our currencies, which over a three-week period had absorbed eighteen and a half hours of a Tynda friend's time. (The bank had discovered an error; it owed Igor twenty-seven kopeks and legally he was not empowered to cancel the debt – I'm not making this up, there is written evidence.) Then I faced the fact that (c) had most appeal; I didn't really want to risk another robbery. Yet I intensely regretted losing this opportunity to discover how a solo foreign cyclist, dependent at sundown on the locals, would fare in the villages of European Russia. My hunch was that the stranger's vulnerability/trust would dissipate the regional wariness. That's how it is almost everywhere else I've been, awheel or on foot, and why should this part of the world be different?

As I freewheeled down to the railway station it was drizzling greyly, which seemed fitting. Thereafter complications proliferated. No ticket was available for that evening; I must wait until 4.40 a.m. Anyway dollars were unacceptable to Russian Railways. As the station's Bureau de Change was not yet in business I must go to a bank, which would certainly not admit Pushkin. But a loaded bicycle, however securely locked, couldn't be left on the street for up to an hour. With difficulty I found the 'Onward Baggage' office only to learn that my 4.40 service had no freight wagon, and to travel coupé a bicycle must be converted into an item slim enough to fit on the overhead luggage shelf. In a non-cycling environment, how to find the necessary mechanic? And the job couldn't be done before I had roubles to pay for it . . . By this stage I was perhaps showing the strain. Apart from my disappointment, I felt physically exhausted – had cycled fifty miles, was out of training. The woman in charge of the Onward Baggage weighing machine looked at me with some concern, then beckoned a porter, a young man with a smattering of English. When pooled with my smattering of Russian, we came to an agreement; while I went to the bank, Pushkin could be left in this guarded zone, temporarily for free.

The Mostbank queue was forty minutes long. Next I searched for the sports shop I had vaguely noticed because a few bicycles hung in its window. But where exactly was it? It was at the far end of Rostov's main boulevard, ulitsa Bolshaya Sadovaya. A bus returned me to the station where I put the panniers in a Left Luggage locker two platforms away from Onward Baggage. Pedalling back to the shop, I persuaded an unfriendly young man to do the dismantling. He then watched me hauling my unwieldy package onto the pavement where I waited for a taxi in a cold downpour.

A freakish event rounded off that grim day. I was on my way to fetch the panniers before settling down in the waiting-room when, going through an automatic door – high and wide, leading from ticket hall to platform – one half of the door forcefully slammed shut, flinging me to the ground. I landed on my left side, three yards from the door, momentarily too winded to stand up and too bemused by the novelty of this situation to wonder if I'd been damaged. The platform was deserted but for a Railway Policeman, standing nearby, who pretended not to notice my prone form. As I slowly picked myself up, registering only minor damage (a bruised upper arm), he strolled away. Turning to survey the door, I saw his colleague standing just inside it; he too must have witnessed the incident but when I tried to interest him in this alarming defect he smirked and shrugged and also strolled away.

The cost of Rostov's 'prestige project' station had not, Tina told me, been admitted and people could only guess who, locally, might have fielded the kickbacks. According to Nestor, most citizens resented it and we agreed that honest architects must have a professional term of opprobrium for such excesses. Ugliness is not the main issue here; even if as beautiful as the adjacent original station (1880s), this extravagance would be unforgivable in the impoverished Federation.

The average Russian train passenger's luggage is awkward and heavy, yet two long, steep stairways led from ticket hall to waiting-spaces – an irrationality comparable to the white elephant BAM and monster dams producing unwanted electricity. While ascending, I overtook a babushka struggling with a weighty load, slowly heaving it from step to step. Three young men were also ascending yet none offered help. When I did so the woman looked bewildered. At the head of the stairs is the first of three vast interconnected waiting-spaces, this one dimly lit and empty – totally empty, serving no purpose. The others hold hundreds and hundreds of small black metal chairs which may all be occupied the day Rostov hosts a World Cup Final. At intervals throughout the night the black and white tiled floors were mopped by elderly women with headscarves and swollen legs and tired eyes. Teams of adolescent boys and girls, wearing blue and yellow overalls and looking quite jolly, spent hours pushing ladders and buckets around and scrubbing white walls and yellow doors. Three cafés sold overpriced junk food and the prowling Railway Police barked 'Nyet!' at passengers who had brought their own sustenance. And high above shone the ceilings – made of something silvery reflecting everybody's movements in a curiously desta-bilizing way. All that mirrored activity overhead drew one's gaze upward, as the flickering of a silenced TV set draws one's eye to its corner.

Other long, steep stairways led down to Platform 1; tubular walk-ways gave access to more distant platforms. Exploring, I wondered how to cope if my train didn't halt at No. 1, how to get my peculiarly unwieldy luggage across pedestrian bridges.

Those dire waiting-spaces further lowered my spirits and I spent the last two hours on Platform 1, strolling up and down under a starry sky and considering the St Petersburg option. Perhaps a week in the Hermitage was what I needed as an antidote to twelve days in Rostov-on-Don. When the 4.40 arrived at No. 3 my luck turned. An Onward Baggage clerk who had earlier befriended me now loaded Pushkin and the panniers on a trolley, raced a long way down No. 1, illegally crossed two sets of tracks, paused to look at my ticket, raced a long way up No. 3 and with a big smile delivered me to my *provodnitsa*.

I slept most of the way to Moscow.

15

A Pessimistic Postscript

IF YOU TAKE your Hermitage seriously, and are limited to eight days, there isn't much time left over for St Petersburg's many other wonders – or, indeed, for more than one-third of the Hermitage itself. In general I'm an inefficient sightseer, wandering and drifting and leaving things to chance. But on the banks of the Néva I changed gear, planned my days, set off before sunrise for a three-hour exploration on foot or by bus, clocked into the Hermitage at 10.0 sharp, left at 5.30 and collapsed in the down-market Dragon Luck bar, almost beside Vladimir Putin's boyhood home and primary school (now a technical college). 'Piter's' up-market bars feel rather unwelcoming; peering through the doorways, it is obvious that everything will be overpriced and a shabby babushka scorned.

As the sheer beauty of this city overwhelmed me, my ambivalent attitude to the fulfilment of Peter the Great's dream went into abeyance. While walking along the Neva Embankment with the Winter Palace on one's left, the University Embankment across the river and the Senate and Synod ahead, I stopped thinking about those countless thousands of workers who were mercilessly sacrificed to create all this in an area previously uninhabited by anyone because of its swamps and diseases.

That said, one inevitably remains conscious of St Petersburg's artificiality. As Alexander II commented to Otto von Bismarck in 1861, 'Russia must not be judged by Petersburg, of all the empire's towns the least Russian one.' When Peter the Great decided to wave his imperial wand and build a city to rival Venice and Amsterdam, where not even a hamlet existed before, he had to depend on Western European architects, sculptors, stonemasons, engineers and 'experts' of every sort. And even today, despite the historic patina acquired in the course of two centuries as an imperial capital, Petersburg's centre

– the beauty that overwhelms – doesn't feel truly Russian. The rest does – and the rest contains most of this city's 4.2 million inhabitants. Early morning bus or tram rides took me, for miles, through districts as wretched as any I had seen in the Russian Federation, districts that gained nothing from the restoration of the centre in preparation for its 2003 tricentennial celebrations. (Shades of Potemkin.)

A Muscovite acquaintance, a young woman met as we queued for ice cream near Palace Square, put it pithily. 'Sure it's lovely,' said she, looking around. 'Only it's not real – here Muscovites don't feel comfortable. It's all an imperial playground, how one man wanted Russia to be – modern, powerful, rich – many big ships, many loud operas! But building a stone capital in a crazy place couldn't change Russia.'

When next I visited my family near Trento, a beautiful little city in the Dolomites that has grown naturally over many centuries, St Petersburg came even more clearly into focus as a paradoxical newcomer to Europe's urban ranks. In Trento one senses the passage (often troubled) of the millennia and the city belongs where it is; was created by its natives or their cultural kin. St Petersburg is an implant, could not possibly have been created by Russians, was visualized by Peter as a 'Europeanizing' turning point for his empire but in fact was a profound obeisance to an artistically more sophisticated civilization. (Or was it, as one of my Muscovite friends insists, 'a gesture of psychological subservience'?) Anyway, Peter might have seemed Greater had he been less architecturally and more judicially influenced by Western Europe.

The Dragon Luck bar, I soon discovered, was popular with university students, the sort who have to count their kopeks. And the ratio of outgoing English-speakers was high; in more than miles, Piter is a long way from Irkutsk and Khabarovsk. One quartet of regulars – deducing 'journalist' from my diary-writing – invited me to their table and quickly we became boon companions. They formed two 'items', in today's (or is it yesterday's?) jargon: Misha and Olga, Lazar and Vera – all reading Politics and Economics, with varying degrees of enthusiasm. On the first evening we talked about me (their choice of topic); after that things got more interesting.

When I reported my pro-Putin findings in both 2002 and '04 – most people praising him for being strong on Chechnya, honest, hardworking, not a drinker – everyone laughed, kindly.

'You were in *Siberia*!' said Olga. 'Now you're in Piter where we *think*! Putin is a mistake, not a leader. He never tried to be a leader, it happened to him by accident. Always, he was being led, doing jobs well because they were the right size for him and he obeyed orders. It's true he works hard but –'

Misha interrupted. 'You're wrong, he led the FSB [Federal Security Service].'

'*You're* wrong!' retorted Olga. 'Really Tatyana Dyachenko [Yeltsin's daughter] led it and he obeyed her. He got voted President because people liked sending the army back to Chechnya for revenge, to punish Chechnya for winning first time – and for terrorist bombs. People didn't know that was going to happen anyway, it wasn't Putin's decision. Again he was good at obeying orders – and lucky. He came in time to get all the praise for being tough.'

Lazar said, 'He's not a bad man, like Yeltsin. He's not corrupt. But he hasn't many brains. That's why he's afraid of power. I'd guess he doesn't enjoy it, not knowing how to use it. I believe he loves Russia, wants to get us respected in the world.'

'You're joking!' said Vera – then echoed the other Olga, the Novosibirsk student. 'Look at his face – it's KGB, like his mind. He loves Russia in a KGB way. Is that how we want to be loved?'

'It's worse than that,' said Olga. 'He's so stupid he thinks Chechnya can be OK in the end if we kill enough Chechens. Lazar's right, he's afraid of political power, can't use it, prefers military power. That's how the last czar behaved, here in Piter in January 1905. It didn't work then and it won't work now.'

Misha said, 'I don't think he's stupid or not enjoying power. OK, he never looked for it, Yeltsin gave it. But now he's got it he won't let go. He'll be a KGB-trained dictator with other KGB minds helping. We need more revolution – a big one!'

By this stage Anatoly had joined us: Lazar's half-brother, in his thirties, studying corporate law. He looked sternly at Misha and said, 'Revolution? No way! So we know our President's not one for human rights and free speech, wants us to do what he thinks best for Russia. But I wouldn't call him arrogant, he only hates being argued with. He believes we need discipline, not being confused by party politics like people in the West. Couldn't he be right? Are we ready for that sort of complicated freedom? Under Yeltsin, with no discipline, we had chaos.'

'And what have we now?' asked Olga. 'He *is* arrogant because he has no plan, doesn't know what's best for Russia, doesn't like arguing because if you've no plan you can't argue.'

'That's why I'm afraid!' said Vera. 'No plan, a vacuum, KGB minds at the top – people with fascist plans all worked out could come and use those minds.'

Misha nodded. 'That's why I say we need more revolution *now*.'

Anatoly looked annoyed, then shrugged. 'I see no danger. It doesn't matter if our President would like to dictate – we've moved on, it couldn't happen. Look at the corporate interests, Russian and foreign, wanting our resources on the open market, not controlled by a dictator. They'd have him assassinated if he seemed threatening. People with oil interests – from anywhere, any nationality – will kill for oil. The West maybe doesn't know that – all can be covered up, smoothed over. But we know it. Chechnya is all about oil. Same in Afghanistan and Iraq – and Georgia and Ukraine, in different ways being kept under control.'

'He seemed threatening when first elected,' said Vera. 'Then he talked like Stalin about "liquidating the oligarchs as a class". That got him in a muddle – same time he was wanting foreign investment so we can have a fast-growing economy. And jailing billionaires puts foreigners off.'

Olga said to me, 'Seen from abroad, he needs to look like a free-market democrat – not to be one, only to seem one. Seen at home, he needs to look too clever for the oligarchs – you don't know how much they're *hated*! Has he enough brains for that tightrope? No!'

'It's good he's not a hypocrite at home,' said Lazar. 'He doesn't pretend to us he likes public political debate and opposition parties and all that.'

On which positive note I took my leave.

Vladimir Putin is very much a Piter boy who has lived mostly in his birthplace, never wished to move to Moscow, as President has surrounded himself with Piter allies and plans to retire to Piter. Peter Truscott, in his shrewd and entertaining study of Putin the politician, *Putin's Progress* (2004), mentions an improbable link between Putin and Rasputin. The former's paternal grandfather (Spiridon Ivanovich, from a village north-west of Moscow) became a celebrated chef in

Petersburg's Astoria Hotel and cooked for many famous guests including Grigory Rasputin, who tipped him generously (one rouble when his monthly wage was 100 roubles).

Putin's father, Vladimir Spiridonovich, was born in 1911 in a rented flat on Gorokhovaya Street near the brooding bulk of St Isaac's Cathedral (one of Piter's few charmless buildings). During the Civil War, when the Whites announced that having taken Petrograd they would hang a Red from every street lamp, fear and famine drove the Putins back to their village of Pominovo where numerous Putin cousins still live.

In 1932 Putin's parents (both aged seventeen when they married in Pominovo) moved to what was now 'Leningrad' and with friends shared a semi-detached house not far from Peter the Great's answer to Versailles: Peterhof. While Vladimir worked in a factory his wife Maria swept streets; war had disrupted her village school education. Then Vladimir was conscripted into the submarine fleet and, at the start of the Great Patriotic War (June 1941), transferred to an emergency branch of the NKVD, forerunner of the KGB.

Vladimir and Maria barely survived the 900-day Siege of Leningrad during which a million out of the city's three million inhabitants died of wounds, cold, disease, and (mainly) starvation. Maria's brother Ivan, a naval captain of the first rank, had access to a few extra rations and was based at the Soviet navy's Smolny headquarters. He probably saved his sister's life but the Putins lost two sons, aged six months and five years. On the battlefield Vladimir was badly injured – permanently maimed; after months in hospital he became foreman of a munitions factory. When the blockade was broken in 1944 his factory allocated him one room, twenty metres square, in a fifth-floor communal flat in central Leningrad – just around the corner from the Dragon Luck bar. And there the Putins lived for the next twenty-five years.

On 7 October 1952 – as Stalin approached death and I prepared for my twenty-first birthday party – Vladimir Putin was born in Snegeryov maternity hospital. Soon after came his furtive baptism in one of Petersburg's most beautiful churches, the Cathedral of the Transfiguration of the Saviour – furtive because his Papa, a fervent atheist since boyhood and a lifelong Party member, would not have approved. The new parents, aged forty-one, had resigned themselves to childlessness and 'Volodya's' birth seemed something of a miracle, at least to his devout mother. (How would she have reacted had she been able to visualize him forty-eight years on, President of all the Russias?) Volodya grew to manhood in that one room where the three Putins slept, lived and washed; there was no bathroom, no running water, just a weekly visit to the public *banya*. In the communal 'kitchen' – a narrow, windowless, unventilated hallway – several families shared one small gas cooker.

This baby was too precious for kindergarten care; at the end of her two-months' maternity leave Maria took a variety of menial part-time jobs near home while Vladimir rose daily at 5.0 a.m. to get to his distant factory on time.

At primary school Volodya didn't do well and became, according to his own account, a pre-pubertal courtyard hooligan named on the police list of lads to be watched. Several of his childhood friends were jailed while still in their teens. Once the local Comrades' Court strongly recommended that Volodya be banished to a 'special boarding school for difficult children' – the Soviet euphemism for borstal. Mama wept and pleaded with the court, Papa guaranteed to sort the boy out and gave him yet another belting. The courtyard scene around Baskov Lane was tough (and still is, from what I glimpsed of it) so the undersized but truculent Volodya decided, aged eleven, to take up self-defensive *samba*, a Soviet judo/wrestling hybrid. For nine years he attended two-hour classes, three times a week, in a gym near the Finland station – and saluted that famous statue of Lenin each time he passed. He was, as he later described himself, 'a pure and utterly successful product of Soviet patriotic education'. In 1972 his trainer advised him to concentrate on judo and four years later he became Leningrad's judo champion, with Olympic potential – but by then he had another priority. This rigorous gym regime, and his father's ascetic example, no doubt explain an enduring aversion to alcohol and nicotine.

In 1969 the Putins could at last afford to buy a three-room dacha, twenty-five miles east of the city, also without piped water; its earth-closet helped to fertilize the fruit and vegetable garden.

Children commonly fantasize about spying for their country – bravely sabotaging vital communications systems, exposing plots to poison-gas the nation, brilliantly deciphering hitherto uncrackable codes. I was given to this myself, at primary school. Volodya started a little later, aged thirteen, when he began to read spy stories. Aged sixteen he was past the fantasy stage and literally knocking on the KGB's door – its Leningrad headquarters on Liteiny Street was less than ten minutes' walk from his home. Only on his third visit did he meet a KGB officer who was unimpressed by his starry-eyed patriotism but gave him the information he sought. To have even a faint chance of being considered for the KGB he needed top marks at university level in Russian language and literature, fluency in at least one foreign language and a law degree with special emphasis on constitutional law. He regarded his own language and literature as a pleasurable hobby and had already done three years of German – but how could a youth with no money, no connections and no exceptional talent get into Russia's most esteemed Law Faculty, founded by Peter the Great? Only ten out of one hundred places were open to high school pupils; military cadets filled the rest.

Now the erstwhile juvenile delinquent became a swot, won his place, continued to swot and at the age of twenty-two was invited to join the KGB, who had of course been keeping him and his family and friends under surveillance for the previous six years. At this stage most new-hatched spies, as members of a privileged though not very well-paid service, quickly acquired a new social circle; old friends might retard their promotion or hamper their unsavoury endeavours. (One of Putin's jobs during his initiation period had him spying on Leningrad's dissident and religious groups.) However, this freshman did it differently, remaining loyal to all his friends then and later. An admirable trait, loyalty, provided you can recognize those circumstances in which it ceases to be a virtue.

For the next ten years Putin plodded along prosaic paths; none led to the realization of those teenage dreams of daring deeds done in darkness. Then, in 1985, came the longed-for foreign posting – though only to dozy Dresden, on the wrong side of the Iron Curtain, where spying was to prove about as exciting as bank-clerking. A few months after Mikhail Gorbachev came to power, Putin and his twenty-seven-year-old wife Lyudmila (they had married in 1983) arrived in East Germany with their baby daughter. However dull, Dresden represented promotion; for the first time in either of their lives they were living in comparative luxury, in their first home. In Leningrad, they had had to share with Putin's parents.

In 1986, soon after the birth of another daughter, Putin was promoted to Lieutenant-Colonel and second-in-command at the eight-man Dresden office. Then came the Fall of the Wall and the Soviet Empire's meltdown, leaving him dazed and adrift. Back in Leningrad in January 1990, his posting curtailed by six months, he was one of many thousands of KGB officers abruptly made redundant by unforeseen events and facing a challenging transition – from being a minor member of the ruling class to being a jobless middle-ranking KGB officer with no powerful friends, an undistinguished CV, a wife and two children and no home. The senior Putins, now living in a three-room flat, made space for the younger generations – an unsatisfactory arrangement, especially as Maria and Lyudmila were not kindred spirits.

Many of Putin's colleagues rapidly slid into the shadowy world of Leningrad's mafia-led free market; but it seems Putin wasn't tempted. As he himself primly put it several years later, 'It was difficult in those days to do business within the parameters of the law.' The implication that things have changed since 'those days' is rather misleading.

Although in theory still entitled to a KGB salary, Putin was now among the millions of Russians going unpaid month after month. Then loyalty brought a reward; an old friend organized his appointment as vice-rector of Leningrad University. This ostensibly administrative job was reserved for retired KGB officers whose main duty was to spy on foreign students. Putin at once settled down to prepare a doctoral dissertation and thought vaguely about a legal career in the private sector.

In 1991 loyalty was again rewarded. Anatoly Sobchak, a former law lecturer now posing as a reformist politician, had just been elected Mayor of Leningrad and needed competent administrators. An old friend from university days recommended Putin to the new mayor who remembered 'Volodya' as an exceptionally hard-working student. In due course Sobchak chose him as one of his three deputy mayors, thus unwittingly putting Putin's foot on the lowest rung of the long ladder to the presidency.

Around this time 'Leningrad' reverted to 'St Petersburg' (by referendum) and in Putin's new office in Smolny, now Piter's administrative HQ, he replaced a photograph of Lenin with a portrait of Peter the Great – while remaining a full member of the Party until President Yeltsin banned it in November 1992. This seems typical; wherever there's a fence, Putin likes to sit on it.

Promotion came rapidly: from being chairman of Piter's foreign relations committee to being Sobchak's second-in-command – first deputy mayor; in our terms, an unelected civil servant.

Anatoly Sobchak was generally accepted by the outside world as someone dedicated to democratic reforms. He revelled in the social side of representing a great city (numerous formal receptions, meeting celebrities at the airport – duties loathed by Putin and his wife) while shirking the monotony of city administration. His second-in-command and other subordinates were left to deal with such matters and soon Putin felt 'in charge'. During his reign, the West invested in Piter as never before or since; he brought major banks to the city, and also Gillette and Coca-Cola. According to Yury Novolodsky, another of Putin's Law Faculty friends who worked under him in Smolny, 'The whole system of government for five million citizens had to be built from scratch in the early 1990s. It's the system we still have and it was created by Sobchak and Putin.'

Putin greatly enjoyed his job, was energized by its importance, didn't mind having to work twelve hours a day six days a week – or being a mafia target. However, the frequency of contract killings in Piter prompted him to sleep with an air gun by his bed. 'Honest Putin' was certainly in a minority in Sobchak's City Hall, notorious for its intimacy with the Tambov mafia, one of Russia's most influential organized crime gangs. From Piter's military colleges Tambov reps regularly recruited cadets trained in martial arts. Increasingly the convivial though moody Sobchak was attracting Fraud Squad attention while his wife, Lyudmila Borisovna, conspicuous in business circles, had a well-deserved reputation for being able to organize useful 'introductions'. In a glorious kettle/pot moment, even Yeltsin eventually conceded, 'Of course not everyone in Sobchak's entourage was clean.'

Probably Putin would have lived happily ever after as Piter's first deputy mayor had Sobchak not lost the May 1996 election. (By then the title had changed: governors were being elected to replace mayors.) The Sobchak re-election campaign had been run by Putin and when Vladimir Yakovlev, another deputy mayor, won by 2 per cent Putin revealed his incomprehension of Western-style democracy by furiously denouncing Yakovlev as a 'traitor'. This lacuna was to become more and more evident in Moscow.

Having lost his mayoral clout, Sobchak took fright and fled from the Fraud Squad, with Putin's assistance, to enjoy a long holiday in Paris. Again Putin was jobless and dazed. The possibility that such a powerful figure as Sobchak might be voted out of office hadn't entered his rigid KGB mind, which explains why he wasn't the best choice to run the re-election campaign. Governor Yakovlev invited him to work with the new administration, keeping his old job, but he spurned the offer knowing he would no longer be 'in charge'.

Soon after, signals came from Moscow hinting at a post in the Presidential administration. Peter Truscott plausibly suggests that the new Governor wanted Putin off the local scene and, being 'close to the Yeltsin family (unlike Sobchak) . . . clearly had the influence to get Putin offered a job in Moscow'. As the months passed, promised opportunities glowed then faded; under Yeltsin, the Kremlin's infighting made for unpredictability. More months passed and Putin's morale sank to its lowest ebb; he seriously considered becoming a taxi-driver to feed the family. Quite often Fate hits a man when he's down and a double blow was delivered during a visit to the family dacha. Putin had saved some US $5,000 – a touchingly non-oligarchic nest-egg – and like all sensible Russians he distrusted banks. The dollars were stashed away for an even rainier day behind his bed, where they went up in smoke when the *banya* stove overheated one evening and the dacha was burnt to the ground.

St Petersburgers stand by one another to an extent remarkable even in Russia where regional solidarity has deep roots. Eventually Alexei Kudrin, former deputy mayor of St Petersburg and now running the President's Main Control Directorate, had a word with Alexei Bolshakov, former first deputy of the Executive Committee of the Soviet Leningrad City Council, now deputy Prime Minister – who had a word with Pavel Borodin, Director of the President's General Affairs department. At last the door to the Kremlin swung open and a revitalized Putin took up his new post as Borodin's second-in-command, with responsibility for state property owned abroad and for foreign economic relations.

In 1997 Putin moved up, replacing Alexei Kudrin, and in 1998 he moved farther up, becoming deputy head of management in President Yeltsin's administration. Now his boss was Valentin Yumashev, a member of 'the family', as Yeltsin's coterie of relatives, friends and advisers was popularly known. In 1994–95 Yumashev had been regularly observed, by Yeltsin's then bodyguard, General Alexander Korzhakov, depositing in the Presidential office a suitcase holding $16,000 in cash, the monthly interest on the President's London Barclays account.

When Putin came to Moscow the coterie's most scandalous member was Tatyana Dyachenko, Yeltsin's daughter, who laboured daily in the Kremlin on behalf of her semi-invalid father. She was married to Aeroflot's Director, Valery Okulov, a retired pilot and bosom pal of Boris Berezovsky, then a valued 'family' member though later repudiated. He controlled the state airline and had originally bought his way into the 'family' by publishing the first volume of Yeltsin's memoirs, *Notes of a President*, and lodging $3 million worth of mainly unearned royalties in that Barclays account.

Tatyana Dyachenko soon noticed Putin as a useful sort of person, not given to questioning orders or launching personal initiatives – an ideal person, in fact, to head the FSB, heir to the domestic security section of the KGB. Its latest chief, Nikolai Kovalev, a former KGB officer, had antagonized the 'family' by setting up well-equipped anti-corruption units. Incidentally, Andrei Sakharov, the dissident nuclear scientist long hounded by the KGB, once described that force as 'the least corrupt Soviet institution'.

Back in the Lubyanka, this time in the Director's office, Putin made the best of a promotion he hadn't wanted but couldn't refuse; he was now much more interested in serving in government or the Presidential administration.

Meanwhile Sobchak had returned to St Petersburg where the Fraud Squad were keeping him under observation. As part of a much-publicized anti-corruption campaign, the Federation's Prosecutor-General, Yury Skuratov, had resolved to curb him. In November 1998, when Skuratov's office issued an arrest warrant, Sobchak was rushed to Piter's best hospital with a heart problem and Putin travelled from Moscow to sit by his old friend's bedside. Yeltsin relates the sequel in the second volume of his memoirs, *Midnight Diaries*:

> Thanks to the holidays, the city was quiet. [7 November is a public holiday.] Using his connections in St Petersburg, Putin made a deal with a private airline and brought Sobchak out to Finland. From there

Sobchak made his way to Paris. Sobchak was ordered not to leave town so he was being followed. But they were not watching too carefully, probably because they didn't think anyone would help a man who was five minutes away from finding himself behind bars in Kresty Prison . . . Later, when I learned about what Putin had done, I felt a profound sense of respect for and gratitude towards him.

Naturally Putin denied having enabled his mentor to abscond but we needn't take this too seriously. The FSB's 'prostitutes in a sauna' ploy, during the 1999 Fimaco scandal, surrounds his probity with a swarm of question marks.

This mind-numbingly complex scandal, widely reported in the international media when first exposed, involved more than eight hundred government and Central Bank officials. Many of the accused bankers, oligarchs and senior officials (including the former deputy Prime Minister, Anatoly Chubais) belonged to Yeltsin's inner circle while quite a number were 'family' members. This however did not deter Prosecutor-General Skuratov and Prime Minister Yevgeny Primakov from doggedly pursuing them, with intent to imprison; Berezovsky was one of the many for whom arrest warrants were issued. Yeltsin and the 'family' were both angered and rattled; this scandal was linked to the August 1998 rouble collapse, which brought Russia to the brink of bankruptcy, and the IMF had demanded an in-depth investigation. Fimaco's directors had 'disappeared' billions of dollars of IMF loans and the paper trail led directly through the Kremlin to the Presidential residence.

Putin then saw to it that an FSB videotape, supposedly showing Skuratov interacting with two prostitutes at *banya*-time, was given to the press and shown all over Russia on State TV on 16 March 1999. The Prosecutor-General, and many others, accused the FSB of forgery but Skuratov's reputation had been demolished, he would have to go soon – and Putin was present as Yeltsin told him so.

The provision of that video at such a sensitive moment proved Putin's loyalty to the 'family' and won their gratitude. The FSB Director became simultaneously Secretary of the pivotal Security Council whose previous Secretary, Nikolai Bordyuzha, had lost favour by openly supporting Prime Minister Primakov's moral fumigations. Less than two months later, Yeltsin sacked Primakov.

In May 1999 the Duma Communists sought impeachment proceedings against Yeltsin but were bought off at $30,000 per head – a trifling sum, in the circles under consideration. Shortly after, Yeltsin registered 18 per cent support in a nationwide opinion poll.

Come the autumn of 1999, the alcohol-ravaged and deservedly reviled Yeltsin had to plan for retirement. Now his sole concern was to put in place a President who would guarantee immunity from prosecution to the 'family'; by then their unfathomable corruption was public knowledge around the world. Sergei Stepashin, Primakov's successor as Prime Minister, was seen as 'promising' – until he defied orders to block various threatening probes and, on a visit to the US, boasted of his resolve to bring Russia's oligarchs to heel or to jail. Within less than three months of his appointment, he had been replaced by Putin. And then, on New Year's Eve 1999, to the bemusement of the whole Federation, this virtually unknown administrator – without intellectual brilliance, oratorical talent or physical presence – was named by Yeltsin as the candidate he would like to see taking over the Presidency in 2000. 'A nobody from nowhere', wrote one astounded Russian analyst – presumably not a St Petersburger.

Yeltsin's stage-managed resignation, as the third millennium began, made Prime Minister Putin acting-President. The Yeltsin immunity decree, dated 31 December 1999, is entitled 'On Guarantees for the President of the Russian Federation and His Family Members after Completion of His Exercise of Power in Office'. Putin signed it in the small hours of 1 January 2000. Peter Truscott reports: 'Yeltsin was awarded a generous pension, state security protection, medical care for him and his immediate family, and retained the Gorky-9 state dacha for his personal use. The cost to the Russian taxpayer of looking after the Yeltsin family is over $1.4 million per year.' In a less grotesque world, the Yeltsin family would be scraping by on those $16,000 per month. (After Putin's election as President, on 26 March, his Duma supporters organized a similar deal for all Russian presidents, current and future.)

Later on 1 January 2000, Putin gave thought to a potential disaster which was also a personal embarrassment. The misdeeds of Pavel Borodin, under whom he had worked in the General Affairs department (his first Kremlin job), were becoming bigger and bolder, reaching a critical mass that could blow apart the new regime. Yet 'loyalty' required that Borodin's exit from the Kremlin should be tactfully arranged. Putin therefore appointed him Secretary of the Russia–Belarus Union, in which capacity, a year later, he attended President George W. Bush's first inauguration. On his way home he was arrested in New York, at John F. Kennedy airport, and charged with bribery and money-laundering. That must have been a big laundry. Geneva's Chief Prosecutor, Bernard Bertossa, had issued a warrant through Interpol charging Borodin and his family with accepting $25 million in bribes from the Swiss-based Mercata Trading and Engineering Company – a shell company owned by Viktor Stolpovskikh, a Russian 'biznizman'. Following Borodin's extradition from the US to Switzerland, the Russian Foreign Office protested and vowed to 'take all necessary steps' on his behalf. When he declined to co-operate with the Swiss authorities Moscow (that is, Russia's taxpayers) bailed him out and on his arrival home the prosecutors could find no evidence against him. Putin had ordered that the case be dropped – and not only out of loyalty. Had it been pursued, tons of ordure would have hit the air-conditioner.

Within days of 'Volodya' becoming Prime Minister his father died, after a long illness; his mother had died the previous year. Ever a loving and loyal son – and here was no ulterior motive – Volodya had made time to visit his parents every weekend, no matter what his official duties might be.

Filial virtues aside, to describe Putin as 'honest' is plainly absurd. If someone repeatedly colludes in massive corruption – though never putting their own hand in the till – how can they be so described? And in Putin's case collusion led directly to the Presidency. Not that this sort of corruption is peculiar to Russia. Marta Andreasen, the European Commission's former Chief Accountant, was sacked for exposing the workings of the Commission's internal financial controls. Those workings enable 'immune' officials annually to defraud EU taxpayers of at least €900 million. US soldiers and UN officials who commit crimes here, there and everywhere enjoy immunity for reasons unclear to the general public. Corporate criminals who bribe, intimidate and reduce whole populations to destitution enjoy immunity – and seek to reinforce it through the World Trade Organization. The US administration enjoys immunity when it sets up prison camps furnished with instruments of torture in defiance of the Geneva

Conventions – or invades sovereign states unthreatening to the US. I could go on . . .

I met no one who could honestly express optimism about Russia's future. Free marketeers are running amok while government support is withdrawn from the poorest. Putin's regime, ever more daringly dictatorial, allows the army to commit crimes in Chechnya of which Western leaders wish to know nothing. Ominously, the septuagenarian Professor Tamara Pechernikova is back in the courtrooms, she who as a young consultant psychiatrist made many KGB-inspired 'schizophrenia' diagnoses of dissidents. Under Putin she and other veterans of the 'compulsory psychiatric treatment' era are again giving evidence, this time in defence of military personnel charged with torturing, murdering and raping Chechen civilians. Meanwhile, in the background, Green groups concerned to avert even more environmental tragedy are having their offices and homes raided, their computers confiscated and their personal property vandalized or stolen by the FSB.

Anna Politkovskaya lists some of the positions held by KGB/FSB officers in 2004, after President Putin's re-election:

> These include key ministries, in which they occupy the key positions: the President's office (two deputy directors, the heads of the staffing and information departments); the Security Council (deputy secretary); the government administrative apparatus; the ministries of defence, foreign affairs, justice, the nuclear industry, taxes and revenues, internal affairs, press affairs, television, radio and mass media; the State Customs and Excise Committee; the Russian Agency for National Reserves; the Committee for Financial Recovery – and so on.

Given its location, I should have been paying $150 instead of $15 a night for my B&B on Nevsky Prospekt, midway between the Moscow railway station and the Hermitage (twelve minutes' walk from both), on the fifth floor of a nineteenth-century mansion block. From my window I looked directly down on what are reputed to be 'the finest sculptural representations of horses in Europe' – Peter Klodt's *Horse Tamers*, cast in bronze, rearing powerfully on the Anichkov Bridge, itself a small gem spanning the short, canal-like Fontanka river. Across the river, on the corner of Nevsky Prospekt and the Fontanka Embankment, stands the Beloselsky-Beloszersky

Palace (1846–48). After the Princess Beloselskaya-Beloszerskaya's death the State inherited her palace and here lived Grand Duke Sergey Alexandrovitch, Alexander III's brother, assassinated in 1905 by Ivan Kaliaiev. The last occupant was a nephew of Alexander III, Grand Duke Dmitry Pavlovitch, one of the organizers of Rasputin's assassination – subsequently exiled to the West and therefore a royal survivor of the 1917 Revolution. At night, from my bed, I could see this palace's wine-red, half-colonnaded magnificence, discreetly flood-lit, and I wondered about Grand Ducal ghosts.

Nearby were the much bigger and stunningly beautiful Stroganov Palace (1750s) on the corner of Nevsky Prospekt and the Moika Embankment, and the austerely elegant Sheremetev Palace (1730s) on the Fontanka's left bank – my favourite, built on land given to General-Field Marshal Boris Sheremetev by Peter the Great and the oldest of the surviving palaces. Throughout the eighteenth century, country estates lined the Fontanka – St Petersburg, though trying hard, wasn't yet city-sized.

My week in St Petersburg coincided with the thaw. All the little rivers and canals were iced over when I arrived and liquidly active when I left. Small icebergs floated slowly down the Neva, sometimes meeting and halting momentarily, then separating again and moving on. Between them, a few St Petersburgers swam briefly and emerged beaming, to the cheers of their friends. If one scrutinized the darkly naked trees, buds were visible. Given another week, Piter would be ebulliently green. Here is no leisurely springtime but a dramatic leap from frozenness to exuberant growth.

My last evening, before catching the overnight train to Moscow (405 miles: eight hours) was spent on Elagin Island, now tiresomely known as the Central Park of Culture and Rest. I wished I had discovered it sooner. These ninety-four hectares (pedestrians only) form St Petersburg's quietest corner; in two hours I saw only three distant dog-walkers. Capricious paths wind through woodland – already crows were building nests in ancient oak trees – and five tiny, irregularly shaped lakes, covering almost a quarter of the island, are linked by narrow curving channels. The aptly named Joseph Busch, a renowned landscape designer, arranged all this while Carlo Rossi was creating the island's only building, originally the summer residence of the Dowager Empress Maria Feodorovna (1759–1828),

Alexander I's mother. Russia's Palladian (with modifications) Elagin Palace is heart-stoppingly beautiful when suddenly seen beyond a lake, through a gap in dense woodland.

The survival of Elagin's stately oaks (and of all St Petersburg's trees) has a special and moving significance. During the Siege no heating was available and Piter's winters are as extreme as southern Siberia's. Yet the starving and freezing citizens spontaneously resolved (without any official diktat) to fell no mature trees. Their preservation was to symbolize 'No surrender!', to proclaim the St Petersburgers' faith in their capacity to defend a city that Hitler had vowed to 'raze from the face of the earth. After the defeat of Soviet Russia there will not be the slightest reason for the future existence of this large city' (Directive from German Naval HQ, 22 September 1941). No wonder Stalin hated Leningrad, felt it to be a city psychologically beyond his reach whose people would always, inwardly, do their own thing. To him the very fact that St Petersburg had bred the Revolution made it suspect; the seeds of another revolution might be germinating beneath its outward compliancy.

In Bosnia, during the 1992–93 winter siege of Bihac – much shorter than Leningrad's but involving dreadful hardships – the citizens also reverenced their venerable trees, a legacy from the Habsburgs. All those ordinary people of Leningrad and Bihac risked (or in too many cases lost) their lives out of respect for trees. Yet now, all over the New Russia, developers can get away with felling whole forests – including 'protected' forests – to make money. Protest campaigns, backed by specialist ecological research organizations, are thwarted by judges who deliberately postpone hearings until the developers have had their way. Then it is argued, 'The trees have gone, why waste court time on this issue?' Even Berg Park in Moscow Province has been obliterated. Pre-Revolution, the Berg family of Pervomaiskoe village lovingly propagated rare trees; most of their estate was ancient woodland and in 1904 they forested the rest, planting five Weymouth pines (the only specimens in all of Moscow Province in 2004), a White cedar (the only specimen in the province) and many other species. Under the Soviets, this estate became a well-cared-for and popular public park, enjoyed by young and old. When developers moved in, to build palatial 'dachas' for Moscow-based oligarchs, local grief and fury knew no bounds and quickly spread far beyond Pervomaiskoe. As requested by the Provincial Prosecutor, the villagers' 'Save Berg!' group (all pensioners) tried to video the illegal felling – whereupon the developers called in the police who beat them up and broke their camera. Intimidation was blatant. The leader of the Ecological Union of Moscow Province wrote to Mikhail Avdyukov, Provincial Prosecutor: 'The chairman of the Pervomaiskoe Rural District Council publicly stated to members of the ecological group elected by the village assembly that he had given their names and addresses to the mafia, which would deal with them if they did not stop their protests.'

Throughout Russia, applications are frequently made, and usually promptly granted, for the 'transfer of Grade One Forests to the category of non-afforested land'. Grade One includes formerly state-protected habitats of rare animals and birds, valuable plant species, parks and reservations. Similar 'transfer' crimes are routinely committed in Ireland; we call it re-zoning. As yet we don't have any above-ground mafia intimidation but it's probably on the way. Recently my country has emerged as a shining example of 'how to grow your economy fast' – so shining that most of the Irish have become too dazzled to see where they are going.

I had come to Elagin to say a private goodbye to Eurasia; the island's western tip overlooks the Gulf of Finland. Having gazed upon its grey waters, restless under a cold green and russet sunset, I turned east and remembered the frozen immensity of the Pacific, overlooked by Vanino – more than 6,000 miles away and all those miles are *Russia*. No longer an Empire or a Union but a troubled and misruled Federation whose people – so remarkable for their warm-heartedness and courage, and their dignity in adversity – deserve better leaders than they have ever had.

Select Bibliography

Amalrik, Andrei, *Involuntary Journey to Siberia*, Collins/Harvill Press, 1970
—— *Will the Soviet Union Survive until 1984?*, Penguin, 1980
Armstrong, Terence, *Russian Settlement in the North*, Cambridge University Press, 1965
Ascherson, Neal, *Black Sea*, Vintage, 1996
Belliutsin, I. S., *Description of the Clergy in Rural Russia: The Memoir of a Nineteenth-century Parish Priest*, trans. Gregory L. Freeze, Cornell University Press, 1985
Bird, Chris, *To Catch a Tartar*, John Murray, 2002
Blum, Douglas W. (ed.), *Russia's Future: Consolidation or Disintegration?*, Westview Press, 1994
Blum, Jerome, *Lord and Peasant in Russia*, Princeton University Press, 1961
Blum, William, *Killing Hope*, Zed Books, 2003
Bobrick, Benson, *East of the Sun: The Conquest and Settlement of Siberia*, Heinemann, 1992
Bolovkhin, Vladimir, *Searching for Icons in Russia*, Harvill Press, 1971
Borovik, Artyom, *The Hidden War*, Grove Press, 1990
Cochrane, John Dundas, *A Pedestrian Journey Through Russian and Siberian Tartary*, John Murray, 1823
Conquest, Robert, *The Great Terror*, Oxford University Press, 1990
Daglish, Robert, *Coping with Russia*, Blackwell, 1985
Elvin, Harold, *The Incredible Mile: Siberia, Mongolia, Uzbekistan*, Heinemann, 1970
Emerson, P. J., *A Political Cycle: The Other Russian Revolution*, De Borda Institute, n.d.
Farmborough, Florence, *Nurse at the Russian Front*, Constable, 1974
Farmer, Paul, *Pathologies of Power*, University of California Press, 2003
Federova, Marina, and Gorbatcheva, Valentina, *The Peoples of the Great North: Art and Civilization in Siberia*, Parkstone Press, 2000
Fisher, H. H., *The Famine in Soviet Russia, 1919–1923*, Macmillan, 1927
Fleming, D. F., *New World Review*, Fall 1967

Forsyth, James, *A History of the Peoples of Siberia*, Cambridge University Press, 1992

Fraser, John Foster, *The Real Siberia*, Cassell, 1902

Glenny, Michael, and Stone, Norman, *The Other Russia*, Faber & Faber, 1990

Golitsyn, Anatoliy, *New Lies for Old*, The Bodley Head, 1984

Gorbachev, Mikhail, *Perestroika*, Collins, 1987

Gray, Francine du Plessix, *Soviet Women*, Doubleday, 1990

Grey, Ian, *Boris Godunov*, Hodder & Stoughton, 1973

Halliday, Fred, *Threat From the East?*, Pelican, 1982

Hawes, C. H., *In the Uttermost East*, Harper, 1903

Haynes, Mike, *Russia: Class and Power 1917–2000*, Bookmarks Publications, 2000

Heinberg, Richard, *The Party's Over*, Clareview, 2003

Herlihy, Patricia, *The Alcoholic Empire*, Oxford University Press, 2002

Herodotus, *The Histories*, trans. Aubrey de Selincourt, Penguin, 1954

Hobsbawm, Eric, *Interesting Times*, Allen Lane, 2002

Hosking, Geoffrey, *A History of the Soviet Union, 1917–1991*, HarperCollins, 1992

—— *Russia: People and Empire, 1552–1917*, HarperCollins, 1997

Jacob, Alaric, *A Russian Journey*, Cassell, 1969

Jarintzoff, Madame N., *Russia: Country of Extremes*, Henry Holt, 1914

Jenkins, Dominick, *The Final Frontier*, Verso, 2002

Jurgens, Urda, *Raisa*, Weidenfeld & Nicolson, 1990

Kagarlitsky, Boris, *Farewell Perestroika*, trans. Rick Simon, Verso, 1990

Kennan, George, *Tent Life in Siberia*, Putnam, 1871

—— *Siberia and the Exile System*, Century, 1891

Kennan, George F., *The Marquis de Custine and His Russia in 1839*, Hutchinson, 1972

Komarov, Boris, *The Destruction of Nature in the Soviet Union*, Pluto Press, 1978

Leggett, George, *The Cheka: Lenin's Political Police*, Oxford University Press, 1981

Lewis, David C., *After Atheism*, St Martin's Press, 2000

Lieven, Dominic, *Nicholas II: Emperor of All the Russias*, John Murray, 1993

—— *Empire: The Russian Empire and Its Rivals from the Sixteenth Century to the Present*, Pimlico, 2003

Lobachev, Valeri, and Pravotarov, Vladimir, *A Millennium of Russian Orthodoxy*, Novosti, 1988

Mackiewicz, S., *Russian Minds in Fetters*, Allen & Unwin, 1932

Mandelstam, Nadezhda, *Hope Against Hope*, Collins/Harvill Press, 1971

Mathossentz, Murad, *The Black Raven*, Policy Research Publications, 1988

Merridale, Catherine, *Night of Stone: Death and Memory in Russia*, Granta, 2000

Newby, Eric, *The Big Red Train Ride*, Weidenfeld & Nicolson, 1978

Pipes, Richard, *Russia Under the Old Regime*, Weidenfeld & Nicolson, 1974

Politkovskaya, Anna, *Putin's Russia*, trans. Arch Tait, Harvill Press, 2004

Portisch, Hugo, *I Saw Siberia*, Harrap, 1972

Rasputin, Valentin, *Siberia! Siberia!*, trans. Margaret Winchell and Gerald Mikkelson, Northwestern University Press, 1996

Ratushinskaya, Irina, *Grey is the Colour of Hope*, Hodder & Stoughton, 1988

Reid, Anna, *The Shaman's Coat*, Phoenix, 2002

Schemann, Serge, *Echoes of a Native Land*, Little, Brown, 1997

Servadio, Gaia, *A Siberian Encounter*, Weidenfeld & Nicolson, 1971

Service, Robert, *Russia: Experiment with a People*, Macmillan, 2002

Shinkareu, Leonid, *The Land Beyond the Mountains*, Hart-Davis, MacGibbon, 1973

Shub, David, *Lenin*, Doubleday, 1948

Smith, Hedrick, *The Russians*, Sphere Books, 1976

Smith, S. A., *The Russian Revolution: A Very Short Introduction*, Oxford University Press, 2002

Solzhenitsyn, Alexander, *The Gulag Archipelago*, Collins/Harvill Press, 1974

St George, George, *Siberia: The New Frontier*, Hodder & Stoughton, 1970

Stiglitz, Joseph, *Globalization and Its Discontents*, Penguin, 2002

—— *The Roaring Nineties*, Penguin, 2003

Stone, Norman, *The Eastern Front, 1914–1917*, Hodder & Stoughton, 1975

Thubron, Colin, *Among the Russians*, Heinemann, 1983

—— *In Siberia*, Chatto & Windus, 1999

Took, Roger, *Running with Reindeer*, John Murray, 2003

Truscott, Peter, *Putin's Progress*, Simon & Schuster, 2004

Van der Post, Laurens, *Journey into Russia*, Hogarth Press, 1964

Volkogonov, Dmitri, *Stalin: Triumph and Tragedy*, ed. and trans. Harold Shukman, Weidenfeld & Nicolson, 1991

Wasilewska, Eugenia, *The Silver Madonna*, Allen & Unwin, 1970

Whitlock, Monica, *Beyond the Oxus*, John Murray, 2002

Williamson, H. N. H., *Farewell to the Don*, ed. John Harris, Collins, 1970

Wilson, Francesca, *Muscovy: Russia Through Foreign Eyes 1553–1900*, Allen & Unwin, 1970

Yates, Athol, and Zvegintzov, Nicholas, *Siberian BAM Guide*, Trailblazer, 1995

Yeltsin, Boris, *Midnight Diaries*, Weidenfeld & Nicolson, 2000

Yergin, Daniel, *Shattered Peace*, André Deutsch, 1978

Index